Hamilton and Philosophy

"Rabinowitz and Arp have assembled sharp and engaged contributors to examine from a rich variety of perspectives one of the most significant cultural events of the decade. A compelling read!"

> —R. BARTON PALMER, World Cinema Program Director at Clemson University, and co-editor of *The Philosophy of Steven Soderbergh*

"Revolutionary or not, Hamilton deserves to be studied seriously. And here we have some smart—and very funny—philosophers to help us out."

> —ROBERTO SIRVENT, Associate Professor of Political and Social Ethics, Hope International University

"Calling all heroes and scholars! Although only half as long as 'the other fifty-one' essays that Hamilton wrote, the twenty-three chapters of this work bring the spirit of the beloved Broadway hit into the classical world of philosophical inquiry. Attacking questions of race, selfhood, freedom, cyborgs, and more, the ragtag volunteer army of philosophers (in need of a shower) who assembled this collection will make you want to talk less and smile more as you pore through their arguments and insights. Don't throw away your shot to read this!"

> —A.G. HOLDIER, Colorado Technical University, Theater Nerd

"Everyone has crazy ideas. Like history being a collection of simple, straightforward stories that are linked together in a way that makes obvious sense. Or that philosophers come up with their ideas in the sterile environment of an ivory tower. Nothing could be further from the truth. The world is a crazy, messy, unpredictable place, especially in American politics. Think I'm crazy? Read Hamilton and Philosophy. *And remember just how crazy our world really is, next time you pull a Hamilton out of your pocket to pay for that morning cup o' joe."*

> —JOHN V. KARAVITIS, CPA, MBA, and popular writer

Hamilton and Philosophy

Popular Culture and Philosophy® Series Editor: George A. Reisch

IN PREPARATION:

For full details of all Popular Culture and Philosophy® books, visit www.opencourtbooks.com.

Popular Culture and Philosophy®

Hamilton and Philosophy

Revolutionary Thinking

Edited by

AARON RABINOWITZ AND ROBERT ARP

OPEN COURT
Chicago

Volume 110 in the series, Popular Culture and Philosophy ®, edited by George A. Reisch

To find out more about Open Court books, visit our website at www.opencourtbooks.com.

Open Court Publishing Company is a division of Carus Publishing Company, dba Cricket Media.

Copyright © 2017 by Carus Publishing Company, dba Cricket Media

First printing 2017

Hamilton and Philosophy: Revolutionary Thinking

ISBN: 978-0-8126-9960-9.

Library of Congress Control Number: 2017939156

This book is also available as an e-book.

Special thanks to Luisa Lyons for all her help.
I know who I married, you're more than enough.

—A.D.R.

To my Mom and Sister, who introduced me to the
joys of musical theater early in life.

—R.A.

Contents

Director's Note

My name is Aaron, and I love to write.
I wish I could rap, but I'm just too white.

Kidding. I would never put you through that. I'm not Mr. Miranda, and this is not *Hamilton: An American Musical*. This is a love letter to Hamilton, and the hit Broadway show that shares his name. It's some notes in the margins of debates that will outlive us all.

Philosophy is a lifelong passion to find the truth. Hamilton was a philosopher, and America benefited immensely from his devotion to knowledge. He soaked up every idea he could find, and handed us a new world, full of freedoms and opportunities. He saw suffering that moved him to action, and through greater understanding he brought some aid to those in need. This book is a tribute to that legacy, and to the philosophies that helped make it possible.

Like many of you, I came to *Hamilton* as a Broadway novice. Despite a lifetime in theater, I was more familiar with rap than musicals. My mind was stuck on a false impression of musicals as broad, saccharine affairs with no intellectual content and a lot of spectacle. *Hamilton*, along with shows like *The Book of Mormon* and *Matilda,* have changed my perception of musicals. I see now that many of them have both intellectual and emotional heft. The philosopher in me loves these shows because they are complex, full of ideas, and built to promote dialogue. This book arose so naturally because *Hamilton* is a philosophical musical. It's unabashedly nerdy. It does not shy away from the love of knowledge. It makes that love cool and accessible. Philosophy is at its best when it does the same, so we are natural allies in social progress.

There's something for everyone in this book. If you already know the show by heart, we'll give you new ways to hear it. If you're new to the show, we're happy to help get you hooked. Perhaps you're not acquainted with the Broadway show at all. Hopefully the ideas here will inspire you to take a listen to the cast recording, or even try and see the production.

We cover the major philosophical themes of *Hamilton,* as explored through the characters in the show. Can you have a happy life and also chase your legacy? Can you be a hero and a slaver at the same time? We look at the morality of honor and epistemic humility, and explore the ways in which Hamilton wrote his own story. Hamilton sees himself as a Macbeth figure, and we explore that comparison in detail. Is Hamilton a great-souled man or a megalomaniac?

Drawing from Eastern sources, we chart the personal philosophies of Burr, Washington, and Eliza, who all share a preference for acceptance over trying to force history. Burr's patience, Washington's perspective, and Eliza's ability to abide make them direct philosophical foils for Hamilton. Is one side right, or is the key to balance these competing perspectives?

In *Hamilton,* dramatic tension builds around the conflict between revolutionary need and the realities of incremental progress. We consider several existentialist strategies for managing this conflict.

The production itself also raises a variety of philosophical questions. The casting call for non-white actors stirred controversy, so we discuss the morality of race and casting. We see also that the blending of cultures and genres reflects the mixing pot that is American history.

Hamilton has received criticism for its reliance on "founders chic," a historical view of the founding fathers that tends to ignore important complexities, so we include several chapters on the nature of history and art. Can a piece of art also be history, or are the two mediums incompatible?

Whether or not *Hamilton* counts as history, no one can deny that *Hamilton* is a historic piece of art. It has reshaped the face of musical theater, drawing people into the world of Broadway who would never have ventured there otherwise. Likewise, *Hamilton* has reinvigorated an interest in history, especially for those who couldn't see themselves in the faces and stories of the founding fathers.

People start with *Hamilton*, but they want more, so they head to the genius lyrics and the wiki pages and Hamiltome. Before long, people find themselves reading *The Federalist Papers* and other primary sources. It's difficult to find art that engenders such an obsession with its source material.

Hamilton is a gateway to curiosity about the past. This book will take that curiosity and point it towards new ideas and philosophers, so that you can continue to deepen your understanding of this epic show and the figures it portrays.

Enjoy!

AARON RABINOWITZ

I

What Kind of a Story?

1

I, Hamilton—Confessions of a Ten-Dollar Bill

CHRISTOPHER KETCHAM

I am limp, wet, and smell of pee.

You're wondering how I, such an important personage in life, could end up in this predicament. I'm made from fine linen and cloth and beautifully fashioned into the magnificent ten-dollar bill, printed on the finest intaglio press.

I started at the mint of course and had a glorious ride in an armored behemoth to a bank where I was separated from many of my identical siblings—identical but for my DNA, my Denomination Number Add.

Well it isn't what they call it in monetary terms but it suits me because the number is mine alone and it does establish me as unique in many billions, just like you. None of my siblings have the same DNA; none of your siblings have your exact DNA—the other kind.

I was separated from my birth mates and stacked in an ATM from which I was quickly dispensed. I will not bore you with the details of my strange existence until a couple of most interesting transactions that occurred relatively recently. Go on, you must admit I have beautiful hair. Take a ten spot out of your wallet and look. I'll wait. Even pissed on I would look quite distinguished, don't you think?

In the first transaction, I was the largest bill changed for the twenty the bartender took for a fill of Mad Dog 20/20, the champagne of fortified wines. Their hands always shake, drunks and addicts, until they get their chosen poison. Shakes me to hell and back sometimes. Well, the old pensioner got his fill and staggered towards home where he was met in the alley by another shaking specter wearing a hoodie. He, the drunk in whose pocket I was resting, fought back but when smacked in the nose by a shortened bat, promptly pissed himself and me and fell to the ground. I, in my sodden state, was quickly transferred to the pocket of the hoodied specter and we commenced a jolly jaunt to his preferred street corner to be palmed for a dime bag of the hoodie's required high.

"Ah, shit, what the hell is this?" demanded the purveyor of bagged goodies. "Stinks of piss. Gimme one that hasn't the smell of a rolled drunk."

The hoodied man protested, bobbing up and down, stomach clenched, teeth chattering. He couldn't get out a word but got the message across that this was all he had.

"Go on, get outa here. I'm not taking no piss-smelling shit. Bad for business and me. Go on, give another or go away." From the shadows came a diminutive man who pointed a pistol at the hoodie who had been fumbling for the bat which he had so industriously used before. As bad ideas go, this one of hoodie's worst, so he ran.

In New York You Can Be a New Man

So, why money in the first place? Say I am a carpenter and you, the farmer, need a cabinet built. You give me a chicken for my efforts. I accept this chicken because I need eggs or Sunday supper. It's a fair deal. You ask me back to build a barn. Here's twenty chickens, you say. What am I going to do with twenty chickens? This barter thing doesn't work anymore.

George Simmel in the early twentieth century realized that money is psychological. It represents the value of my work on your barn but in something that has value to everyone where chickens only have value to some people. If you gave me money for building your barn I could get a new hammer, get my cart fixed, and have a new dress made for my wife. Chickens, what am I going to do with twenty chickens?

The first money was made of precious metals. Nobody is going to argue with getting gold or silver. Bite on it first. If it doesn't leave a tooth mark it isn't gold. However, gold is heavy and can be stolen and melted down into other things. Not very practical. Paper is lightweight and can be easily transported and can be made to foil counterfeiters, at least to some extent. It can get stolen as well, but what can't?

However, paper isn't gold. People won't buy into paper as being the same as gold. We need a solution . . . Let's tell the people that if they don't believe that the paper is valuable we have gold in the federal treasury to back it up. This is why we have Fort Knox.

However, there's only so much gold. If I, an ordinary citizen, try to buy it up I am going to raise the price of gold the treasury needs to purchase in order to back paper money. That could get very expensive and require an increase in taxes. That won't fly. So, let's make gold a crime to hoard (other than jewelry and such) and put a fixed price on it so that we always know what it will cost.

Well you know what happened. Our economy got so big that we couldn't buy enough gold. President Nixon convinced us that you and I and the government could derive value from our huge economic engine so that we could print all of money we need to print. If we had to buy gold at some point we could. Essentially, he convinced us we could back money up without the gold because we had become the most powerful economy in the world.

The philosophy of money changed from being backed up by gold to full faith and credit in the US. Paper money became an idea with an economy attached. Today money is as Simmel predicted, a purely psychological thing. However, you have to believe the politicians for this to be true. Horrible thought, isn't it?

Money is fungible. It's legal tender for any transaction, legal or not. While there are laws against transactions that exchange money for illegal purposes, it matters nothing to commerce nor the transaction nor to the people who exchange money. Money works, period. There's even an official calculation for the underground, underworld, black-market economy. Money is laundered, as I promptly was in a sink at a flop and then ironed to dry and sprayed with room freshener. Not even faded, but my linen was not as starched as it once was, that is, when I entered the ATM. We, the hoody and I, ran together back to the street corner where the deal was done. After that many more hands touched me and I was laundered again, but not in the same way . . .

I have become the favorite in the substance abuse economy. Pills, often the first choice of those who want to get high, have become incredibly expensive. Heroin is cheap. A dime bag will get you high. I move quickly through acquisition by dastardly means or otherwise; then go from pocket to palm. I am piled up and counted and exchanged for more heroin and the cycle continues. Some of my brethren have bought Ferraris for traffickers and others flowers for the deceased, gunned down because the ambitious soul had encroached on someone else's block of street corners.

It's more than a bit disconcerting when heroin addicts palm me, a Hamilton . . . for a dime bag on the street corner. I try to shout, "Hey, do you know where that needle's been?" They don't hear; they just slide that clammy palm over what the sour-faced man has in his and walk away with their next high. Easy come; easy go. Well that's always the way with money, especially paper money these days. Who's got a pocket filled with coins anymore? The meters even take plastic.

There's some consolation. Doesn't matter whether its heroin or weed, I'm still their bill of choice, though junkies probably never look at me or think about what I did to deserve financing their moment of ecstasy. They don't know that my namesake was born on the island of Nevis in the Caribbean. See, he was a poor immigrant like many of them. He was born where they made the drug of choice back then, rum. Guess who worked the fields? Slaves of course.

Can't say it's much different here on street corners in grimy neighborhoods where many are homeless or call abandoned buildings a place to nod off. Slaves died young then. The new slaves to heroin and crack and bath salts and all the other stuff that gets slid across my face thousands of times a day all die young too. Which is worse? You tell me. So I still got value to some even though I am financing a kind of death wish.

Raise a Glass to Freedom

Got only myself to blame, however. We were strapped for cash. The revolution wiped out the treasury and we had no international credit. The first try to make a workable regime, the Articles of Confederation, made the federal government too weak to do anything. We needed something better.

Madison and I wrote the Federalist Papers to convince people that we needed a stronger federal government. We did just that when we rewrote the Articles of the Confederation into the Constitution of the United States. We as a nation, however, were quite broke. We needed to consolidate all of the state and federal debts from the war. I did that and formed a central bank in order to establish ourselves as a legitimate country and to get some international credit which was sorely needed. That, sadly, was not enough.

What we needed more than anything was tax revenue. You must understand the philosophy of the country at this time. As a colony we had no say in British politics, no vote. King George just taxed us for everything because it was easier trying to get revenue from a colony than parliament. We fixed his wagon by rebelling.

After the war, everyone was leery of taxes. The philosophy of the country was for freedoms without government interference, hence the weak federal government. It simply didn't work.

I knew that everyone would be wary of most taxes, so I decided to tax the distillation of whiskey. Whiskey's had as bad a reputation as rum and was something that the former colonies produced in abundance. Even Washington was a distiller of some renown. I figured that at least I would get the temperance folks on my side with such a tax. I didn't quite get that whiskey distilling was so important to the locals, especially rural locals who fought tooth and nail against the tax. They called it the Whiskey Rebellion. While it was a rebellion of sorts, the much more powerful Protestant church leaders and abolitionists weren't sympathetic to the distillers. We got no push back from them at all. Sure the consumers of alcohol didn't like paying more, but as we saw much later with prohibition, money isn't a big object for those who need a drink.

I wasn't like the abolitionists who wanted whiskey gone. I just wanted a fair share in tax revenue for every bottle or jug produced. Got us out of debt then, and we have NASCAR now thanks to bootleggers who souped up jalopies to outrun revenuers who were hell-bent on collecting my tax.

Funny thing about the sin called alcohol. You let it be and you get alcoholics, broken homes, drunk drivers, abusive behavior and death at an early age. You make it illegal and you get Al Capone and bootleggers. You tax it and say the money is going to kids and old people, and others just shake their heads because they know those who are buying liquor are financing their own death with it too.

Sure, booze is a cost to society, but a tax does offset some cost even though it isn't all on what you might call the moral up and up. Let's face it, we don't get any tax revenue with heroin and the other stuff I get palmed for these days. We let addicts die, tie up all our police to look for the stuff, let modern day Capones sell it for obscene profits, and throw users in jail. Once they go in, they never really get out again because society doesn't want them back.

Sometimes I wish I could just turn back the clock and figure out something less divisive to tax, but I'm sure that someone would have figured out how to tax alcohol and we wouldn't be in a much different place than we are today. Besides, Colorado's started it all up again by legalizing and taxing marijuana.

Excuse Me, Miss, I Know It's Not Funny but Your Perfume Smells Like Your Daddy's Got Money

Money, as we have seen, is psychological. Money is also political and has to conform to the philosophy of the government and people. We were a new nation after the war for independence. We wanted our own currency, the currency for a free people. We abandoned the pound for the dollar.

However, we kept one thing that other countries had done, pictures of leaders on the bills. We didn't have kings or queens so we had to figure out whose face was going to be on each bill. Washington, of course, but then there were many more who had and were contributing to this new philosophy of freedom. There were a lot of great early choices, but who gets their picture on what bill or what coin? It's all political, but as you know politicians are not the brightest lanterns on the wharf.

Well, I didn't get the worst of it. Look at Lincoln, his face is on the penny and who wants pennies anymore? He gets left behind more than any other because nobody wants him. Sure he's also a five-dollar bill, but you need two of him to buy what I do. I do take some pride in that, of course.

I'm really the only finance guy in the whole American monetary collection. Think about it. You've got Lincoln who won the

Civil War and freed the slaves and he's the penny nobody wants anymore. Yes, I'll say it again: his face graces the five but that makes a big wad of bills should you need anything more than one bag of groceries. Besides, why palm two of him when you can palm one of me. George Washington's dollar not long ago bought you a soda from a vending machine (if you rubbed it real flat on the corner of the machine) as did Jefferson's nickel but that was a really long time ago, even before Roosevelt asked whether anyone had a dime or got his picture on it. Why Washington's quarter has been called two bits, I'll never know but you and I both know he had more than two Jeffersons to rub together.

You Want a Revolution?

Well, a real controversy is brewing, and I don't mind saying that I am ecstatic about it. You see Old Hickory, that bastard Andrew Jackson, who tore down my central bank because he couldn't get his way, well he's about to disappear from the twenty. No matter, his was the most counterfeited anyway. You do the nasty and you reap the rewards. So much of him around the world is fake it's hard to keep track of what's real. Mark of a true politician.

Speaking of politics. They used to burn old and mutilated bills. Not very green is it? Instead of burning old bills, now they just shred us and turn us into compost. Can you say greenback?

I can't stop thinking of that no-good Jackson . . . Who do you think packed up all the Cherokee and sent them west on their trail of tears to reservations in what is now Oklahoma? Jackson, yeah that one. Reservation for money; reservations for Native Americans. We do like parking money and people, don't we?

Well, we won't have to burn Jackson in effigy much longer because they are about to scrape Old Hickory from the twenty and replace him with Harriet Tubman. Harriet was a railroad baron, actually ran the first American subway they called the Underground, which Britain promptly stole to name their tube, I'll have you know. Well certainly Harriet's Underground was not filled with steel carriages, rather barefoot escaped slaves who seemed to be able to find her and her safe houses all up and down the east coast even into the abolitionist north. Why safe houses in the slave-free north? Because, thanks to the 1857

Dred Scott Supreme Court decision, a southern slave owner could reclaim his runaway slave anywhere in the United States.

So Harriet is going to be on the twenty and don't that beat all? Certainly, there was some money that changed hands to run that railroad, but she wasn't getting rich like Cornelius Vanderbilt who built a railroad empire all across the Northeast. Why not him, if we're giving pictures on big bills for railroad work? Well, you're going to just have to ask someone else. Me, I'm not going anywhere and that you can take to the bank.

There is precedent, for a woman that is, on money. We have Susan B. Anthony of women's suffrage fame who got the vote for women in the 1920s. I guess since women hold most of the big wealth in this nation, it was appropriate to put her face on a dollar coin. That may be stretching it a bit unless the politicians are thinking they can get the woman's vote by putting a woman on a coin which just about nobody wants or hands out anymore. Doesn't make sense, does it? Think about it, you used to be able to put fistfuls of Susan B. Anthonys into slot machines, but they only work with plastic now.

Yo, Who the F Is This?

Some of you may also be wondering how Sacagawea got on the other dollar coin. Now you'll probably think I'm crazy but I'm going to tell you no one else deserves a face on money more than Sacagawea, besides me. Toting an infant on her back, she guided Lewis and Clark west from the Missouri river across the country to the Pacific Ocean in what is now Oregon, and back again. She did this at the dawn of the nineteenth century and Lewis and Clark reported back to Jefferson just what it was we got for his Louisiana purchase.

Think about it, she led the way to our westward expansion and the huge economic push that brought our country to prominence later that century. Sacagawea has done more for commerce than anyone else I know. She invented the west. She was the first pioneer even though she was a Native American and entitled to go anywhere she wanted. Well, before 1492 anyway. Go figure.

Lest you think I'm forgetting the others, Kennedy on the fifty-cent piece, Grant on the fifty-dollar bill, and Franklin on the hundred. There, I've said it. There were larger bills like the thousand and a few miscellaneous larger ones that never were circulated, and an ill-fated two-dollar bill but that's about it for faces on money.

One thing more about Franklin being on the hundred. With inflation and all that he likely will be me in a few years; a dime bag will be a hundred bag. Things change with the times. What is more interesting about Franklin being on the hundred is that he not only said things like "Early to bed and early to rise makes a man healthy, wealthy, and wise," and "An investment in knowledge pays the best dividends," and other illustrious platitudes, but he was also in his own right quite the entrepreneur, when he wasn't having dalliances with the ladies at court in France. However, he also said, "Wine is constant proof that God loves us and loves to see us happy." Happy? I think maybe we got the happy thing all wrong. Giving that burden to God, well . . .

How do we choose the face that will occupy our coins and bills? Is it all political or is there a distinctive philosophical message we want to convey to our kids? Hmmm. Why then choose a crude rube like Jackson who hated Native Americans and central banking?

Even me! I died in a duel. There is enough violence today without bringing back dueling. Jefferson was a slaveholder and so was Washington. Married Kennedy had umpteen mistresses and married Franklin bedded umpteen more as ambassador to France. FDR, well he practically invented socialism with the New Deal which goads Republicans even today.

What message are we telling our children? It's all about politics and who wins, not what's right? Well, I didn't win . . . the duel that is. Besides, everyone else is dead too—but that's a requirement. Wouldn't want the press hounding you into your grave asking you why you deserved your face on a bill. Doesn't matter to the British because they plaster Elizabeth's face all over their bills. They do think differently, don't they?

Hamilton Doesn't Hesitate, He Exhibits No Restraint

I feel good about my position in the hierarchy of money. It feels comforting to be wanted and to be needed and even better now that Jackson is going bye-bye. However, I do fret that nobody has given my fellows Madison or John Adams the head nod.

The father, John, not John Quincy Adams because he was such a boor the public couldn't wait to elect Jackson. I suggest we be very leery whenever another member of a so-called dynasty is offered up to be our next president.

Thank God there are no vice presidents on anything because I can see some heartless bastard putting Aron Burr, that hapless oaf and toady of Jefferson who, by the way, murdered me, on a bill larger than mine. Well, let's give him a really big bill, one of those that never gets circulated—like a one-hundred-thousand-dollar bill. Fade into oblivion you ignominious cur.

My time's up. Here I am in the back of another rumbling armored beast on my way back to the Federal Reserve where my DNA will be retired. I'll be spread around a bit more but more likely in someone's garden to grow fat red tomatoes for salads, hopefully not poppy plants for narcotics. Not to worry though about my impending demise, they are making more of me as we speak.

What if they ask me to name names, to tell all about those who've touched me? Money can't talk. That's the beauty of me. I just keep on keeping on, and to you and to me, I am one in a billion but the same value to people all over the world. Sure, I've got my DNA and that's traceable but who's got the time? Once I get out into society the first and last hands on me are anonymous. Somebody or nobody, it matters not to me. So I will go quietly, silently with my lips sealed into this goodnight.

So long, and remember me for all that I've done for you.

2
Who's the Hero?

JOE CHAPA

Hamilton: An American Musical casts its villain, the self-aggrandizing political hack, Aaron Burr, against Alexander Hamilton, the true statesman who devotes his life to the future of the republic. Or does he?

The play is structured around a life-long friction between Hamilton and Burr. From the opening moments, we're invited to see Burr as the villain. Burr will say and do whatever needs saying or doing to climb the political and social ladders.

When they first meet, Burr cautions Hamilton, "Don't let them know what you're against or what you're for," and immediately following that exchange in "My Shot," Burr chides the group of young revolutionaries, "Geniuses, lower your voices. You keep out of trouble and you double your choices." In response, Hamilton paraphrases the famous quote of a *different* Alex Hamilton when he demands to know, "if you stand for nothing, Burr, what'll you fall for?" Hamilton is committed to a cause and is willing to give up his life. Burr is committed to nothing but his own gain.

Hamilton seems at first to be the true servant of the revolution, and later, the republic. But a one-dimensional "villain" poised against a one-dimensional "hero" doesn't make for a very good story—and *Hamilton* is a great story. The complexity of the characters comes out when we dig just a little deeper.

Burr is not *simply* a power-starved villain. In "Wait for It" and "Dear Theodosia," we get a glimpse at this villain's humanity. Burr's love and devotion for Theodosia appears genuine. Though the details didn't make their way into the musical,

Theodosia and Burr were married following the death of Theodosia's first husband in 1781. Shortly after they were married, they gave birth to a daughter whom they also name Theodosia. *Hamilton* captures Burr's love for his daughter well when Burr tells her that they bled and fought for her, and that she will come of age with the young nation.

Meanwhile, Hamilton is no saint. Even as he chides Burr for his lack of integrity, we get a glimpse at that Hamiltonian pride that will prove to be his downfall. Hamilton is ambitious and "desperate to rise above his station" ("Cabinet Battle #2"). Even as he serves Washington in their joint struggle for American independence, he is posturing for his role after the war. During his youthful courtship with Eliza, Hamilton swears to God that she will never feel helpless, and yet he violates Eliza's trust during his affair with Maria Reynolds.

It's not obvious that Hamilton has chosen the right kind of life any more than Burr has.

Aristotle's Three Lives

Aristotle has something to say about how we ought to live. The fourth-century B.C. Greek philosopher and founder of his own university offers his reader three possible approaches to life: the life of pleasure, the life of honor, and the life of contemplation. Aristotle defines the good life as the life of contemplation. It's the fully human life—the life that cultivates uniquely human traits like reason, love, and character. Hamilton's life certainly seems more virtuous than Burr's, but does it really meet Aristotle's standard for the good life?

Those who follow the life of pleasure seek instant gratification. This is the life of the epicurean; the hedonist who seeks to fulfill short-term desires, even at the expense of long-term advantage. We might think here of James Reynolds, who extorts the Treasury Secretary by pimping his own wife. James Reynolds wants money; and he will obtain it at any price. James Reynolds uses Maria's sexuality and the Secretary's reputation to get rich quick, and so epitomizes the life of gratification. Both Aristotle and Miranda expect their audiences to dismiss this life as obviously not the good life.

The second life Aristotle proposes, the life of honor, is more difficult to assess. Aristotle's concern isn't over honor itself—

surely honor is a virtue. Instead, he cautions against living the political life in order to gain honor because, as Aristotle says, honor of this kind "seems to depend more on those who honor than on the one honored."

Think here of any sleazy politician. He flip-flops on the issues, he panders to the crowds, and he commits himself to nothing, always leaving the politically expedient option open. The historical Aaron Burr summarized this approach to life nicely when he said, "Never do today what you can do tomorrow. Something may occur to make you regret your premature action." After all, someone who never commits to anything will never be wrong.

Aaron Burr, Honor Seeker

Aristotle's "life of honor" describes Aaron Burr perfectly. Burr waits to see "which way the wind will blow" ("Non-Stop"). When asked a question "he obfuscates. He dances" ("The Election of 1800"). He switches parties to obtain General Schuyler's senate seat in New York and is always willing to sell out friends and colleagues if it will yield personal gain. Washington wants a free country. Hamilton wants a strong central government. Burr simply wants *personal power*—to be "in the room where it happens" ("The Room Where It Happens").

Even if Burr is the archetypal honor-seeker, that doesn't mean that Hamilton is safe from Aristotle's criticism. Aristotle is careful to explain that honor itself is good, but the *pursuit of honor* can get us into trouble. Aristotle asks whether we're trying to be honorable for honor's sake, or whether we're trying to be honorable because we want everyone to *see us* as honorable.

Plato, Aristotle's teacher, tells a story that illustrates the distinction. Suppose you had a ring that could turn you invisible whenever you wanted, so that you could get away *with anything*. What would you do? The characters in Plato's dialogue disagree about the answer. Some claim that a just person will still be a just person even if he has the power to do whatever he wants without getting caught. Others argue that the just person and the unjust person would both behave unjustly, because people only act justly to gain public praise and avoid public shaming.

Aristotle answers Plato's question by arguing that the *truly just* person acts justly for the sake of justice. The virtuous person, according to Aristotle, doesn't just behave virtuously for some external or societal reason. She *takes pleasure* in behaving virtuously. As a result, the virtuous person acts honorably for the sake of honor, acts courageously for the sake of courage, and acts virtuously in general for the sake of virtue itself, whether he has an invisibility ring or not. Does this describe Hamilton?

Hamilton's Motives

Does this great man, this aide-de-camp to Washington, Congressman, Attorney, Treasury Secretary, and founder of America's Bank do great things because they are great things? Or does he do them because he wants to be known as a man who does great things?

Hamilton answers these questions in his own words throughout the play. When he's young, he wishes for war. He tells Burr in their first meeting, "I wish there was a war! Then we could prove that we're worth more than anyone bargained for" ("Aaron Burr, Sir"). In the very next song, he proudly proclaims, "we are meant to be a colony that runs independently" ("My Shot"). Here we get our first taste of Hamilton's parallel priorities. If we were to ask Hamilton why he wishes for a war, an honest answer would have to include *both* motivations. He wants a free and independent United States, but he also wants to show the world his value.

Throughout the war, Hamilton pleads with Washington for a command. Once again, we are tempted to laud this man for his bravery and service to the cause. But Aristotle challenges us to ask *why* he is so brave and *why* so bold in his service.

Willingness to sacrifice your life for the greater good certainly seems laudable. But Hamilton may take it to an unhealthy level. He fixates on his own death and jokes with Burr that maybe the two of them should just die to secure their respective legacies, like General Mercer. In "Right Hand Man," Washington notices Hamilton's eagerness to die for his cause and admonishes the young officer, saying that dying is easy, while living is harder. For all Hamilton's martial virtue, we are left to wonder whether he is virtuous for the sake of virtue itself, or for the sake of his reputation and legacy.

The Reynolds Pamphlet

"The Reynolds Pamphlet" is an ensemble piece that stands out against the rest of the music in the show. The song balances the style of contemporary gossip, replete with frequent uses of the two-syllable "day-um," against "highlights," from Hamilton's actual 1797 published pamphlet, "Observations on Certain Documents."

Through these contrasting styles, Miranda asks the audience to probe Hamilton's complicated psychology. Hamilton intends to clear his name of any charges of illegal activity, but in publishing a detailed account of his affair with Mrs. Reynolds he catalogues his *immoral* activity. The character Eliza, Hamilton's faithful and adoring wife, responds that in publishing Eliza's letters and telling the whole story of the affair, Hamilton cleared his name but ruined their lives.

So why, we are left to wonder, does this fiercest of politicians, obsessed with his own public reputation, go to such great lengths to prove himself an adulterer? It would seem that Hamilton cared more about how others judged his professional and political life than how they thought of his personal life. Hamilton figured that history was more concerned with his performance in public office than in his marriage. Given his permanent fixture as an American Founding Father, it seems that he was right.

Once again, Aristotle would express concern over Hamilton's interests here. In addition to the pain Hamilton had already caused his wife by engaging in the affair, he caused her even more by publicizing it. Is Hamilton clearing his name for the sake of honor itself? Or is he clearing his name so that others will perceive him as honorable?

The Duels

Hamilton's defense of "honor," if that's really what it is, takes on a lethal quality on the dueling ground. The play is bursting with the dueling theme: Laurens and Lee, Phillip and Eaker, and of course, the final duel between Hamilton and Burr. We may have even been given a hint of Hamilton's fate in "Satisfied."

Hamilton introduces himself to Angelica saying, "You're like me. I'm never satisfied . . . I have never been satisfied." The lyric is brilliant for its triple meaning. Angelica's initial rejoinder, "I'm sure I don't know what you mean. You forget yourself," gives Hamilton's line a sexual tone that foreshadows the oddly intimate relationship the brother- and sister-in-law would share in the following decades. The reference to satisfaction also probably alludes to Hamilton's explosive quill; writing "like he's running out of time." No matter what Hamilton's accomplishments may be, they are never enough to satisfy him.

But there is a third meaning as well. In "The Ten Duel Commandments," Laurens explains that the duel is a challenge that "demands satisfaction. If they apologize no need for further action." This reference to "satisfaction" in the dueling context alongside the reference with Angelica at the beginning of the play suggests that it was Hamilton's need for "satisfaction"—that is, to defend his personal honor at all costs—that led to his death.

In the end, we're left with Hamilton and Burr on the field of "honor," if that's really the right word for it, preparing for the duel. In the final honor-seeking contest of his life, Hamilton's priority scheme is not unfamiliar. In the Reynolds scandal, Hamilton caused additional pain to his family by publicizing his affair in order to save his good name (at least professionally). There is a similar dynamic here. In order to preserve his "honor," Hamilton is willing to sacrifice all, leaving his wife a widow and his children as fatherless as he was in his Caribbean youth. Once again, it's not Hamilton's love of honor itself, but rather his desperate need to have others bestow honor upon him, that drives his decisions—and this time, it brings him to an early grave.

Honor and Praise

We return to Aristotle—this time to his helpful distinction between honor and praise. Lots of things are praised, Aristotle argues, but "for the best things there is no praise, but something greater and better." This is real honor. So perhaps, for all Hamilton's strivings after honor, we find that he has, in fact, only sought after praise. But if Burr is also seeking after praise, what is the difference between Burr and Hamilton?

Burr spent his life trying to secure a legacy. So did Hamilton. Burr thought that his legacy would be best served in the military and in politics. So did Hamilton. Burr did his very best to safeguard his "good name" in the pursuit of these goals. So did Hamilton. The difference seems to be that Burr was mistaken about what would bring him lasting praise. Burr wanted to be "in the room where it happens," to get as close to the seat of power as possible. But Hamilton recognized that in the future—indeed hundreds of years in the future—we would celebrate the virtues of honor, courage, loyalty, integrity, and honesty.

Hamilton lashed his own future to that of the republic, as did Washington, Jefferson, Madison, and the other Founding Fathers. If the country succeeded, Hamilton would also succeed. If it failed, he would fail with it. Even though Hamilton secured for himself this lasting, though perhaps belated praise, he did so at some cost. On the "field of honor" with Burr, he won the badge of courage, but lost his life, liberty, and any possibility of pursuing happiness.

Aristotle identifies something higher than lasting praise. For him, the best thing is precisely that which Hamilton sacrificed: Happiness. Happiness for Aristotle is not a fleeting feeling or a passing reaction to one's circumstances. Aristotelian happiness is nothing less than fulfilling what it is to be human. It's not the life of pleasure, nor of honor. It's a life of virtue and not merely the appearance of virtue. It is made in deep and lasting friendships. It is the life of wisdom and moderation. It is life-long learning and the desire for understanding. It is excelling at that which is uniquely human. It is Aristotle's third life, not gratification nor honor, but *the life of contemplation.*

If neither Burr nor Hamilton can show us this kind of Aristotelian flourishing, where can we find it? Thankfully, there is another character in this historical drama who fits the bill. If we can't find human excellence in Hamilton, we must find it in His Excellency, the General. Washington plays the part of the Aristotelian virtuous sage to perfection. He has all the courage of Hamilton but all the discretion of Burr; all of Adams' love-of-country but all of Jefferson's understanding. There were some, specifically those who had served under Washington's command, who wished for the President to become a new monarch. Washington spurned these advances with a vengeance. Could Hamilton have passed on such a legacy?

In fact, it is Washington's strong hand on Hamilton's shoulder throughout their professional friendship that steadies the brash, young politician. Washington keeps Hamilton by his side for the sake of the country, despite Hamilton's demands for combat. Later, Washington convinces Hamilton to use diplomacy with Congress to get his debt plan passed. In "Stay Alive," Washington is willing to allow Lee and Conway to "rake his name through the mud" without complaint, recognizing that "history will prove them wrong," despite Hamilton's demands for "satisfaction" on the dueling field.

The absence of Washington's authoritative moderation after his death likely contributes to Hamilton's early end. Hamilton is no longer reined in by Washington's deliberating wisdom. Hamilton's anger, pride, and fierce defense of his legacy lead him to the dueling ground at Weehawken, never to return.

Miranda pulls from Washington's personal letters to give Washington these lines: "like the Scripture says: 'Everyone will sit under their own vine and fig tree and no one shall make them afraid.' They'll be safe in the nation we've made." And citing the final lines of Washington's historical 1796 farewell address almost verbatim, Washington sings "I promise myself to realize, the sweet enjoyment of partaking, in the midst of my fellow-citizens, the benign influence of good laws under a free government, the ever-favorite object of my heart." We can almost hear the echoes of Aristotle who wrote that "peace . . . is the end of war, and leisure of toil."

Hamilton wished for a war. Washington, like Aristotle, wished for peace. Hamilton was a great man and ought to be remembered as such, but, if you're looking for a role model who seeks war only for the better peace it promises, and who pursues honor for its own sake, you won't find it in Alexander Hamilton or Aaron Burr. Instead, look to the nation's foremost father and greatest patriot, George Washington.

3
Cyborgs in Revolutionary Manhattan

Maggie Jackson

If I were to call Alexander Hamilton, Secretary of the Treasury and Broadway sensation, a *cyborg*, you'd probably give me a weird look. When the word "cyborg" comes to mind for most people these days, they're more likely thinking of Iron Man's rocket-blasting hand cannons than the old white dude on the ten-dollar bill, or the young, Latino men who have played him onstage. None of those guys, as far as I'm aware, have ever been conclusively proven to be part robot. Yet.

"Cyborg" is a word out of science fiction, and not out of American history, right? A cyborg is "a cybernetic organism, a hybrid of machine and organism." So, to apply the word quite seriously, as I want to here, seems a bit counter-intuitive. But is it?

If we move past the flashy, shiny metal exoskeleton of the cyborg's popular image, there's a fascinating philosophical question in the existence of a creature that is part human and part machine, but never conclusively either of those things. Our society is structured around black-and-white binaries: man-woman, gay-straight, good-evil . . . and of course, human-machine.   *smart Bureaucrat*

Think of the story of John Henry and the steam drill, or the harrowing tale of Dave and HAL in *2001: A Space Odyssey*. Henry fought to show that man was still relevant in the age of the machine, and Dave simply tried to *survive* in a world controlled by machines. Hell, every time a computer is subjected to the Turing test, we must once again grapple with the discomforting idea that the technology we create is also creating *us*.

21

The very *existence* of the cyborg as something that is at once human *and* machine but also neither is, we might say, blasphemous. It's antithetical to the binary-centric point of view we are taught, and yet it exists. *We* exist.

Because, surprise! You, my friend, are a cyborg creature. Are you reading these words right now on your tablet screen? Your phone? Are you reading these words off of a page that I wrote on my computer, which was then sent via email to my editor, then submitted electronically to the publisher, who produced, shipped, and promoted this book via printers and vehicles and the Internet? Congratulations; the technologies through which you're encountering these words right now are inescapably a part of you—which means that you are a cyborg.

And if, simply in this act of reading, you are transgressing the boundary between human and machine that has been so widely understood as essential and inviolate, what might become of the other opposing forces that have shaped the way you understand yourself in relation to the world around you? If the walls that separate what you *are* from what you are *not* were never really walls at all but rather simply optical illusions, what, in the end, *are* you?

In the midst of this identity crisis, we find the cyborg as a useful philosophical figuration. In her "Manifesto for Cyborgs," Donna Haraway describes the cyborg as "about contradictions that do not resolve into larger wholes" and "about the tension of holding incompatible things together because both or all are necessary and true." Far beyond the RoboCops and Cybermen who are most easily recognized by the term today, Haraway's cyborg is a creature of irony, intimacy, and perversity. The cyborg is happy living as a contradiction in a world that is structured around clear-cut distinctions. We humans feel immobilized and panic-stricken because of our contradictions, and society tells us that if we're uncertain or conflicted, we shouldn't act or express ourselves. The cyborg, on the other hand, is free to express its complex self. It goes 'non-stop' in situations where we binary-centric humans are told to simply 'wait for it."

Fans of *Hamilton* are already familiar with the sort of conflict that brings about a cyborg. Alexander Hamilton, that bastard-orphan-hero-scholar, is certainly a cyborg, and throughout his story he encounters other characters who have varying levels of comfort with their own contradictory natures. The play *itself* is a hybrid product of historical fact and modern fiction. It's a story about some old dead white dudes told by a cast comprised almost entirely of young people of color. *Hamilton* takes references from all over the archive of American musical theater and from every corner of the densely-packed library of hip hop and rap. This cyborg is acted out live, night after night, for an audience of only a thousand people, and yet has become a cultural phenomenon whose scope reaches far beyond the four walls of the room where it happens.

Hamilton holds together multiplicities and cultural tensions intrinsic to American society, but does not seek to resolve those tensions. Instead, it gains its extraordinary energy from the fusion of seemingly incongruous ideas. *Hamilton* insists that something may be full of contradictions and still be worthy of attention. As a product of a society that increasingly cannot fit itself inside traditional understandings of who we are and where we come from, *Hamilton* suggests we may be able to live with the very real possibility that we will never be satisfied.

The Absent Made Present

The cyborg may be a constructed philosophical idea, but it is an idea born of lived experience, rather than mere academic speculation. In trying to get past how society forces our identities and experiences into false binaries, the cyborg is a consequence of "lived social relations," which are "our most important political construction, a world-changing fiction." In *Hamilton*, we see the men and women who created America drawn on a far more human scale than the monumental one that we're accustomed to. When Christopher Jackson stands before us as George Washington, an almost mythic figure, whose name has become synonymous with the notion of representative democracy itself, and attests to the uncertainty and loneliness, the pressure of leadership and the burden of history, he becomes an ordinary man dealing with extraordinary circumstances. His fears of death and dishonor are fears we all share.

For a country where systemic racism is an enormous and undeniable part of our history and our current political climate, seeing the foundational myth of the United States embodied by people of color is *essential*. It is a physical manifestation of that original, supposedly self-evident but oft-failed truth: that all are created equal. In *Hamilton,* the ideals of equality and freedom upon which America was founded transcend the ugly realities of our racist past and present. We're not so different, the casting of *Hamilton* asserts. We all want the same things.

And yet, at the same time and no less crucially, to have Christopher Jackson standing before us as George Washington reminds us, constantly and irrepressibly, of the deafening silence that exists and persists in how the story of America is so often told. Jackson may be inhabiting Washington with humanity and empathy, but his presence on the stage is a reminder that, had he been alive at the founding of our country, Christopher Jackson may have *lived* at Mount Vernon, but he would never have been the master there. The same is true of Daveed Diggs as Thomas Jefferson, when he name-checks the only historical person of color, Sally Hemmings, who is ever mentioned within the text of the play.

When we see these giants of history, so familiar from their monuments of white marble, being embodied by men that, had they been contemporaries, they very likely would have regarded as property, we cannot help but experience a tense, contradictory kind of double-vision. These men, who wrote and talked and fought so passionately for the ideals of life, liberty, and the pursuit of happiness were also the perpetrators of systemic racialized violence on a massive scale, leaving deep scars on the American psyche that trouble us still. The casting choices at work in *Hamilton* demand that we see and recognize both at the same time.

This essential, uncomfortable double vision is precisely where the cyborg lives. "Liberation," it argues, "rests on the construction of the consciousness, the imaginative apprehension, of oppression, and so of possibility." The lack of the perspectives from people of color in American history is still a problem today. Having these famous white figures from history embodied onstage by people of color allows the ideals upon which the country was founded to transcend the thorny and divisive issues of race and racial difference, while also making it impossible and irresponsible to ignore the absence of people of color from those founding myths. Seeing in *Hamilton* the lack of diverse narratives in our founding myths, we can understand the oppression that is still being perpetrated through this historical silence.

As the cyborg tells us, there's always possibility in the recognition of oppression. While it sucks to recognize that the history we think we know is so full of violence and the silence that comes from the suppression of non-white voices, hearing those voices raised in *Hamilton* might help us to imagine a future in which the delineations of race that plague America still could dissolve, while still not ignoring their current reality. The cyborg founders shown to us by *Hamilton* demand that we hold the reality of continued racial inequality in America and the concomitant historical silence together with the ideals of freedom and equality upon which the United States of America was founded. Because both are necessary, and both are true.

Two Traditions in Balance

A balance of conflicting ideas is essential to understanding the music in *Hamilton*, which is built out of two wholly American traditions that have diametrically opposed racial histories. The rich and complex archives of American musical theater are referenced *heavily,* with allusions to everything from traditional musicals like *South Pacific* and *The Producers* to off-Broadway hits like *The Last Five Years.* Lin-Manuel Miranda's love of both historical and contemporary musical theater are evident in every second of *Hamilton*'s lyrics and score. Similarly, his intricate stylistic and lyrical references to rap and hip-hop artists from Sir Mix-a-Lot to Mobb Deep to Lauryn Hill give nuance and complexity to the plot and characterization, for those in the know. *Hamilton* occupies the unprecedented spotlight that it enjoys partly because of the seeming contradiction of a hip-hop musical. A contradiction that is a direct result of the separation of music preferences along racial lines.

We as a culture look at the racial segregation in music, between hip hop and musical theater, and we falsely conclude that the experiences of white people and people of color are somehow mutually-exclusive. But *Hamilton*'s very popularity seems to contradict that conclusion. The music in *Hamilton* is not mainstreamed or watered down, nor does it lose its generic integrity for being used in a way that might be considered outside of its original context. "My Shot" is no less an "I Want" song for being an impressively verbose and erudite rap, just as the

Cabinet Meetings are no less rap battles for establishing an important second-act conflict.

Hamilton is both steeped in the history of hip hop and faithful to the traditions of American musical theater, but it would be impossible to reduce it to either one of these genres. Rather, the musical styles work together to increase the depth and complexity of the story and characters, drawing from traditions that are *both* quintessentially American, even though they are so often painted as contradictory. In telling the story of the founding of America, the histories and traditions of *all* Americans are included as true.

Both Human and Digital

Alexander Hamilton and so many of the other characters of *Hamilton* are cyborgs. They may not have cool bionic arms (except for maybe Hercules Mulligan?) or even the ability to access the Internet via their phones, but they are creatures of contradiction. And we who encounter them would not be able to do so without being cyborgs, ourselves. If you stood me in the middle of Times Square and told me to find my way to the Richard Rogers Theater, I would not have even the first idea of which way to go without getting out my phone, because I have never actually been there. I haven't been among the thousands of people who have crowded around to see the Ham4Ham shows in hopes of winning the ticket lottery, and I certainly don't have the kind of Beyoncé-level influence that it currently takes to get an actual *seat* in the actual *room* where *Hamilton* happens. I am, in this regard, the very Burr-est of Aaron Burrs.

And yet, I know every word to every song, even "Congratulations," and that one isn't even *in* the show anymore. If I were to see Renée-Elise Goldsberry or Phillipa Soo or Leslie Odom, Jr. walking (inexplicably) down the street in the little Middle-American town where I currently reside, I would likely recognize them and freak out accordingly. How? Have I some sort of witch-magic specific only to theater? Am I just a very geeky kind of psychic? I mean, that'd be really cool, but in reality, it is of course just the fact that I have access to the Internet that allows my fannish devotion to everything *Hamilton* to be so complete, even from halfway across a continent.

The fact that this particular Broadway show is such a big deal, and the reason that the tensions and contradictions inherent in its performance and writing are so provocative, is because of the technologies of dissemination that people like me can use to access the play, which might have once existed only as an exclusive, in-person experience. Recordings of the Ham4Ham shows that the cast performed for months outside the theater in New York found their way to YouTube, where avid fans who had already consumed the cast album waited hungrily for more content.

Tweets and Snapchats and online interviews from the cast allowed those of us who couldn't see the show live to experience, in some small way, a mediated version of the immediacy and intimacy that is most easily found in live theater. As the play gained traction and notoriety, in no small part due to the success of its cast album, more people began to seek out these little bits of second-hand "live-ness," which in turn caused the demand for tickets for physical seats in New York to steadily increase. *Hamilton* may have started out as only a play—the kind of entertainment that is experienced exclusively live and in-person—but social media, streaming, and the other far-reaching affordances of the technologies that make cyborgs of us all have made it into a cultural touchstone like no other musical in history. *Hamilton* simply wouldn't be *Hamilton* without the Internet.

The contradictions continue, though. Theatrical productions that are performed by real, breathing human beings every night for a different crowd of other real, breathing human beings are never the same twice, while the cast album that I play over and over again on my iPod remains technically the same upon each new encounter. The recorded Ham4Ham shows that I can watch on YouTube may have captured one moment of spontaneous energy and give me some approximation of the feeling of seeing the performance live, but upon each new viewing I will be able to anticipate the progression of events, thereby eliminating that original frisson of "live-ness."

Just as *Hamilton* would not have become the phenomenon that it is without the technologies that has extended its influence so broadly, the fact that it is, fundamentally, a theatrical production is essential to the dynamism and energy that keep those of us who love the story searching for yet another new way to experience it.

Hamilton is both a play and an album, an in-person experience and a media phenomenon, so it can be universal in the reach of its message, the energy of its music, and the conviction of its performances. The contradictory energy of *Hamiton* can spread through the synapses of the cyborg's mediated nervous system, allowing even those who will never be able to experience the play in-person the chance to be profoundly impacted. At the same time, the mutable, ever-changing nature of live theater ensures that, even for the most devoted *Hamilton* aficionado, there will always be a new, different performance to experience. The cyborg-like melding of human experience and digital conveyance expands and reinforces the integrity of the room where it happens.

The Wide-Enough World

"Blasphemy," the cyborg insists, "has always seemed to require taking things very seriously." If *Hamilton* is blasphemous in its embrace of its own contradictions, its refusal to fit neatly into the boxes of "Broadway" or "hip hop," "recorded" or "in-person," "truth" or "fiction," it is because it gains its incredibly impactful energy from the sincerity with which it treats its contradictory elements. Instead of simply asserting as fact the history of America, *Hamilton* insists that we acknowledge the absences and silences in the story we often choose to tell about this country. It insists that we recognize the irony of a "land of the free" that has also been the home of slaves, while at the same time embracing wholeheartedly the American dream that we might all be able to rise up and leave our fingerprints, no matter how lowly or insignificant we might at first appear.

The language of *Hamilton* is steeped in the histories of two fundamentally American musical forms, embracing and honoring the complexity of each, blending them together in such a way as to elevate both without ever insisting that one give way to the other. The popularity Hamilton has gained through the technologies of distribution and social media democratizes the experience of live theater, while the show itself is constantly dynamic and evolving, ensuring that, from one night to another and in every new online video the world of *Hamilton* will never be the same.

We don't live in a world where anything at all is easy to define. And that is, in no small part, because we're cyborgs. The phone in my pocket, on which I can read the Constitution, or watch the VMAs, or feverishly check one more time that tickets to the Chicago production haven't gone on sale yet, opens up the possibility of a world where *my* truth is not *the* truth.

Since I am a cyborg, whenever those contradictions, that tension, the irreconcilable perversity of parts that don't resolve into wholes gets to be too overwhelming, I can simply put in my headphones, close my eyes, and let *Hamilton* remind me that I will never be satisfied.

And that might be okay.

4

That's Edutainment!

Myron Moses Jackson

Alexander Hamilton is one of the most exceptional and controversial of American heroes. Ron Chernow's 2004 biography and Lin-Manuel Miranda's brilliantly successful 2015 musical have now put Hamilton's historical legacy at the center of national awareness.

From performances at the White House to receiving all the top accolades in the arts and humanities circles, including being nominated the most times ever at the Tony Awards, *Hamilton: An American Musical* has given historians, artists, political scientists, sociologists, and the rest of us much to rethink and reconsider.

Renewed interest in Hamilton's life is not that surprising once we consider how essential the role of symbolic adornment is for American consciousness and discourses. If anything is certain in our agitated climate of "liquid modernity" (a term popularized by philosopher-sociologist Zygmunt Bauman) it is the *difficult* realization that none of our precious cultural forms—not even history—are untouchable or immune from our passion to be meddlesome, as a means to cultivate uniqueness or novelty.

For this reason, *Hamilton* is an example of what I call "novel hybrids." Creations such as *Hamilton* intertwine pop cultural themes with a classical aesthetic form like a musical and may only be categorized or checked off in a box labeled "Other." The dynamic intermixing of identity and symbolization of novel hybrids highlights the ironic tension between American life and identity, compared to the symbolic capital America sells to the world. *Hamilton* is a child of our cultural atmosphere. It speaks to our social infrastructure that will demand shifts in the way we must re-think education and the flexibility of cultural norms.

Sincere cultural lessons come through when we're brought into contact with "counter-ignorant systems." Humans naturally develop blind spots as members of a group or class. People develop systems to take advantage of human nature, so that individuals remain intentionally ignorant of others as "foreign" or "sub"-cultures. Cultural purists or experts who suffer from this kind of prideful hysteria work to censor the kind of open-ended breeding that *Hamilton* creates and symbolizes. American identity in the twenty-first century is still haunted by a diseased racial consciousness, including blind hatreds, often rooted in extremist ideological creeds. Most American prisons, cities, and schools remain self-segregated. Given how various social conditions shape the US, the importance of entertainment cannot be overlooked in maintaining the pluralism that Americans claim to value so highly.

I interpret edutainment as partaking in cultural rituals, in ways that allow for freedom and do not press for an over-investment of selves as participants or spectators. The sharing of culture occurs more through cross-breeding of high and low cultures spawning novel hybrids as forms of edutainment. When it comes to touting an orientation toward the world as open, many exaggerate the extent to which they live out a commitment to the love of freedom. How Americans actually live and socialize may be misconstrued, given the richness of its varied symbols and values. Appearances often do not match the realities. Racial animosities persist more in Americans' actual experience, but ironically less in their virtual integration.

The Revolutionary Revival

The irony of a work like *Hamilton* lies in its Jeffersonian style—something that reflects the particular time and generation of the people for which it is performed. Jefferson's political savvy to tap into the "streets" or rumor-mill and gossip of sex, lies, and scandals of corruption, along with his secret relationship with Sally Hemings, speaks more to the infotainment trends spreading throughout global cultures.

Perhaps Miranda's *Hamilton* is a similar feat pulled off by America's first great "copier and paster" or redactor of the modern age, which resulted in Thomas Jefferson's Bible. Jefferson threw out what was not necessary and only left the essentials in the message of the gospels. As Peter Sloterdijk suggests, redaction allows us to discover the usable in the unusable: "In his scissor-work, the redactor must have been convinced that he possessed the criteria by which to distinguish the utilizable from the non-utilizable in the bequeathed text." In other words, we need not be believers any more but can merely be sympathizers. *Hamilton* is a portrayal of what is essential to the revolutionary roots of America and it is not property-owning white males with a specific hereditary!

This kind of novel hybrid forces introspection. That is the educational advantage that novel hybrids offer over singular types of art, history, politics, and other forms of experience. No art tradition is unquestionably superior or without need of reconsideration, but something special emerges from the entwinement of anemic types that are brought together and resuscitated in public consciousness.

It's no wonder that Miranda's production has single-handedly brought a spark to lagging cultural traditions. Historians, curators, librarians—it is difficult to tell who has benefited most from *Hamilton's* power of revival. Novel hybrids perform a resuscitating function for flagging art forms. They bridge together history and class or social status in uncanny ways. With a more fluid exhibition the purity of form is evaporated and our traditional sense of art criticism are no longer relevant. As a way of reawakening a desire for learning, schools and teachers have raved about taking students to *Hamilton*. Keeping today's hyper-absorbed students focused on historical events is a tall order. Educators are encouraged to find lures such as *Hamilton* that tap onto rituals that engage students.

Openness through Art

Appropriating our experiences through entertainment fosters an imaginative free play between our actual and possible selves. Entertainment involves the *transmission of feelings*. The effect goes below the level of consciousness, but not below the level of imagination. Imagination trades on feeling, as well as conscious decision. There is hope that more people will be able to resonate with the suffering of others through empathy and imagination.

We can develop social capital through the cathartic powers of entertainment. The ritual provides an emotional cleansing and possibly even a sense of fulfillment. People usually speak of music as therapeutic and certainly it can be, but there is more. Entertainment stimulates discourses and activities. It generates the symbols and interpretations that can help to ease social apathy and ignorance.

Experiencing entertainment calls for recognizing the inherent limitations in our own views. Those who are entertained may not experience a conscious alteration, but the ritual itself alters the culture. Americans, regardless of differences in backgrounds and talents, can contribute to entertainment rituals and cultural hybrids.

Despite self-segregating attitudes, American domestic trends don't provide a complete picture of our social relations and social spaces. In our homes and gadgets we interact with others as virtualized selves, at mediated distances. Sports, music, or movies have become a hallmark of the fabric of cultural identity along with the possibility for diversity in our cultural forms. The entertainment rituals act as conduits for the cultural pluralism we are so anxious to achieve. It is through these mediums that most people, including minorities, are open and tolerant in ways they do not otherwise tend to be. Entertainment helps us achieve our goals of openness and a liberty.

A New Man for a New World

The dramatic form allows for possibilities to be entertained according to a plethora of aesthetic rhythms. As philosopher Alfred North Whitehead famously wrote, "it is more important that a proposition be interesting, than that it be true. The importance of truth is, that it adds to interest."

This quest for novelty is given a very high premium in American events, especially in the hype surrounding them. Our infatuation with valuing the new over past mediums of education and entertainment produces two effects. First, a kind of "tyranny of the moment" dominates the scene, with a social prejudice looking for what's "cool" or hip. Novel forms of familiar cultural artifacts have strong appeal and add to the levels of loyalty and intensity consumers have already established with existing songs, movies, product brands names, and so on.

As more of our political exchanges and rhetoric take on those aspects of infotainment associated with celebrity and sensationalism, perhaps *Hamilton* serves both functions in an interesting manner. Caught in the first sex scandal in American politics along with the rivalries that ensued is nothing if not good TV. James Callender's "investigative" journalism, which led to Hamilton's hasty public response, was the first major lesson in how gossip and media innuendo would be a guiding force for American politics. Hamilton's "social media" response was not well received and became a matter of public ridicule. The circumstances around Hamilton's life, even more so than Jefferson's, helped to fuel that lustful American pastime of watching the dramatic scandals of our leaders or stars unfold! The *Saturday Night Live* spoof was a desirable replacement of the duel to settle the "beef" of these types of episodic minidramas. Novel hybrid entertainment cultivates a persuasive agency like the kind conveyed in the pamphlets and *Federalist Papers*. Entertainment has become a leading source of education and self-understanding for our age. In his famous *The Letter to D'Alembert on the Theater* Rousseau writes that the value of spectacle or "entertainment" is too often ridiculed and misinterpreted for moral, religious, and other inhibitive purposes.

Hamilton has been chastised for its exaggeration and lack of accuracy, but to merely glean its meaning from this narrow exactness will miss the unique attractiveness and cultural intensity this hip-hop musical taps into. How much should a work of culture align with the accepted historical record of events is undeniably fascinating. Regardless of how one judges this question, it is equally undeniable that perhaps no group has more to be thankful for this festive American event than the historians themselves. Our narrow and incubated cultural attitudes and experiences will be tested under a relativized, custom-designed pragmatism.

Never Gonna Be History

It seems premature to write off *Hamilton* as a failed form of art, history, politics, or as an ill-suited portrayal of critical race and gender theories. *Hamilton's* motivations lie in the cultural diffusion and pluralism that it promotes as a novel hybrid—not a political message of liberal tolerance or post-racial euphoric societies.

The musical *Hamilton* is much more than a great work of art or visionary piece of interpretive history, it is a monumental shift in the cultural terrain of how we "remix" familiar and widely known symbols. Each form and class is brought to an uncomfortable confrontation with the other, for the sake of mutual growth and relatedness. Like that vexing power of food, the rituals in which we are willing to laugh and cry together with strangers has become the ultimate classroom or public academy, in our age of hyper-cinema and transmedia rituals.

What makes *Hamilton* unique is how it weaves together rituals and identities, which would have been historically impossible. It is as if our social expectations have been destroyed through a great flood, and the permanence of the separation of high and low cultures is no longer divinely sealed. The social distance between the stage and the cheap seats has shrunk. Miranda has ushered in an epoch of novel hybrids that will encourage cultural artifacts rooted in montage and synthesizing processes.

Hip-hop opera as history resonates with an age built on the nuances of edutainment. Novel hybrids as cultural recreations also make us *re-think* the ways we categorize genres or historical methods. Hybridized cultural objects and processes become liberating forms of self-examination and knowledge.

American power has not prospered by means of building banks or military-industrial complexes, but by embracing the ancient rituals of the amphitheater—circuses, modern stadiums, baseball fields, and multiplexes. It is ironically those social conditions that Hamilton found most repulsive and threatening, which have become the chief virtues of American enterprise. Although this may easily seem tragic from a traditional perspective, there are really deeper ironic relations that this kind of inversion speaks to.

Democratically free nations are always more exposed and must face the free-play of hidden or unforeseen relations that explicitly deny ultimate legitimacy to what I call a "privileged observer." That is federalism in a nutshell! Divided or decentralized government is much more than checks and balances or separation of powers—these are merely legal and political concerns. For the wider purposes of cultural value, federalism works to resist that false pretense of superiority of quality or judgment. This is not only the case for philosophers, historians, and presidents, but also for art critics especially.

Embracing Edutainment

It is high time we promote edutainment as a cornerstone of the American character and the possibilities it presents are vital to our global development and thriving. Miranda's *Hamilton* reveals the novel and intermeshing ways we retell the stories of the past.

It was never fashionable, not even in circles of historians, to contend that President Lincoln was gay, until poet Carl Sandburg's 1926 biography. Similar to the Jefferson-inspired Reynolds affair, that led Hamilton to grab his pen too quickly and presume to know what his audience of accusers wanted to hear, we have become a people obsessed with gossip and scandalous politics when it comes to sex, corruption, or conspiracies. Ours is a time of historical re-appropriation under a cultural fervor saturated in futuristic whims.

With any eye toward futuristic possibilities, we see ourselves as unbound from the shackles of traditional expectations. No dominant structures or forms are required for any media to conform to, whether one seeks to promote conservative or progressive tendencies. Cultural novel hybrids able to negotiate this ideological terrain will have a better chance to reach wider groups for whatever reason others find interesting and worthwhile. Anyone who is able to spread this kind of cultural literacy acts as a kind of persuasive agency, in a manner similar to the project carried out in *The Federalist Papers*. These performances have the capacity to teach and learn with the audience, as a collective recreation that serves as some of the most effective and impactful means for large democratic societies.

It's a mistake to consider or even debate the issue of whether a new-age musical should be interpreted as theater or history, political, economic, or otherwise. Identities and values are being intermixed between the characters in a story of new possibilities, which are symbolized to convey new and interesting meanings that compel us to re-think our interpretations of what it means to be an ironic American. No genuine reason exists to deny that the Founding Fathers could have been women or people of color. The uniqueness of the cast and performance brings us to that fundamental human condition: that we are the animal destined to *entertain* the impossible in the midst of what is.

Nations may be able to *coerce* others politically, economically or religiously, but they will only be able to *persuade* culturally—that is, be accepted or rejected solely on the merits of an individual's preferences regardless of influence or agenda. Entertainment is the vessel that serves this aim. It is highly conscious, but ritualized as a vehicle used to symbolize one's love of freedom; to engage through entertainment means that it may or may not contribute anything to the value of the individual, but it can add to the collective worth.

Edutainment has captured our "interest," even if you have never seen the show. Its cultural value is without question. Critics have bemoaned that the musical is "pure fantasy" and there is some truth to this appraisal. But such outright praise or condemnations misses the way these cultural artifacts serve as harsh or unbearable lessons. They may send you a strong revelation that the post-racial society and consciousness we often like to speak of is still a fictionalized American dreamland.

Creating novel hybrids is not an innocent, romantic endeavor—it entails the exploitation of high and low cultural themes for its own gain. *Hamilton* is a symbol of American *potential* for respect, generosity, and openness to the dignity of vanquished people. Its major message is that the vanguards of freedom are manifest when the "illegitimate" become legitimate.

II

Self-Made
Greatness

5
Megalomaniac or Megalopsychos?

Jason T. Eberl

Fans of Lin-Manuel Miranda's historical musical masterpiece *Hamilton* know all about fourteen-year-old Alexander Hamilton's confession that he wished there was a war. In the musical, Hamilton repeats this wish in his first meeting with Aaron Burr, after learning they're both orphans ("Aaron Burr, Sir").

War ensues, and both Hamilton and Burr prove themselves courageous and honorable on the battlefield. Later, they become political rivals, as their friendship devolves around Hamilton's idealism versus Burr's self-serving pragmatism. Hamilton's idealism might be considered self-serving as well, as he clearly seeks glory both on the battlefield and as part of the inaugural presidential cabinet.

In "Cabinet Battle #1," Thomas Jefferson complains about Hamilton's centralizing financial plan, "Now place your bets as to who that benefits—the very seat of government where Hamilton sits." A champion of the rights of individual states, Jefferson doesn't want to see a powerful federal government, with a potentially tyrannical Treasury Secretary, in control of everyone's financial fate. Jefferson's accusation that Hamilton is power-hungry is not without foundation; yet, Hamilton's power-grab didn't necessarily spring from self-serving motives. As Chernow reports in his biography of Hamilton, even when in control of the national army, Hamilton resisted the temptation voiced by Burr to use its power to take over the government, claiming that to do so would be immoral. Burr counters that "all things are moral to great souls."

The classical Greek philosopher Aristotle (385–422 B.C.E.), in his writings on ethics and politics, recognizes the existence of a type of person who is "great-souled"—or *proud*—and whose talents and abilities go beyond those of his fellow human beings: the *megalopsychos*. In his *Nicomachean Ethics*, Aristotle describes the *megalopsychos* as fundamentally "concerned with great things" and as someone who "thinks himself worthy of great things, being worthy of them." The danger faced by the *megalopsychos* is becoming so disconnected from society that others can only relate to him in one of two mutually exclusive ways: they either worship him as "a God among men," or exile him as a threat to their way of life. This danger becomes acute if the *megalopsychos*, puffed up by excessive pride, places his talents and abilities at the service of his own ends and not the greater good, thereby becoming a *megalomaniac*: a person merely obsessed with his own power.

Looking for a Mind at Work

Angelica Schuyler and her sisters are prowling the streets of New York City, looking to meet young idealistic revolutionaries. Angelica's well-bred, intelligent, and a beguiling charmer. She eventually meets Hamilton and their conversation immediately sparks her attraction, having found someone at her own level to match wits with ("Satisfied"). She, of course, surrenders her infatuation to the love of her "helpless" sister, Eliza. But what was it about Hamilton that so attracted her initially, evolving into a lifelong exchange of intimate letters that sometimes involved "comma sexting," as Miranda calls it? If Angelica were looking for a "great-souled man," what was it she saw in this "bastard orphan" from "a forgotten spot in the Caribbean"?

We noted earlier that Aristotle describes the *megalopsychos* as believing himself to be "worthy of great things." This is the essence of *pride*. Pride is often thought to be a *vice*—a negative character trait one ought to avoid. Aristotle, however, considers pride, appropriately defined, as a *virtue*—a character trait one ought to strive to cultivate.

Earlier in his *Nicomachean Ethics*, Aristotle defines virtue as "a mean between two vices, one involving excess, the other deficiency," oriented towards "what is intermediate in passions and in actions." Consider one of Aristotle's favorite examples: *courage*. A courageous person is neither a coward nor rash. General Charles Lee betrays his deficiency of courage when "he shits the bed at the Battle of Monmouth" ("Stay Alive"), ordering his men to retreat when Washington wants him to press the attack. This led to a rare outburst of angry cursing on the part of the usually reserved and well-mannered Washington, calling Lee a "damned poltroon"—even Lafayette was taken aback!

Hamilton's friend John Laurens, on the other hand, falls victim to his "intrepidity bordering on rashness," as Washington once described him, when he violates orders and is struck down leading an ambush against a superior British force that wasn't even engaged in combat. Laurens threw away his life in an inconsequential battle that occurred after the main fighting of the Revolution had already concluded. To be clear, the courageous person isn't fearless, but rather feels an appropriate amount of fear consistent with a desire for self-preservation. Nevertheless, they're willing to risk their life for the sake of the greater good when a prudent assessment of the situation gives confidence that they can actually achieve their objective. Washington's leadership, Hamilton's ingenuity, Mulligan's espionage, and Lafayette's "practical tactical brilliance" augment their collective courage throughout the Revolution to realize its dramatic conclusion at the Battle of Yorktown.

Each of these courageous patriots can thus be deservedly prideful, feeling an appropriate degree of merit for the good they've accomplished. As a virtue, pride is contrasted with another virtue, *temperance*, characterizing a person whose deeds are of little merit and who appropriately thinks oneself to merit little. Eliza exemplifies this virtue insofar as her personal accomplishments, while of great merit, don't rise to the level of her husband's and she thus appropriately says about herself, "I have never been the type to try and grab the spotlight" ("Helpless"). In the half-century following Hamilton's death, Eliza kept shifting the spotlight thrust upon her to her husband's legacy and the revolutionaries who fought at his side.

A person who lacks pride has the vice of *undue humility*, thinking himself, Aristotle says, to be "worthy of less than he is really worth." Washington seems to toe this line by sometimes undervaluing his importance as a leader, both when he confesses his early military failures to Hamilton and especially when he decides not to run for a third term as President; as we'll see, though, his leaving the presidency actually exhibits greater virtue than Hamilton may have been capable of mustering.

Finally, having too much pride leads to the vice of *vanity*, when, as Aristotle puts it, someone "thinks himself worthy of great things, being unworthy of them." Burr's obsession to "be in the room where it happens" fosters his opportunism. Switching political parties in order to attain Philip Schuyler's senate seat, along with his personal maxim not to "let them know what you're against or what you're for," demonstrates Burr's constant striving after offices that arguably go beyond his abilities or merit. Rather than conduct an honest self-examination after losing the presidency to Jefferson, Burr externalizes the blame towards Hamilton, asserting that, looking back on his failures, the common thread was Hamilton's disrespect ("Your Obedient Servant"). Burr proclaims, just before their fatal duel, "This man has poisoned my political pursuits!" ("The World Was Wide Enough"). Not taking accountability for your own failures or weaknesses is the essence of vanity.

Throwing Verbal Rocks

In his *Posterior Analytics*, Aristotle cites Socrates as an example of a *megalopsychos*, whose well-deserved pride is exhibited at his trial when, facing either death or a more reasonable counter-sentence he may propose, Socrates proclaims that he deserves to be fed for the rest of his life in the finest Athenian restaurant where Olympic victors are normally fêted. Striking a similar, and assuredly self-referential note, Hamilton writes in *The Federalist No. 36*,

> There are strong minds [another way of translating *megalopsychos*] in every walk of life that will rise superior to the disadvantages of situation and will command the tribute due to their merit . . .

Does Hamilton measure up to Aristotle's description of such a person?

The chief trait of the virtuously proud person is they're concerned foremost with *honor*, but only, Aristotle notes, "in accordance with their deserts." As Chernow records, Hamilton once described himself as possessing a love of fame, the ruling passion of the noblest minds, which would prompt a man to plan and undertake extensive and arduous enterprises for the public benefit.

He was extremely self-aware of his natural gifts and talents and didn't refrain from proclaiming them: "I probably shouldn't brag, but dag, I amaze and astonish. . . . My power of speech: unimpeachable" ("My Shot"). Yet, he maintained a forward-thinking aim to use his abilities to further the common good, shown in his genuine concern to improve the country's finances. Finally, Chernow notes Hamilton's admission that he engaged in the duel with Burr in order to maintain his public reputation so that he might be in a position to serve America's needs in the future.

Though concerned primarily with honor, the virtuously proud person only seeks honor bestowed by those equally virtuous, disdaining honors bestowed by, as Aristotle describes, "casual people" or based on "trifling grounds." Though Hamilton was extremely sensitive to public violations of his honor—once throwing out two dueling challenges the same day—he disregarded any insults due to his support for unpopular laws he deemed necessary, such as the excise tax on whiskey that led to a violent rebellion in western Pennsylvania. He counsels Burr to focus more on his legacy than upon the fickleness of common opinion ("The Room Where It Happens"). Later in his life, Chernow records, Hamilton tells Washington that "It is long since I have learnt to hold popular opinion of no value." While exceedingly concerned about how honorable men like Washington view him, Hamilton has little regard for the often-shifting and ill-founded views of the masses.

Meriting honor from virtuous equals presumes that you are indeed a person of good character yourself. Aristotle claims that "the proud man, since he deserves the most, must be good in the highest degree." Hamilton fails to rise, however, to the highest level of virtue. Although innocent of the accusation that he engaged in financial speculation with public funds, Hamilton nevertheless disgraced himself by his affair with Maria Reynolds. In his admission to his political foes, he distinguishes his public virtue from his private moral turpitude: he has failed in private morality but not in public service ("We Know"). Hamilton's affair leads to disastrous consequences for both his political career and domestic tranquility when he

publishes his ill-considered confession in the infamous
Reynolds Pamphlet.

In this defensive diatribe, Hamilton reveals the tragic flaw
of his character, stemming from the same foundation as his
virtue: "I wrote my way out . . . I picked up a pen, I wrote my
own deliverance" ("Hurricane"). This is the essence of *hubris*,
which Aristotle, in his *Poetics*, considers the fulcrum upon
which dramatic tragedy turns. According to Aristotle, in
tragedies "the change in the subject's fortunes must be not
from bad fortune to good, but on the contrary from good to bad;
and the cause of it must lie not in any depravity, but in some
great fault on his part." As Angelica surmises, like the equally
hubristic and ill-fated Icarus, Hamilton had "flown too close to
the sun," and so his fall was his own fault ("Burn").

Hamilton embodies many other qualities Aristotle attrib-
utes to the virtuously proud person; yet he still falls short in
several ways. For instance, Aristotle states that the *megalopsychos*, while not fond of danger, will "face great dangers, and
when he is in danger he is unsparing of his life, knowing that
there are conditions on which life is not worth having."

Hamilton's courage in battle is indisputable, as exhibited by
his and Hercules Mulligan's securing cannons before they
could be taken by the British, with Hamilton running back
under fire to retrieve his musket. He was described once,
Chernow notes, as possessing "a sort of frenzy of valor," which
served him well when he led his troops to storm a British
redoubt during the Battle of Yorktown. Chernow describes a
dramatic scene in which "Hamilton, hopping on the shoulder of
a kneeling soldier, sprang onto the enemy parapet and sum-
moned his men to follow." Unfortunately, the musical's choreography doesn't depict this particular display of bravado.

Aristotle further describes the *megalopsychos* as generous in
conferring benefits, but "is ashamed of receiving them; for the one
is the mark of a superior, the other of an inferior." From an early
age, Hamilton had learned the need to be *self-reliant*. When he
did benefit from others' largesse, such as when local businessmen
in St. Croix started a fund to send him to be educated, it wasn't
out of pity but rather as an investment in "a young man, of great
renown" who had proven himself talented through his post-hur-
ricane essay. In turn, the later prosperous Hamilton was generous to friends or relatives in need, which ironically contributed to

his downfall as his affair with Maria Reynolds began when she entreated him and he "gave her thirty bucks that I had socked away" ("Say No to This"). Even virtues, when taken in isolation and not in concert with others virtues—such as *prudence* or *temperance*—can sometimes lead to bad actions.

One key trait of the "great-souled man" that Hamilton lacks, however, is the *self-awareness* and attendant *humility* to refrain from activities at which others excel and, as Aristotle describes, "to be a man of few deeds, but of great and notable ones." Hamilton strove to excel in every possible way he could, even when it might not have constituted the best use of his gifts and talents. When Washington approaches Hamilton to be his secretary, Hamilton balks that he'd rather "fight, not write" even though his "skill with a quill" is undisputed ("A Winter's Ball"). Although he proved himself to be a capable and valiant soldier, Hamilton too narrowly focused on military glory as the path to honor, telling Washington, "If you gave me command of a battalion. A group of men to lead, I could fly above my station after the war" ("Meet Me Inside"). Hamilton's overstepping of bounds continued in Washington's cabinet when he involved himself in establishing diplomatic relations with Great Britain before Jefferson had assumed his post as Secretary of State, the latter having to remind Hamilton in "Cabinet Battle #2" that he doesn't hold that office.

Hamilton also falls short of the great-souled individual when it comes to forgiving those who wrong him. Aristotle contends that "It is not the part of a proud man to have a long memory, especially for wrongs, but rather to overlook them." Hamilton had a quick temper when confronted by slights against his public honor and a long memory for grudges, sending Burr "an itemized list of thirty years of disagreements" ("Your Obedient Servant"). Yet, he could forgive people for the sake of important goals. At the start of the Revolution, he stood in front of a mob intending violence against the Tory—meaning loyal to Great Britain—head of King's College, exhibiting his conviction, as Chernow phrases it, of "the superiority of forgiveness over revolutionary vengeance." After the war, Hamilton defended the legal rights of Tories against what he, as related by Chernow, termed the "little vindictive selfish mean passions" of those who couldn't see the long-term benefits of adopting a more forgiving stance.

With respect to speech, Aristotle states that the *megalopsy-chos* is not a gossip and "not an evil-speaker, even about his enemies, except from haughtiness"—in other words, the virtuously proud person will not lob petty insults, but give voice only to valid criticisms of others. Hamilton's polemics fall short in this area, telling the loyalist Samuel Seabury, "My dog speaks more eloquently than thee! But strangely, your mange is the same" ("Farmer Refuted"). Later, he publicly calls President John Adams a "fat mother—[BLEEP]er" ("The Adams Administration").

Under the protection of pseudonyms, Hamilton traded public insults readily with his political enemies. Even Jefferson laments, "We smack each other in the press, and we don't print retractions. I get no satisfaction witnessing his fits of passion" ("Washington on Your Side"). In his later years, Hamilton apparently regrets his ill-mannered loquaciousness; Chernow relays Hamilton's advice to his son James, "A prudent silence will frequently be taken for wisdom and a sentence or two cautiously thrown in will sometimes gain the palm of knowledge, while a man well informed but indiscreet and unreserved will not uncommonly talk himself out of all consideration and weight." It sounds like Hamilton finally took to heart some of the good aspects of Burr's advice.

Hamilton's quick-wittedness, while fun to watch as he rap-battles Thomas Jefferson, represents the opposite temperament Aristotle accords the virtuous: "a slow step is thought proper to the proud man, a deep voice, and a level utterance; for the man who takes few things seriously is not likely to be hurried, nor the man who thinks nothing great to be excited, while a shrill voice and a rapid gait are the results of hurry and excitement."

Upon arriving in New York, Hamilton immediately seeks "an accelerated course of study" ("Aaron Burr, Sir"), and is described at that time, Chernow relates, as walking "with a buoyant lightness, and his observant, flashing eyes darted about with amusement." His demeanor doesn't change as he grows older. Chernow records descriptions of Hamilton's "courtroom theatrics" as he appears to be "agitated with intense reflection . . . His lips were in constant motion and his pen rapidly employed . . ." At his peak, he puts forth prodigious effort and speed in publicizing his opinions about the new US Constitution—writing "non-stop" like he's "running out of time." By contrast, Washington exhibits the prudential deliberateness Aristotle commends. Chernow, in his biography of Washington, records Hamilton reporting that the first President "consulted much, pondered much; resolved slowly, resolved surely."

Speaking of physical appearances, Hamilton can also be faulted for his *vanity*, fastidiously adorning himself with fine clothing and outward display, which Aristotle derides. Jefferson taunts that Hamilton "Smells like new money, dresses like fake royalty, desperate to rise above his station" ("Cabinet Battle #2") and that "he primps and preens and dresses like the pits of fashion" ("Washington on Your Side"). In sum, Hamilton certainly bears certain essential marks of the *megalopsychos* Aristotle describes, primarily his concern with honor, his courage, and his disdain for popular opinion in preference for what's right and true. Yet, he falls short in several key areas, most notably his adulterous affair, his sometimes hot-tempered pen, and his vanity. His overall virtue shines brilliantly, however, when compared to Burr's jealous striving.

To Thrive When So Few Survive

The virtuously proud person is, again, one who *merits* the honor they rightfully seek. On the other hand, Aristotle notes, a person who *acts* proudly, perhaps believing themselves to merit pride due to their being "well-born" or having been smiled on by fortune in other ways, will *despise* a person of good character who genuinely merits pride, even if not well-born or fortunate. Aaron Burr fits this mold, both well-born—"My mother was a genius. / My father commanded respect" ("Wait for It")—and able to complete his course of study in two years at Princeton due to both his intellect and his father being the college's president. When Burr approaches Washington in the hope of becoming his right-hand man, he provides his resumé and then begins to offer "a couple of suggestions" regarding military strategy. Washington, however, can read Burr immediately "on a chemical level," as Miranda puts it, and summarily dismisses him when Hamilton walks in.

Even in their romantic pursuits, Burr's cockiness comes from his unearned social status—"I'm a trust fund, baby, you can trust me!" ("The Schuyler Sisters")—whereas Hamilton lowers Eliza's expectations while emphasizing his natural gifts and the merits of an uneasy life: he owns no wealth, but does have "my honor, a tolerance for pain, a couple of college credits and my top-notch brain" ("Helpless"). In his jealous musings, Burr constantly references Hamilton's less prestigious roots, asking how "the bastard orphan son of a whore" keeps becoming more and more successful ("A Winter's Ball"). Most revealing about Burr's discontent is his sense that Hamilton is simply more conniving than he is: "Hamilton doesn't hesitate. He exhibits no restraint. He takes and he takes and he takes. And he keeps winning anyway" ("Wait for It"). As Burr himself noted earlier, morals, laws, and other rules of society don't apply to one who is great-souled; the *megalopsychos* rewrites the game to his own advantage.

The fundamental difference between Hamilton and Burr is that Hamilton *knows himself,* and with merited pride pursues public honors for his service to the public good. Burr, by contrast, constantly strives after whatever will put him "on the up and up again" ("Schuyler Defeated"); and, being a chameleon all his political life, ends up not really ever knowing himself. Chernow records Burr's pathetically revealing self-description, written in the third-person: "He is a grave, silent, strange sort of animal, inasmuch as we know not what to make of him." For all his faults, Hamilton at least was able to live out the classical Greek maxim endorsed by Socrates: "Know Thyself."

Not only did genuine self-knowledge distinguish Hamilton from his longtime "frenemy," but they differed in how they proclaimed *truth* to others. Although Hamilton often veered too far into the realm of unforgiving polemics against his political opponents, he never *slandered* anyone by claiming something he wasn't certain was true of them—most especially Burr. When Burr angrily calls Hamilton out for having publicly called him "amoral" and a "dangerous disgrace," Hamilton unapologetically confesses: "Burr, your grievance is legitimate. I stand by what I said, every bit of it. You stand only for yourself. It's what you do. I can't apologize because it's true" ("Your Obedient Servant"). Hamilton thus exemplifies a key trait of the *megalopsychos* as described by Aristotle: "He must also be open in his hate and in his love (for to conceal one's feelings is the mark of timidity), and must care more for truth than for what people will think, and must speak and act openly."

A final point of contrast between Hamilton and Burr can be seen in their relation to Washington. Burr, ever the opportunist, seeks to flatter Washington in order to obtain a post with him: "I admire how you keep firing on the British from a distance" ("Right Hand Man"). He later rues Hamilton's being "seated at the right hand of the father" ("A Winter's Ball"). Hamilton, on the other hand, initially resists serving merely as Washington's secretary, and even leaves his service for a time due to a falling-out based on mutually perceived disrespect.

Yet, these two men can't help but be drawn to each other's respective virtues. As Aristotle puts it, the *megalopsychos* "must be unable to make his life revolve around another, unless it be a friend; for this is slavish, and for this reason all flatterers are servile and people lacking in self-respect are flatterers." Aristotle defines *perfect* friendship as shared between persons "who are good, and alike in excellence; for these wish well alike to each other *qua* good, and they are good in themselves." Despite the various ways Hamilton fails to perfectly exemplify a "great-souled man," he nevertheless shares sufficient virtues with Washington for the two of them to forge a lifelong friendship that neither could've shared with someone like Burr.

He Holds a Pen, He's a Threat

Thomas Jefferson and James Madison shared a distrust of Hamilton's allegedly "monarchical" ambitions for the office of the President and his potential rise to it. In his famous six-hour speech at the Constitutional Convention, Hamilton proposed what Madison described as an "elective monarch." This accounts for Madison's and Jefferson's glee when it becomes clear that Hamilton is "never gon' be President now" ("The Reynolds Pamphlet"). Never doubtful of Hamilton's abilities, they feared that, if he attained the presidency, he could become what Aristotle calls in his *Politics* "a God among men." Aristotle asserted that "for men of pre-eminent excellence there is no law—they are themselves a law."

Hamilton indeed appears many times to be a law unto himself. His choral introduction proclaims, "Will they know you rewrote the game?", later echoed by Burr as a jealous lament ("Alexander Hamilton"). Hamilton doesn't play by the rules of a game crafted by others; instead, he *writes* the rules with his prodigious pen: "And in the face of ignorance and resistance, I wrote financial systems into existence" ("Hurricane"). So the Virginians have good reason to fear Hamilton's growing power when in office and his continuing influence afterwards.

To avoid the undemocratic calamity of an uncontrollable lawmaker, Aristotle observes in his *Politics* that "Democratic societies ostracized or banished from the city for a time those who seemed to predominate too much through their wealth, or the number of their friends, or through any other political influence." "The Election of 1800" shows how Hamilton continued to exert significant political influence even after his sex scandal, his falling out with John Adams, and his move "uptown" after his son's death.

Writing one of his many polemical editorials, in a moment of prescience, Hamilton chose the pseudonym "Camillus," a Roman general with wisdom and virtue. Camillus's people didn't see that he had their best interests at heart. Like Socrates, Camillus fearlessly proclaimed unpopular truths and suffered exile; though Socrates wasn't just exiled but *killed* by the people of Athens for his expression of unpopular truths. While Burr's motives for killing Hamilton were more personal, one wonders whether the world was indeed *not* "wide enough" for a man of Hamilton's excessive abilities, ambitious drive, and sometimes hot temper.

Faced with the question of what to do with someone who is "pre-eminent in excellence" Aristotle concludes in his *Politics* that, if exile or death is not an option, "The only alternative is that all should happily obey such a ruler . . . and that men like him should be kings in their state for life." As a genuine *megalopsychos* capable of rewriting the game, President George Washington carved out a third option by teaching the American people "how to say goodbye." Washington's choice may have "perplexed" Hamilton as much as it did King George III.

Who knows to what extent Hamilton would've virtuously limited his executive power if he'd attained the presidency or otherwise continued to exert an inordinate influence on American politics? Perhaps Burr did Hamilton's legacy a favor by ending his life when he could still be properly lauded as a *megalopsychos*, preventing him from potentially turning into a *megalomaniac*.

6
They Think Me Macbeth

KATE BOSSERT

In the song "Take a Break," Alexander Hamilton quotes one of Shakespeare's most recognizable speeches: "Tomorrow and tomorrow and tomorrow / Creeps in this petty pace from day to day." Hamilton assumes that his sister-in-law, Angelica Schuyler, will catch the reference "without my having to name the play." But just in case, he name-checks Macbeth in the next line.

Angelica probably would have guessed on her own, though. Shakespeare's Scottish play was familiar to well-read Revolutionary Americans. Thomas Jefferson includes Shakespeare's plays on his list of essential books for a private library, and he singles out *Macbeth* as one not to miss. In a 1771 letter to Robert Skipwith, Jefferson explains that reading about "any atrocious deed" is good for the practice of virtue because it helps us learn to distinguish right from wrong. He is sure Macbeth's atrocities will inspire "great horror of villainy" in every reader "of feeling and sentiment."

So, when Hamilton admits to Angelica, "They think me Macbeth," he knows no one's paying him a compliment. Macbeth's no nice guy. He's a murderer and a tyrant, fueled by self-confessed "vaulting ambition." In Shakespeare, Macbeth's unbridled appetite for political power leads him to kill King Duncan, along with his friend Banquo and a slew of others, including innocent children. His conscience causes only momentary hesitation—fleeting and early on. But the ruthless Lady Macbeth convinces him to abandon his scruples, famously encouraging him to "screw your courage to the sticking place." A bloody reign of terror ensues before Macduff can

53

stop him. Macduff finally returns from exile and bumps off Macbeth after the impossible happens and Birnam Wood "moves" to Dunsinane.

To a modern audience, it might be a little confusing to compare the relatively benign-looking man on the ten-dollar bill to a raving, bloodthirsty, eleventh-century Scot. But in Lin-Manuel Miranda's musical, Hamilton's detractors see something suspicious in him. They think his "non-stop" work ethic is a little too much like Macbeth's will to power. Hamilton's scrappy determination, so instrumental during the fight for Independence, now looks like a threat to liberty.

The sticking point is the question of managing state debt. Hamilton refuses to compromise on the issue, disrupting what should be a democratic process and turning it into a contest of wills. "Take a Break" comes shortly after Hamilton has it out with Jefferson in "Cabinet Battle #1." In the cabinet meeting, Hamilton is digging in his heels over his financial plan and being a real "pain in the ass." (Literally: he threatens to show Jefferson "where his shoe fits.") Washington roundly scolds him for not playing nice and orders him to "figure it out."

At the top of "Take a Break," Hamilton needs to decide whether he will follow orders from his commander or, like a bullying Macbeth, do it his way instead. He's aware that he's got Macbeth-potential. As Miranda himself has put it, Hamilton starts "dream casting the play with his frenemies too." When Hamilton explains to Angelica that "Madison is Banquo," he depicts himself as betraying his friend for political gain. Hamilton has just had a falling out with Madison over the financial plan. Although we don't see their fight play out on stage, Hamilton is casting himself as the aggressor and Madison as the victim.

Macbeth, of course, kills his closest friend Banquo in a preemptive strike, all because the witches prophesy that Banquo's sons will wear the Scottish crown. Hamilton says that Jefferson is Macduff, and "Birnam Wood is Congress on its way to Dunsinane." The parallels are there again: Jefferson, finally back from France, looks poised to play Macduff, with Congress on his side. Hamilton worries Jefferson is the emerging hero who will handily defeat him.

But is Hamilton a tyrant in the making? Is tyranny even possible in a government where, as Washington warns, Hamilton either gets the votes or gets voted out?

The Founding Fathers obviously had no time for tyrants. They had worked to escape the tyranny of the British monarchy and weren't interested in recreating the same problem on this side of the Atlantic. The obvious first step was to get rid of monarchs altogether. After all, the Greek word *tyrannos* originally meant "monarch." When it came to kings and tyrants, one naturally led to the other for the Founding Fathers.

But for classical philosophers, eliminating tyrants wasn't as simple as abolishing monarchy altogether. Kings sometimes served their purposes. As Plato points out in *The Republic*, there's a difference between irrational tyranny and rational kingship. It's not *kingship* that makes the tyrant—although it certainly gives him an excellent platform. It's the tyrannical character that's the real root of tyranny.

Platonic Tyranny

Macbeth's tyranny flourishes not only because the monarchial system allows for his swift consolidation of power—but also because he allows himself to be ruled by his personal appetites. In *The Republic*, Plato says that all of us actually have tyrant potential because our animal brain would make us slaves to our desires, no matter how base or depraved. Most of us manage rational self-restraint: we realize that not all of our desires are worth it. We make decisions about what desires we can reasonably pursue and which ones we probably shouldn't for the sake of the common good. But people like Macbeth don't appeal to reason—and that's when a tyrant's born.

The Platonic tyrant has no self-control and no conscience. His personal desires require immediate satisfaction, and he's bound by no law. As Macduff notes in Act 5 of Shakespeare's play, "Boundless intemperance is the root of tyranny." And Macbeth's lawlessness is on display for all to see. He's "bloody, / luxurious, avaricious, false, deceitful, / Sudden, malicious, smacking of every sin / that has a name."

Miranda gives us a clear-cut example of Platonic tyranny in his depiction of King George. A cartoonish villain, George clings mercilessly to power. He'll do anything to keep it, no bones about it, giddily admitting in the song "You'll be Back," that he'll "kill your friends and family" if you stand in his way. George can't even fathom a representative government. In "I

Know Him," he's flummoxed by Washington's self-imposed two-term limit, asking if it can be true: "I wasn't aware that was something a person could do."

Miranda's characterization of George is consistent with John Adams's own historical depiction of the British monarchy. In his personal correspondence, Adams repeatedly quotes *Macbeth* to describe the British abuses. In an essay published in the *Boston Gazette* in 1765, he explicitly compares the monarchy to Lady Macbeth, a pitiless mother who tore her children from her nursing breast before she "dash'd the brains out." It's not hard to imagine Miranda's George doing the same, all while merrily humming "Da da dat dat da ya da!"

While Hamilton seems a far cry from George and his maniacal ruthlessness, they do share an appetite for power. At the very least, Hamilton is reticent to lose his position in the new government. "I'll lose my job if we don't get this plan through Congress," he frets. But he's also conflicted about the best way to move his financial plan forward. Jefferson wants to compromise, but Hamilton thinks they need the "bold strokes" that his plan offers.

At this point in the libretto, Miranda had a mind to emphasize how Hamilton's continued inflexibility had the potential to mirror Macbeth's own self-destructive determination. In his liner notes, Miranda admits that he originally intended another *Macbeth* quote for "Take a Break," but the reference was so obscure that he went with the more familiar "Tomorrow and tomorrow and tomorrow" passage instead. The omitted quote comes from the end of Act 5, just before Macbeth commits another brutal murder: "They have tied me to a stake," Macbeth soliloquizes. "I cannot fly, but bearlike I must fight the course." Macbeth is saying he's at a point of no return—he's come this far, and he won't turn back now. If he lets up, he'll lose the power he's achieved. But the image carries even more significance than that.

Macbeth is comparing himself to a bear in the bear baits—a common entertainment in Shakespeare's time. Bear-baiting involved tying a bear to a stake and setting dogs on it to see how long it could defend itself—a brutal, bloody pastime. Macbeth is saying that he's ready to fight like an animal in order to stay in control. He proves it seconds later when he thrusts a sword through Young Siward. But, in the very next scene, the dogs get fiercer: Macbeth finds himself face to face with Macduff, and then it's all over.

Hamilton could have been the bear. He could have gone for blood, acting like Plato's base animal. But, it wouldn't have gotten him any further than it got Macbeth, even if he had survived, because Hamilton and his colleagues had already established a way to leash political beasts.

The American system, replete with its checks and balances, makes Platonic tyranny nearly impossible. Representative democracy means that tyrants can't have it their way unless they have the votes. And as Washington tells him, Hamilton needs to "convince more folks" if he wants to keep his job. Overthrowing tyrants turns out to be much easier than persuading citizens. "Winning's easy. Governing's harder," Washington explains. And in "Take a Break," Angelica gives Hamilton the same advice. He has to meet with Jefferson and persuade him to compromise: "Don't stop till you agree." Like Washington, Angelica urges diplomacy, not belligerence. So, Hamilton checks his low blows and negotiates instead.

Keeping his cabinet post means learning to give and take. That's the system that the Founding Fathers put into place. No one person can have their whim in American government since the Executive, Legislative, and Judicial branches counterbalance each other. Of course, Hamilton already knows how the system's supposed to work. He helped lay the foundation for the new republic—and, as Burr tells us in "Non-Stop," Hamilton wrote a staggering fifty-one essays in defense of the Constitution.

Aristotelian Tyranny

Hamilton is willing to talk it out, but that doesn't mean he's completely devoid of tyrannical potential. As Shakespeare scholar Rebecca Bushnell points out, Aristotle thinks that Plato's definition of tyranny is a little too one-dimensional when it comes to describing actual tyrants. So, it's no surprise that Miranda's Platonic tyrant, King George, comes off a lot like a cartoon. Unlike Plato's tyrant, Aristotle's doesn't completely embrace depravity. The Aristotelian tyrant retains the capacity for reason, and he understands why it's sometimes necessary to at least *pretend* to be virtuous for the sake of maintaining power.

In the *Politics*, Aristotle agrees with Plato that tyrants are driven by their appetites, but he says that maintaining power is different than achieving it. Winning's easy. Governing's harder. Tyrants have to look like they're playing by the rules if they want to hold on to the power they've achieved. So, outwardly, the Aristotelian tyrant must appear to be virtuous, just, and responsible, even if he's still playing the villain in private. In the best-case scenario, pretending to be virtuous long enough tends to make you virtuous. In other words, a tyrant who gets used to making ethical choices—even if he's making them for his own benefit—can develop a habit of virtue. He can become a good guy again, or sort of a good guy, which is better than nothing.

As Bushnell points out, the possibility of redemption adds a complexity to Aristotle's tyrant that's missing from Plato's version. Whereas Plato's tyrant embraces bestial instinct, Aristotle's is still capable of rational decision-making. He might be a hypocrite, but he knows he has to do damage control. The public won't tolerate him otherwise.

Shakespeare's play gives us an example of Aristotelian tyranny, too. In Act 4 of *Macbeth*, Macduff coaches Malcolm, the assassinated king's heir, in how to be an Aristotelian tyrant. At this point in the play, Malcolm is trying to test Macduff's character. He wants to see how Macduff will react if he thinks Malcolm is depraved. So Malcolm poses as the embodiment of the Platonic tyrant. He tells Macduff that he can't control his sexual desires: "Your wives, your daughters, / Your matrons, your maids could not fill up / The cistern of my lust."

But, Macduff is sure there's no devil in hell who's worse than Macbeth, with his "bloody-sceptered" villainy writ large. Believing Malcolm's self-description, Macduff argues that so long as Malcolm has the presence of mind to disguise his vices, he can safely take back the throne and restore Scotland: "You may / Convey your pleasures in spacious plenty / And yet seem cold—the time you may so hoodwink." In other words, as long as Malcolm walks the straight and narrow in public, no one ever needs to know about his private dalliances. Macduff is coaching Malcolm to be an Aristotelian tyrant—the lesser of two evils. Fortunately for Macduff, Malcolm later reveals he's actually a virtuous prince with not a lustful thought in his mind.

Hamilton's problem is that his private dalliances do become public. He succumbs to his appetites when he has an affair with Maria Reynolds. In the song "Say No to This," Hamilton blames himself for his lapse in judgment: "How could I do this?" he laments. In Miranda's notes on the libretto, he comments that it was important for Hamilton to recognize his own culpability in this scene. Hamilton admitting fault was "more compelling than blaming Maria." Recognizing fault is also something that Aristotle's tyrant has to do. He must understand how he'll be perceived by those who expect better of him. This way, he knows how and when to practice public relations.

When Hamilton realizes that his political rivals know about the affair—that the dirt on him could go public—he's quick to get ahead of the exposé. He effectively orchestrates his own press release, not only admitting to the affair but also sharing every sordid detail. The cynical reading of the Reynolds Pamphlet—and the one that Hamilton's wife, Eliza, takes in "Burn"—is that Hamilton's tell-all is the calculated strategy of an Aristotelian tyrant. She reads the pamphlet as a desperate political survival tactic. Hamilton's words are "obsessed with his legacy" and nothing else: the self-obsessed Hamilton is "paranoid in every paragraph." Angelica had warned Eliza that Hamilton, driven by ambition, would "do what it takes to survive." Her prophecy seems to have come to tragic fulfillment. Eliza's accusations seem fair, too, given what we see of Hamilton's decision-making process in the song "Hurricane."

Hamilton's only concern at the end of "Hurricane" is how to preserve his carefully manicured reputation. Unable to hide the affair, he decides to share everything with the public—to "overwhelm them with honesty." Honorable penitence is the "the only way I can protect my legacy," he concludes.

But Hamilton never pauses to consider the effect of the pamphlet on his wife or family. As Eliza explains, "In clearing your name, you have ruined our lives." And what's more, honesty isn't enough to save Hamilton's political career. As Jefferson, Madison, and Burr chorus in "The Reynolds Pamphlet," "he's never gon' be President now."

A New Kind of Tyranny?

This would all suggest, then, that Hamilton proves to be neither a ruthless Platonic tyrant nor a calculated Aristotelian one. And this might seem like good news—but as Miranda presents it, Hamilton's failure to recover from the Reynolds affair still has the tinge of tragedy. Miranda's musical entertains the possibility of a third kind of tyranny, one that Hamilton succumbs to, even though he resists it at first.

In "Take a Break," Angelica encourages Hamilton with Lady Macbeth's infamous advice, "Screw your courage to the sticking place"—another moment when Miranda directly quotes Shakespeare's tragedy. When Lady Macbeth speaks this line in Shakespeare, she's urging Macbeth to kill King Duncan—to buck-up and commit a brutal murder for political gain. But when Angelica sings the line, she's practically urging the opposite. She's begging Hamilton to stay away from politics. She wants him to have the courage to "take a break" and "run away with us for the summer" (possibly even inviting him to have an affair with her, but Miranda leaves this deliberately ambiguous).

Yet Hamilton says *No* to his Lady M, flat-out refusing Angelica's pleas. He won't disengage from politics because the stakes are too high. He "wrote financial systems into existence," and he needs to seize the moment to see them through.

Miranda seems to argue that America's better for Hamilton's selflessness. This "ten dollar founding father" was willing to put aside his personal desires and sacrifice for the greater good. It's not that Hamilton doesn't want to spend time with his family. In "Take a Break" he is delighted by nine-year-old Philip and seems genuinely to enjoy his time with his wife and children.

The most charitable reading of Hamilton is as a selfless public servant. His ambition to participate in the political process, to choose Congress over summer vacation, is not for his legacy alone. Neither is it, as Burr speculates in "The Room Where It Happens," only because he's enamored with gaining "unprecedented financial power." He might be interested in both, but he also professes to be invested in advancing the public's best interest. In "Cabinet Battle #1," he tells Jefferson that if they can be aggressive and competitive, "The Union gets a boost." When his negotiations finally succeed, he justifies his ruthless behavior on account of his desire to build something that will outlive him. Here, we could read Hamilton as thinking about his own reputation after death, but we can also understand him as thinking bigger than himself. Hamilton knows he's acting at a pivotal moment in American history and that his success could impact the Union for generations to come.

Hamilton's Macbeth moment, then, is actually the temptation to check-out. Hamilton could take a trip upstate—but he doesn't. Miranda suggests that we have a Federal bank, along with a national capital in Washington, DC, as a result of Hamilton's staying in the game.

The tragedy comes when Hamilton can't resist his personal appetites the second time around. He says no to Angelica, but not to Maria Reynolds. News of his affair is too scandalous to overcome, and just as Washington had warned earlier, Hamilton's unbridled appetites lead to his premature removal. Then, just a few songs later, his personal rivalry with Burr ensures that he's lost to history far too soon.

Miranda leaves us pondering what Hamilton might have achieved had he lived and remained politically engaged. In this way, Miranda leaves us wondering, too, about the real threat to American liberty. In theory, representative democracy hamstrings Platonic tyrants and mitigates Aristotelian ones, but only if enough of its citizens participate actively and earnestly in the system. If we "take a break," we become our own tyrants.

7
Smartest in the Room?

CHERYL FRAZIER

In almost any classroom or business room, there's that one person who leaves us wondering: why do you assume you're the smartest in the room? Typically this "obnoxious, arrogant, loudmouth bother" talks without actually saying anything of importance, something that would make Aaron Burr beg them to "talk less and smile more."

However, Hamilton turns that world upside down. People's opinions of Hamilton vary greatly. Some think he's a bright young man, while others just wonder "Yo, who the eff is this?" But regardless of their responses to his verbosity, it's hard to deny that Hamilton is saying things that matter.

Some people think that intellectual humility is a virtue. As a virtue, it's supposed to guide our behavior. But how should this virtue be understood? Can you show intellectual humility and still be really confident about what you know? Enter Alexander Hamilton. Is Hamilton's forward, confident behavior intellectually virtuous? Or is it better to sit back, stay quiet, and wait for it like Burr?

Virtue and Vice

Aristotle (384–322 BCE) thought part of the project of being a human was to develop *virtues*, or capacities to do things well. These virtues were often paired with vices, or extremes that took the virtue too far. For example, if honesty is a virtue, and a good trait we should try to develop, then the corresponding vices are being too honest and not being honest enough. The first extreme is a vice of excess, meaning you've exhibited too much of the given virtue. The second extreme is a vice of deficit, where you didn't exhibit the virtue strongly enough. Aristotle thought we should try to find a "golden mean," or demonstrate virtues in *just the right amounts*.

Take drinking alcohol, for example. Drink too much, and you become a bumbling idiot who brags about sex with horses (looking at you, Hercules Mulligan). Drink too little, and you miss out on raising a glass with Hamilton and company. But knock back the right number of pints of Sam Adams and you're a virtuous drinker.

Virtue Is Not a Word I'd Apply to This Situation

When it comes to being humble, Hamilton and Burr are on opposite ends of the spectrum. Hamilton is loud and confident, sure that his way is best, whereas Burr prefers to wait and see how things play out before taking action. Regarding *intellectual* humility, the virtue for being humble about your thoughts, knowledge, and beliefs, neither seems to strike the perfect balance.

As psychologists and philosophers Peter Samuelson, Matthew Jarvinen, Thomas Paulus, Ian Church, Sam Hardy, and Justin Barrett discuss in a 2014 article from the *Journal of Positive Psychology*, there are two components generally attributed to intellectual humility: an epistemic (knowledge-based) component and a social dimension.

The epistemic dimension of intellectual humility focuses on our fallibility and the evidence we have for our beliefs, taking into account the following kinds of issues:

- *Do I have enough evidence to believe some proposition x?* For example, do I have enough evidence to believe the proposition "Grass is green"?

- *Am I confident enough in my belief that x is true?* Am I confident enough in my belief that the statement "Grass is green" is true?

- *Am I open to other positions that may conflict with or disprove x?* If someone said "Grass is not green" would I be open to hearing their reasons for that belief?

- *Are my views sufficiently coherent? Are they clear and reasonable?* Do my beliefs about grass and color make sense with my other beliefs about the world?

- *Am I able to be wrong? Is my knowledge fallible?* Do I accept that I could find out that grass is actually blue? Or do I insist that it has to be green no matter what?

Conversely, the social dimension explores our abilities as knowers relative to other people, asking questions like:

- *If someone claimed to know some fact x, would I take them seriously?* If someone claimed to know that grass is green, would I take them seriously?

- *Do I give enough weight to the views and evidence of others?* Do I think about what other people know about grass?

- *Am I biased to doubt any groups of people?* Do I automatically dismiss views about grass from anyone who isn't a gardener, for example? Do I only listen to the opinions of certain people?

- *Do I think I'm smarter than others, or more often correct, without first considering the evidence they give me in support of their views?* Do I assume that I know everything there is to know about the color of grass, and ignore anyone who disagrees with me?

Samuelson et al.'s definition of intellectual humility, then, is a virtue between the vices of *intellectual arrogance* and *intellectual diffidence*. Arrogance, or excessive pride, marks a deficit of humility—saying you know more than you really know or have evidence to know—while diffidence/modesty comes from being excessively humble about your knowledge.

If you accept this view you get what's called a *proper beliefs* definition of intellectual humility. This means that you're doing it right if you're appropriately confident in your beliefs. This will vary from situation to situation, but generally it amounts to having the right amount and right kinds of evidence to support your views.

Consider the battles leading up to and discussed in the song "Stay Alive." The American army was weak, discouraged, and quickly losing numbers. Local merchants denied them equipment and assistance, and they were so short of food that they had resorted to eating their horses. Congress encouraged the weakened American soldiers to aggressively attack the British forces, reflecting a poor understanding of military strategy and the realities of war. In contrast, George Washington's strategy of outrunning and outlasting reflected good military intelligence. Washington hoped his troops would win, but took into account the facts at hand and the likelihood of survival. Had he overestimated their ability and held firm to the belief that his men could win the war with an aggressive, quick-paced strategy, his failure of intellectual humility could have been deadly.

Although the *proper beliefs* view seems quite plausible, philosophers Dennis Whitcomb, Heather Battaly, Jason Baehr, and Daniel Howard-Snyder argue that it isn't specific enough and lacks a behavior-guiding component needed for an account of intellectual humility. As they explain, there are two main problems with the proper beliefs account.

> Forming proper beliefs isn't routine and doesn't mean that all of your beliefs will be well-formed. You can have solid, virtuously-formed beliefs about one subject but form other beliefs without paying attention to ways in which your beliefs might lack evidence or contain errors. In other words, humans aren't perfect. Hamilton, for example, seemed to have proper beliefs about the values of his country, but his beliefs about how to best defend that country demonstrated an irrational desire to quickly become the nation's hero. As Washington pointed out, those fantasies of dying like a martyr were not in the best interest of Hamilton nor anyone around him.

> Just because you have your head on straight regarding whether your beliefs are proper or not doesn't necessarily mean that proper behavior about those beliefs will follow. Even if you recognize that your views are ludicrous, that doesn't ensure that you will act like a civilized, open-minded person. Burr prided himself on being more intellectually humble than Hamilton. He consistently encouraged Hamilton to slow down, arguing that Hamilton's intellectual hubris would be his doom. It seems clear that Burr understood that he didn't know everything, and should be quick to listen and reflect. Despite all this, Burr regularly criticized Hamilton's beliefs, demonstrating the very inconsistency that Whitcomb, et al. find so troubling with the "proper beliefs"

account. While he had the right beliefs mentally, Burr acted on them in the wrong ways by refusing to be open to beliefs that differed from his own. In other circumstances, he was too timid and diffident about his beliefs and refused to share them with others. For example, during the election of 1800 Burr was criticized by Hamilton for not strongly believing in anything or taking a strong political stance.

The theme running through both of those problems is that proper beliefs about intellectual humility do not actually make us act or think humbly. Merely having proper beliefs still leaves room for the arrogance of Hamilton *or* the diffidence of Burr. It's really hard to acknowledge that our beliefs are misguided or inconsistent. Likewise, it's unfortunately easy to think that the things you believe are justified and true. Especially for people as educated as Hamilton and Burr, admitting you are wrong is rocky, unfamiliar terrain. However, failing to develop epistemic humility could mean disaster.

Owning Your Limitations

Whitcomb, et al. propose an alternative account of intellectual humility, *limitation-owning intellectual humility*, which hopes to resolve these issues. They recognize that people are imperfect. We are packed with strengths, but with those strengths come weaknesses. While we may be confident in our abilities to write like we're running out of time, we may also talk too much at the Constitutional Convention. Their account centers on being intellectually humble in that we recognize and *own* our *intellectual limitations*, be they ignorance, mistakes or faulty memory, or intellectual character flaws.

The first step is admitting you have a problem. In order to work around your limitations you must first recognize that you have them, but this can't be taken to the extreme. If you only see your limitations, it may be impossible to move forward or develop beliefs with any degree of certainty. Whitcomb wouldn't ask Hamilton to think of himself as stupid, or to stop seeking an accelerated course of study at Princeton. After all, if Hamilton hadn't seen himself as smart and capable enough to write his way out of unfortunate circumstances, he might have never become our ten-dollar Founding Father. However, having the appropriate attentiveness to his intellectual limitations might mean learning that he needs to take a break, to finally heed Burr's advice and talk (just a little) less.

Owning your limitations entails more than just acknowledging that they exist. Instead, it requires that you develop four sets of *dispositions,* or mindsets and behaviors:

1. cognitive or mental

2. behavioral

3. motivational

4. emotional.

As Whitcomb, et al. understand them, *cognitive* responses involve believing, accepting, and reminding yourself of your intellectual limitations regularly. Part of this entails taking responsibility for the consequences of your actions and beliefs.

Standing across the Hudson at dawn, Burr took this important step as he recognized that he should have known the world was wide enough for him and Hamilton. Although his realization came too late, following a fatal strike between Hamilton's ribs, it shows the importance of realizing our biases. Often, our actions are not life-or-death matters, as the art of dueling has faded out of style. However, having the appropriate cognitive response to intellectual limitations is a handy tool for everyday life, even beyond the dueling ground.

Behavioral responses are equally important in owning your limitations. Many of the questions explored in the social and epistemic dimensions of intellectual humility can lead to appropriate behaviors. Upon noticing that you fail to give appropriate consideration to others' input and beliefs, for example, you can adjust your behavior in ways that allow you to remain humble. Listening to and closely considering evidence that cuts against your beliefs, deferring to experts when you don't know the answer, and getting more information are just a few ways in which you can develop the appropriate behavioral responses. In general, though, the behavioral component of owning your intellectual limitations requires you to be open to *others* about your flaws, and to actively work to develop and maintain proper, consistent, and well-supported beliefs. For example, in the Cabinet Battles Thomas Jefferson and Hamilton both failed to have the appropriate behavioral responses because they got aggressive and hostile toward their opponent. As Hamilton pointed out, the other cabinet members didn't have a better plan for the government—they just hated Hamilton's. Both people failed to consider their opponent's arguments, and instead assumed they knew what was best for the country.

Building on behavioral responses, a third type of disposition necessary for intellectual humility concerns our *motivational* responses. These go a step beyond the recognition entailed in behavioral responses, instead requiring you to actually care about and want to fix your limitations. This often comes in the form of recognizing and taking seriously your limitations, rather than just acknowledging that they exist. Washington epitomizes this as he addresses the nation, admitting that he is too sensible of his defects to not recognize that he probably messed up a lot during his presidency. In one last address to the country, he asks for forgiveness for his past mistakes and demonstrates a willingness to move forward and correct those mistakes.

Finally, intellectual humility helps us have the proper *emotional* responses to our limitations. While it's easy to feel scorned from past events, and threaten to send a fully armed battalion to cope with these sentiments, it's much more difficult to rationally and calmly respond to mistakes. However, in so doing, you're able to effectively respond to your limitations without being bogged down by regret, anger, and hostility.

What Comes Next?

Limitation-owning intellectual humility provides guidelines by which you can assess your belief-making processes and intellectual behavior, giving a more practical account than a *mere* proper beliefs account. However, Whitcomb, et al. fail to fully explore the practical aspects of Samuelson, et al.'s version of intellectual humility, and a full revision of that initial account might not be necessary. In developing their proper beliefs notion of intellectual humility, Samuelson, et al. assessed clusters of traits that an intellectually humble person might share with a wise or intellectually arrogant person. One standout trait that was important in the concept of an intellectually humble person was the notion of open-mindedness.

In their study, Samuelson, et al. found that people considered open-mindedness to be an epistemic quality of an intellectually humble person. This means that an intellectually
humble person is open-minded with regards to education and
learning; they're willing to explore new concepts and terms,
and are able to expand their knowledge based on new information. However, this open-mindedness show's there is a behavioral component to the proper beliefs view. In order to form
proper beliefs, the study reflects that people must be willing to
seek truth—a behavior that can guide in a similar way to the
limitation-owning account.

Further, the proper beliefs view is founded upon social qualities that are similarly action-guiding. For example, being a
good listener and sharing information are qualities Samuelson,
et al. identified as belonging to intellectually humble people,
something that the limitation-owning account seems to overlook. The limitation-owning account prides itself on being able
to guide behavior in a way that previous accounts could not,
but in so doing overlooks a critical consideration of the aims of
Samuelson, et al.'s project. Their work sought to identify
descriptors of different types of people—intellectually humble,
wise, and intellectually arrogant—and to describe how the
behaviors of each related to one another.

Many of the behavior-guiding principles in the proper
beliefs account were described in terms of characteristics someone with proper beliefs might already possess, rather than
looking at intellectual humility as a work in progress. It's
admittedly important to consider and work to correct *your own*
flaws, but the proper beliefs view adds a refreshingly *other-
directed* set of characteristics that are equally significant. Both
views address crucial elements of intellectual humility. The
proper beliefs view lists the behaviors an intellectually humble
person demonstrates when interacting with other people. The
limitation-owning view explores what internal changes and
behaviors are necessary for epistemic humility.

Hamilton and Burr's ultimate downfalls come not only in
being unable to acknowledge their own failures of intellectual
humility, but also in being unable to communicate effectively
with a broader community of people. They were politicians and
lawyers, people whose lives were devoted to studying and fighting and killing for the nation they got to build. In order to make

significant progress, each man needed what the other man had—in one case, the ability to listen and observe, and in the other, the ability to fight confidently for what you believe in. As we interact with others, we leave behind a legacy that outlives us. We have the power to behave as we choose, to talk nonstop, or just wait for it, or something in between those extremes. As Burr pointed out, we keep living—"We rise and we fall and we make our mistakes"—and it's up to us to decide how humbly we interact with the world. Ultimately, though, a system of intellectual humility that helps us maintain a healthy balance between arrogance and diffidence seems to be key.

III

Leaving Your Mark

8
Legacy or Happiness?

CARRIE-ANN BIONDI

Many people wish to leave their mark. As Alexander Hamilton famously puts it, "I wanna build something that's gonna outlive me." We want to be remembered rather than forgotten after we die.

But remembered for what? And at what cost? Legacies typically come with a hefty price tag that few are willing to pay: extraordinary amounts of time spent on difficult tasks while facing major obstacles.

Alexander Hamilton was no stranger to this human longing. We see his burning desire to "rise up" in the world vividly depicted in *Hamilton: An American Musical*. This Broadway sensation brims with memorable events in the all-too-brief life of this Founding Father. One that stands out—lifted above the fray as a slow-motion bullet heads across the stage—is the moment before Hamilton dies in a duel with Aaron Burr. Facing the death he knew would one day greet him, Hamilton ponders the meaning of a legacy: "Legacy. What is a legacy? It's planting seeds in a garden you never get to see. I wrote some notes at the beginning of a song someone will sing for me." These lyrics poignantly capture Hamilton's remarkable life, as he dies not knowing what the future holds for the country he helped create. He can only hope that the place where he could earn a legacy through hard work and ingenuity will continue to make that possible for others.

These lyrics invite us to wonder about the purpose of a legacy and what it takes to achieve one. Hamilton's words make it sound like the flowering of our legacy occurs after we die. If legacies are what we leave behind, does this make our life incomplete, since we don't live to see our purpose realized? You'd never know whether all of that hard work and fun forgone was for nothing. So, does striving for a legacy preclude happiness? Some may choose to sacrifice happiness to secure a legacy, but it's a false dichotomy to think that you have to choose between them. One can achieve greatness and happiness.

Legacy versus Happiness

Thinkers from Aristotle and Plato to John Stuart Mill and Michel de Montaigne have wondered whether personal happiness must elude them in this life while they seek great accomplishments through political office and public deeds. At first, Hamilton's answer appears to be "Yes." He sings about how he has "never been satisfied." That's a big part of what drives him to achieve. As a youth he wished for war to prove his worth and make a name for himself. He not only wants his children to tell his story, but also imagines that he'll be immortalized in history books. Little did he know that one day his name would be emblazoned on a Broadway marquee and sung by countless thousands of adoring fans.

Hamilton works like he's "running out of time." The specter of death is always lurking around the corner as he races to complete the next major task. It's not just his own mortality that presses upon him. After receiving news of the death of his best friend and abolitionist-in-arms, John Laurens, a shocked and saddened Hamilton retreats, saying, "I have so much work to do." Hamilton sounds a note that resonates with the French Renaissance philosopher Michel de Montaigne, who urges us always to have death upon our lips and in our thoughts, and proclaims: "I want Death to find me planting my cabbages, neither worrying about it nor the unfinished gardening."

Hamilton's work ethic, that scorns both ease of life and fear of death, contrasts sharply with Hamilton's buddies, who we meet at the local tavern, drinking and swapping stories. It's not until Hamilton comes along with his drive, vision, and charisma that they set aside their beers and sexual pursuits and leap into action for the revolutionary cause. We also see him resist the charms of his wife, Eliza, and sister-in-law

Angelica, as he refuses to "take a break" from pushing his plan for a national bank through the US Congress.

It's unclear whether *Hamilton* really aims to show that pursuing a legacy prevents happiness in this life. Legacy-making isn't much fun, since it involves lots of thankless work, but it's rewarding. Achieving something big and worthwhile, whether it's winning a war or creating a financial system or founding a new nation, takes a lot of dedication. You've got to work eighty hours a week, turn down invitations, and learn in your "spare time" whatever it takes to do the task at hand. Hamilton did *all* of that and more, including writing fifty-one of the *Federalist Papers* that secured ratification of the US Constitution. Not a lot of time in there for gardening, backpacking through Europe, or taking long walks on the beach.

In contrast, living in the moment by partying with friends and vacationing with the family is not exactly the stuff of legend. These activities are pleasant and easy ways to pass the time. One can look back fondly at memories of sunsets in far-away lands and be amused at having attempted the Coney Island hotdog-eating contest. However, these are insufficiently great in nature or scope to build a legacy on. Setting aside a desire to get into *The Guinness Book of World Records*, do you really want future generations to remember you as the person who downed eighty-two Sabretts in less than four minutes? This is not the kind of fame that Hamilton sought.

Competing views of what counts as a life worth living create this apparently irreconcilable conflict between legacy and happiness. What is the better way to think about happiness? "Nothing of value comes easy" or "All work and no play make Jack a dull boy"?

History's Eyes on You

According to the Greek philosopher Plato and the English philosopher John Stuart Mill, the burden falls to the capable few to achieve great things like foster progress, set up a just state, or advance civilization. Trailblazers must live up to their public duty no matter how onerous the personal cost, else the world will be swallowed in chaos and barbarism. What's the loss of one man's happiness, if the world is saved by his sacrifice? Posterity will not look back favorably on shirkers.

In Plato's *Republic*, Socrates and his friends discuss the nature of justice and how best to set up a state. Socrates defends the view that only Philosopher-Kings have the knowledge and virtue to rule a state well. So that they aren't tempted to become corrupt, he would deny them material goods beyond the basic necessities provided by the state. Philosopher-Kings are also compelled into these political positions rather than left to a private life contemplating the eternal, transcendent truths they have been educated to grasp. Socrates's reason is straightforward: "The law produces such people in the city, not in order to allow them to turn in whatever direction they want, but to make use of them to bind the city together." Those least eager to rule are more likely to preserve Justice and Goodness in a stable political order.

John Stuart Mill seconds this approach. Mill's theory of morals, Utilitarianism, claims that happiness is the ultimate good, but it is the happiness of everyone rather than individual happiness that matters most: "As between his own happiness and that of others, utilitarianism requires him to be as strictly impartial as a disinterested and benevolent spectator." Say that you are faced with the options of happily getting to see *Hamilton,* or unhappily ruining your fancy clothes and missing the long-awaited show to save the lives of three drowning people. Utilitarianism calls for saving those people. Sometimes, you need to take a hit for the team. In exchange, the overall happiness is maximized and you'll be remembered as a hero.

General George Washington knows when to play upon these noble sentiments. During the difficult Valley Forge winter of 1777–1778, the Continental Army is on the brink of defeat. A frustrated Washington laments that "any hope of success is fleeting" because "the people I'm leading keep retreating." He turns the tide by persuading Hamilton to forget his fantasy of "dying like a martyr" and join Washington's staff to help him strategize and lobby Congress for much-needed money and supplies. Then, to rally his demoralized, starving troops and quell an imminent mutiny, Washington arranges for a re-enactment of Joseph Addison's rousing play *Cato*. This play—Washington's favorite one—was based on the life of Cato the Younger, who fought for republican freedom against the tyrant Julius Caesar. Cato ultimately chose death before dishonor, by committing suicide rather than live under Caesar's yoke.

Honor, patriotism, virtue, liberty, legacy. According to Cato, these values are worth more than a life of servile submission, where people are promised bread and circuses as trade-offs for their lost freedom.

Hamilton and his friends—Laurens, Marquis de Lafayette, and Hercules Mulligan—sing about how they might not live to see their glory, but "will gladly join the fight" for America's freedom. They already have a hunger for greatness and willingly face death, believing that the beneficiaries of their actions will tell stories of their noble deeds after they're gone.

Dueling Legacies

Before Lin-Manuel Miranda's masterpiece came along, most people recalled only that Hamilton had been killed in a duel with sitting Vice-President Aaron Burr. Contrary to popular opinion, the duel between Hamilton and Burr was about more than defending their honor. The collision course between the two men was years in the making. Central to this fatal event are opposing views of legacy—its proper object, the motivation for achieving it, and the means by which to secure it.

Hamilton and Burr both desire a legacy, to achieve lasting fame, but in this matter the two men couldn't be more different in every way. First, Hamilton, the orphaned immigrant who starts out with almost nothing but his wits and drive, has to create his own legacy. Burr, on the other hand, has "a legacy to protect" that he inherited from his ancestors. Burr's ancestors include his formidable grandfather, famous Puritan preacher Jonathan Edwards, and his father, reverend Aaron Burr, Sr., who was president of Princeton University (then known as the College of New Jersey). Burr had a lot to live up to.

Second, Burr seems interested in his reputation, in simply being known. He wants to be "in the room where it happens"—whatever important "it" of the day it happens to be. The content of "it" doesn't matter. What does matter is that Burr gets to exert power and influence over the course of world-historical events, and it's his name that's remembered. Burr's attitude is similar to Thrasymachus's in Plato's *Republic,* where he maintains that "Might makes right" and history is written by the winners. On the other hand, Hamilton wants to be known for doing things of genuinely great value. Concerned with not sullying his "good name," and not merely with making a name for himself, he takes "a stand with pride" on behalf of the public good. He doesn't see pursuit of a legacy as a zero-sum game of either/or—"it's him or me," in Burr's words. Hamilton believes, instead, that the legacy you leave behind must be one worth seeking, one that's good for everyone.

Hamilton and Burr also disagree over the best way to secure a legacy. Burr has unprincipled ambition to gain what he wants, while Hamilton insists on principles even when doing so is unpopular or painful for him. For Burr's part, the musical depicts him as switching political parties only because he thinks that he can win election to the New York Senate that way, which he does. He also connives with Thomas Jefferson to dig up dirt on Hamilton so as to discredit him. Burr eventually kills Hamilton through an avoidable duel. These are the deeds of a man willing to win at any cost.

Hamilton acts in many principled ways for the sake of his legacy. He wears his heart and beliefs on his sleeve, and sticks by them with integrity, unconcerned with popular opinion. He makes a principled stand for many important values, including: defending a British Tory's right to property and due process, upholding an accused man's presumption of innocence during America's first murder trial, arguing for the abolition of slavery, and generally defending individual rights against the tyranny of the majority. And when accused of mishandling public funds as Treasury Secretary, Hamilton pens what has come to be called the Reynolds Pamphlet. In it, he recounts the details of how he used his private savings to pay off James Reynolds to keep quiet about Hamilton's affair with Reynolds's wife, Maria. This accounting clears him of any charges of cronyism or embezzlement. He believed that publishing the truth about his affair, though it was personally embarrassing, was the only way he could protect his legacy as an upright public servant.

Stop to Contemplate the Roses

Bewildered by this legacy business that consumes Hamilton and Burr, Eliza Hamilton is shown three times in the musical as resistant to her husband's ambition. When Hamilton is temporarily sent home from the war, Eliza is pregnant. She implores him to settle for a quiet family life, telling him that at this point in the Revolutionary War he's lucky to be alive. If he could be content with staying alive at home, with her providing him "peace of mind," she assures him "that would be enough" and that they "don't need a legacy."

Unconvinced, Hamilton not only returns soon to fight in the war, but later leaves his private job as a New York lawyer and steps up to serve in public office as President Washington's first Treasury Secretary. Eliza attempts to prevent him from making this move, but she might as well try to distract a hurricane. Finally, pained and embarrassed by Hamilton's choice to save his public reputation as Treasury Secretary by revealing his affair with Maria Reynolds, Eliza bitterly points out how her husband's obsession with his legacy has ruined their lives.

These scenes make it seem that Hamilton's nonstop pursuit of a legacy is purchased at the expense of personal happiness—both his and Eliza's. Eliza's call to stop and smell the roses, to be content with a tranquil life, has a rich philosophical tradition. It also comes in two varieties: experiential and contemplative. Both versions share a rejection of the grand, earthly pursuits needed to secure a legacy. They argue, instead, that the human good is located elsewhere.

The experiential variety is often defended by Epicureans. Epicurus and his followers recommend a simple life of easy hedonism. We know only our first-hand human experiences, comprised of various mental and physical pleasures. A meaningful human existence is created by each person out of the sum of these ephemeral experiences, so we should savor the sweetness of the peach or the colors of the fading sunset before they are lost to the oblivion of death. Pleasure should be pursued in moderation, though, so as to avoid both mental anxiety of addiction and the physical pain caused by overindulgence.

The contemplative variety usually comes from a religious perspective. Genuine human happiness is achieved by an intensely personal path involving purification of the soul through meditation and reflection on spiritual matters, mortification of the flesh, and disdain for both material goods and political activity. Successful pursuit of this good cannot be achieved in this life, but is crowned with the reward of eternal bliss granted by God in an afterlife.

The False Choice between Legacy and Happiness

Hamilton may disagree with his wife about whether family life and success as a New York lawyer are enough. But this doesn't mean that he's unconcerned with personal happiness. He's just not content with experiencing only life's simple pleasures. An individual may be unsatisfied with the status quo, but this isn't the same as being unhappy. His view of the self and human happiness—and hence his ideas about the role of legacy in one's life—fundamentally differs from Eliza's. Overall, Hamilton's approach to pursuing a legacy is more along the lines of a third alternative defended by Aristotle. On this view, being ambitious for something more is not only compatible with experiencing the good life, but is required for it.

Aristotle argues that individuals have complex natures, with biological, emotional, and intellectual capacities. Individuals achieve their highest good of *eudaimonia* (flourishing) by actualizing fully these capacities through virtuous activity in accordance with reason. It's fitting for the "great-souled man," who is morally excellent, to seek honor through actions of great worth. Two of the greatest creations, on Aristotle's view, are a person's character and a political society that allows each and every person the possibility of actualizing themselves.

This leads Aristotle to say that although the good for individuals and the state is the same—flourishing—that of the state "appears to be greater . . . and more complete both to achieve and preserve; something more beautiful and more divine." You might read this as advocating for the common good over the individual good. But it avoids the false alternatives of "legacy or happiness." What makes the flourishing of the state *appear* to be greater than and opposed to personal flourishing is that it's more demanding in terms of moral virtue, skill, and effort. However, those who pursue and succeed at such legacy-worthy action have reached the heights of self-creation, thus achieving personal happiness at the same time.

Hamilton's own life and beliefs did not fully escape the false dichotomy of legacy versus happiness. It's true that he would today be diagnosed as a workaholic, and his personal life was marred by the deaths of his mother, best friend, and eldest son as well as the torrid affair he made public. Despite these facts, he created a highly self-actualized character. He experienced significant marital bliss with his beloved Eliza before and after the affair, and was reported to be a fun and loving father who doted on his children. He also lived to gather some of the fruits of his carefully tended garden: victory in the Revolutionary War, ratification of the US Constitution, and creation of a national bank to stabilize the American economy, to name just a few major achievements.

Even though Hamilton's bouquet was a mixed one at the end of his life, cut short by Burr's bullet, it is possible to pursue a legacy without forgoing happiness. So "Do not throw away your shot." Plant seeds *and* smell the roses that bloom along your journey. Just make sure that you can handle the inevitable thorns and grow flowers worth gathering. Posterity will both be grateful for the legacy you leave them and "raise a glass" that you lived well.

9
The Right Way to Win Over Posterity

Thomas Wilk

Alexander Hamilton was obsessed with his legacy. As a "bastard, orphan, son of a whore and Scotsman," he spent his life doggedly trying to rise up, to leave his mark on the world and be remembered by posterity.

Hamilton became a leader of the revolution, an invaluable adviser to Washington, and the architect of a financial system that solidified the union. He was an extraordinary human being whose legacy permeates all our lives to this very day. But his overriding concern for how his story would eventually be told also led him into folly.

He alienated many of the Founding Fathers. In his response to the Reynolds Affair, he put his legacy as a public servant above the wellbeing of his family and left his wife Eliza devastated. He raised a son who died in a duel defending his father's honor and met the same fate defending his own.

Given these mixed results, we might wonder if a concern for our legacy is morally virtuous or a serious liability. Is someone who is so preoccupied with how he'll be remembered more likely to make moral errors as he tries to shape the narrative to his liking? It's easy to see how this could happen. An ambitious man like Hamilton takes risks. Sometimes things pan out in his favor. Sometimes they don't. In recovering from the mishaps, his chief concern is the preservation of his public reputation, the raw materials from which his legacy will be constituted.

The *Reynolds Pamphlet* is an excellent example. Hamilton tells all about his sordid marital affair, publishes the letters

Mariah Reynolds wrote to him, and describes how he brought this woman into his marital bed. He publicizes his personal impropriety in the hope of burnishing a mark from his image as a dutiful public servant and ardent champion of the new nation. His obsession with maintaining his place in the history books leads him to overlook how his immoderate confession of marital impropriety will affect his family. Is this obsession with how posterity will appraise you, with how you'll be remembered, bound to lead to such moral catastrophe?

To judge on the basis of just one case would be its own kind of folly, so let's look at another. Washington is also a man concerned with how his story will be told. In some ways, he and Hamilton are birds of a feather. Both suffer from certain social anxieties. In Hamilton's case, these stem from his lowly beginnings in the West Indies. Washington's origins were not so humble, but, because his father—a justice of the peace and county sheriff—died when George was just eleven, he didn't receive the same English education as his older brothers. This fact haunted him. As he rose among the Virginia gentry, he fretted that his lack of formal education would undermine his progress, yet he fervently yearned to make something of himself, to leave his mark on the world.

Like Hamilton, Washington sought military glory as a remedy to these anxieties. He was a risk-taker who would put himself directly in the line of fire. Writing after his only military surrender as the commander of Virginian troops at Fort Necessity, he confided to his brother, "I have heard the bullets whistle; and believe me, there is something charming in the sound." He went on, as we know, to take command of all Virginia troops during the French and Indian War and, eventually, to lead the Continental Army. His military successes and knack for leadership made him a natural choice for the Presidency.

Even such monumental achievements still could not quash his anxieties over how he would be judged by history. As biographer Joseph Ellis writes, "most of the prominent leaders of the revolutionary generation recognized that they were making history . . . but none of them . . . were as earnest in courting posterity as Washington." His memoirs and voluminous correspondence all bear the marks of a man deeply concerned with the telling of his story, which he worked tirelessly to ensure would be to his liking.

Unlike Hamilton, Washington was not led to moral lapses by his obsession with legacy. He aimed to control his narrative but he didn't destroy any relationships, or fight any duels to do it. So, obsession with legacy can lead to greatness that is sometimes but not always accompanied by moral mishap. What's the key difference between Hamilton and Washington? Why was one drawn to shady behavior while the other was not?

We can see our way to answering this question by getting a grip on what a legacy is and why it is something that someone might worry about. When someone is appropriately concerned with their legacy, they are exhibiting what Aristotle called a *virtue of character*. They are doing something that is morally praiseworthy. The difference between Hamilton and Washington emerges when we pay attention to what kind of concern for legacy is *appropriate*.

The distinction between appropriate and inappropriate concern is not one of degree but of your understanding of the object of that concern. For Hamilton, what mattered most was that his name would go down in the history books. For Washington, what mattered was that he would do great things worthy of being remembered by history. Hamilton was concerned primarily with the story, Washington with the deeds that the story would be about. Washington exhibited appropriate concern for his legacy, and this kind of concern is a virtue of character, but what does it mean to have a virtuous character to begin with?

Aristotelian Virtue

When philosophers talk about character, we usually have one guy in mind. Aristotle (384–322 B.C.E) claimed that ethics has to do with the development of character traits that will help us to live a good life.

Aristotle begins with the question of what a good life for a human being would be like. In his *Nichomachean Ethics*, he argued that such a life is one of *flourishing*, or what he calls *eudaimonia*. The life of an oak tree is going well when it is being the best that an oak tree can be. Tall, strong, green-leafed, and maximally reproductive. The life of a human being is going well when he or she is being the best that a human being can be.

What matters is fulfilling your human potential. A person who is flourishing in this way, whose life is filled with all the goods of human life, must have certain character traits that are conducive to living this good life. Aristotle calls these traits— like bravery, temperance, and magnanimity—excellences or *virtues of character*. The virtuous person is the person who exhibits all the virtues of character, and good actions are just those that the virtuous person would choose.

Most people exhibit some but not all the virtues. The Founding Fathers all had their foibles. Jefferson had the virtue of writing extraordinary prose, but he was terrible with money. Madison had the vision to foresee the need for a strong central government, but worried far too much about the length of his commute. We are all works in progress, hopefully being molded and molding ourselves into better people as we go along. We do this, according to Aristotle, by mimicking the actions of virtuous people until we develop our own habits of acting virtuously. We become virtuous by practicing at being virtuous. But this presents a bit of a problem. How are we to know who's virtuous? Whose habits are we to emulate?

Aristotle's answer to this conundrum is called the *Doctrine of the Mean*. Virtues, Aristotle claims, are states of a person between extremes of excess and deficiency. These "mean" states are defined through reason and prudence, and are relative to each individual. Discovering what these states are might sound tricky. Luckily, he gives us some examples. Bravery is a virtuous state in response to frightening circumstances. Being excessively fearful is cowardice, but one who is lacking in fear is rash or foolhardy. Similarly, with respect to conversational prowess being witty is a virtuous thing. Excessive wit spills over into the vice of buffoonery, while lacking wit all together makes a person boorish.

The Doctrine of the Mean says that we should find the mean between two vices, and then act in accord with that mean to lead a good life. Now, we want to know whether appropriate concern for legacy is a virtue, but before we can ask that, we need to have a more precise idea of what a legacy is.

Planting Seeds in a Garden You Never See

What is a legacy? The concept has at least two important meanings. In the first, it is something tangible that you leave to someone after your death. A healthy stock portfolio, a prized art collection, or a shed full of old golf clubs might be the legacy that your father leaves to you. In the second sense, a legacy is something more ephemeral. It's deeply tied to your identity; the thing that springs to mind when others think of you in the future. An author's novel might be his legacy, as a general's victory in battle might be hers. This kind of legacy can also be "passed down" to posterity, but in a less literal way. It's the story by which you are remembered, the shared recollections of your community and their estimation of the value of your life.

These two senses of legacy are related. Some tangible thing that you leave to future generations might be integral to your identity. It might be something you are remembered for and, as such, it might be taken as evidence of the kind of person you were. It is in this sense that leaving a legacy is "planting seeds in a garden you never get to see." You dedicate yourself to a project like the building of a nation or the writing of a great work of literature with the hope that it will earn you the respect of friends, family, and strangers in this life and in perpetuity. This integrated sense of legacy is the driving force in *Hamilton*. The characters each hope to be identified in one way or another with the project of building a new nation. They want to be remembered for their contributions. They hope it will be their legacy.

What's a Legacy Good for, Anyway?

But what's it all for? Why do any of us care how we'll be remembered? One way to answer this question is to think about the related idea of respect. Perhaps having concern for your legacy is a species of concern about being respected. Just as we desire respect for the things that we do, we want to leave a legacy that reflects the totality of our lives.

Respect, like legacy, can have multiple meanings. The philosopher Stephen Darwall has identified two important ones. He calls the first *recognition respect* and the second *appraisal respect*. We grant someone appraisal respect when we judge her to have done well with regard to some standard of achievement. Winning at Wimbledon or defeating a grandmaster in tournament chess will earn you appraisal respect, which we could also call esteem. Recognition respect, on the other hand, is respect that you're owed because of certain facts about you. Someone who holds some appointed office, like a judge, might be owed respect merely *because* she holds the office rather than for any particular things she has accomplished.

Appraisal respect or esteem is the notion of respect that will be useful for us. If we can understand why we desire esteem, we might make some headway into understanding why we yearn for a legacy. In most cases, we want to have a good reputation, to be esteemed, because it will benefit us as we live our lives. Others will be more willing to work with us to achieve shared goals. Perhaps more importantly, we will also find ourselves in a position of some power and authority because of the esteem we have earned. We'll be able to make more demands on others, to bend them to our will. Think of how celebrities can easily get tables at booked-up restaurants or how a man like Hamilton, having gained military honors, could win the attention of women like the Schuyler sisters. Maybe concern over legacy is just desire for esteem after death.

If that's right, then what Hamilton and Washington want is just to be esteemed, even once they're dead and gone. But why would anyone care if they're esteemed when it no longer does them any good? Dead people can't cash in on their esteem to wield authority or call in favors, after all. I think we can find a clue, once again, in Aristotle. He argues that we cannot pronounce whether a life has been a good one until after a person's death since "life includes many reversals of fortune, good and bad, and the most prosperous person may fall into a terrible disaster in old age." Given this, it is not so strange to think that the virtuous person would be concerned with how he or she is remembered. Being concerned with your legacy is just worrying over being esteemed not for a single act but for the totality of your life, and such esteem can only be had once that life is complete.

So, concerns over legacy and esteem are related, but distinct. Someone who's concerned to win the esteem of her colleagues has a short-term goal in mind. She wants the social capital that comes with that esteem. On the other hand, someone concerned with her legacy is playing the long game. She's worried about how others appraise her deeds but not for instrumental gain. Instead, she aims to be the sort of person who lives a life that her community will eventually recognize as praiseworthy because, in being this kind of person, she exemplifies true virtue. If this is right, then there is room for concern for legacy as a virtue of character. Someone who's concerned in this way is just worried, in a broad way, about living a virtuous life, a life worthy of posthumous esteem from his or her community. Washington, as we'll see soon, does seem to exhibit just this sort of concern. Hamilton presents a more questionable case.

The Virtue of Concern for Your Legacy

If appropriate concern about legacy is a virtue, then, according to the Doctrine of the Mean, it would have excesses and deficiencies like all virtues. This is not a definitive test for something's being a virtue, but it's a helpful exercise as we try to map this terrain. Someone who isn't at all concerned with her legacy, who doesn't care one wit about how her community will assess her life's projects after she's gone, lacks something essential to being fully human. She just doesn't care if the things she has done in her life are worthy of praise. A deficient concern for legacy is the mark of a person who isn't driven to do good in her life, to make the world a better place, to serve her community, or to achieve anything more than the ordinary.

On the other hand, someone who is overly concerned with her legacy also misses the mark. This person exhibits a kind of obsession with how others will assess her life when she's gone, to the point where she not only undertakes praiseworthy deeds but also does things to project and protect the story she wants to have told. Her concern shifts from actually living a virtuous life to merely being remembered as one who did so. Therefore, a good life is achieved through an appropriate concern for your legacy: not too much or too little, but just the right amount of the right kind of concern.

Washington's Mature Concern for Legacy

Our Aristotelian theory of appropriate concern for legacy helps us to see why two men who are both deeply worried about their legacies take different paths as a result. Washington's concern for his legacy comes out in a few places in the musical. We learn in "Right Hand Man" that, like Hamilton, the young Washington sought his glory in battle with a "head full of fantasies of dyin' like a martyr."

But unlike his younger self, the mature Washington is worried about more than merely getting his name into the history books. His mature desires are given expression in "One Last Time," where Washington waves off Hamilton's prodding to run for a third term as President. He sees more clearly what will be best for the fledgling nation. America has lessons to learn. It needs to be warned against partisan bickering, but this could only be done by someone above, or perhaps beyond, the partisan fray. Only a president who has abdicated the office could lecture the new nation on this cause. Washington sees that his project can best be served by removing himself from a place of prominence, even if he might have increased his own fame by holding onto power.

Washington understands that in saying farewell, he teaches the nation how to say goodbye. This new nation is an experiment in democratic self-governance. Having, for the most part, lived under the autocratic power of the princes of Europe, America's citizens have no experience with the peaceful transfer of power from one administration to the next. Washington must set the precedent that a president will not maintain a grip on power until his death but will step down after an appropriate time in service to ensure that political power is not concentrated in the hands of one person or family. His mature concern for legacy leads him to take the good of the project as his primary concern. If America prospers, if it outlives him, then his legacy is secure even if he is not aggrandizing his present public image.

Washington's mature concern for legacy is a virtue. It motivates him to undertake a project that's deemed praiseworthy by both his contemporaries and posterity, not because it is in some way spectacular (though it may be), or difficult (though it was), but because it is good. It is a project that really is deserving of praise, and his legacy will be secure because the success of his project will contribute to the well-being of his community both now and in the future. What really makes his concern virtuous, though, is that it also contributes to Washington's own flourishing insofar as service to one's community is a component of the good life, as Aristotle also claims. Washington's mature concern for legacy motivates him to plant the seeds of a prosperous nation, even as he retires "under his own vine and fig tree."

Hamilton's Naive Concern for Legacy

Hamilton is like the young Washington, headstrong and fool-hardy. Unsatisfied as Washington's *aide-de-camp*, he yearns for battle and a command post. He is certain that he can secure his legacy by taking huge risks and making great personal sacrifices. This attitude never fades as he ages. Years later, when a Manhattan street is named in his honor, Secretary Hamilton and Senator Burr discuss General Hugh Mercer's legacy. "The Mercer legacy is secure," say the two men, "and all he had to do was die." This seems to confirm Hamilton's belief that a glorious death in battle is the way to capture one's place in history, but Washington knows that "dying is easy . . . Living is harder." It is through living that you accomplish great deeds. An early death might win you a street named in your honor or your image on a ten-dollar bill, but a true legacy requires a life's work.

Hamilton's greatest offenses in the name of legacy arise amid the Reynolds Affair. His obsession with crafting his story led him first to a cover-up and then to the writing of the tell-all pamphlet that wrecked his relationship with Eliza. Obsessed with his legacy, "paranoid in every paragraph how they perceive" him, Hamilton undermined the very projects in which he had invested his life. He failed to consider how his rash actions in retelling his story would harm those closest to him. He thought he could maintain his public image and his legacy by demonstrating that his folly was a personal one not connected to his public office, but he failed to see how doing this would undo any perception of him as a virtuous character that others might have had.

Hamilton's naive concern for legacy is a vice of excess, an obsession. It undoes his projects and, in the end, his life. This is not to say that he failed to achieve great things. He rose from nothing to be a leader of a new nation and crafted a financial plan that would solidify the bonds between the states. His life, however, is not one that we are apt to judge as *eudaemonic*; he did not flourish. He injured those around him, he made rash decisions, and, in the end, he died a tragic death. These flaws all are rooted in his obsession with making a name for himself and crafting his narrative for posterity. He was more worried about the story that would be told than about the deeds that the story would be about.

Our theory of appropriate concern for legacy does seem to help us understand why two men, both obsessed with their legacy, are led to such different deeds by their obsession. The difference between appropriate and excessive concern for your legacy is not just a difference in degree. Washington and Hamilton could both rightly be said to be obsessed, but Washington was obsessed with doing good works for which he might be remembered. This was a mature and appropriate way to be concerned about his legacy. Hamilton's concern, on the other hand, was naive. His obsession was not with the good of the deeds but primarily with the story that would be told. He though only about himself rather than the world he was helping to shape. Hamilton's concern over his legacy is purely egocentric, and this is what led him into moral error. In the phrase, "my legacy," we could say that Washington's focus was on "legacy" while Hamilton's was on "my."

The Lesson

Concern for your legacy is a virtuous trait when that concern is properly aimed at doing good work that will, in the long run, earn you a good reputation. If you think too much about the stories that will be told once you're dead and gone and about how best to craft them to your liking, you've doomed yourself to Hamilton's fate.[1]

---

[1] I'd like to thank Steven Gimbel, Ryan Wilk, and Rose Ann Wilk for providing valuable feedback on an earlier draft of this chapter and my partner Kate Mereen for all of her support in this and all of my projects.

10
One Eye on the Future

ANDY WIBLE

Alexander Hamilton has long been remembered for organizing and co-authoring the *Federalist Papers*, signing the constitution, being the first Secretary of the Treasury, and emblazing the ten-dollar bill. Recently his rap has extended to a reflective and captivating biographical musical.

Hamilton may by now be the most popular Founder of the United States, and yet much of the musical's allure lies in exploring the flawed character that led to his early death. Hamilton is a modern-day star whose personal life is as important as his public contributions.

Alexander Hamilton and his wife Eliza never could have imagined that Hamilton's legacy would be shaped two hundred years after his death by a Broadway musical. As Washington says in the musical, we don't have control over how we will be remembered. Yet most people care deeply about their legacy, whether it's manifested in their children, their charitable donations, or their work. Hamilton's mix of great and reprehensible actions provides plenty of fodder for the musical about his life, and his wife Eliza worked feverishly after his untimely death to make sure his legacy was a positive one.

So, was Eliza right to work so hard preserving a positive legacy for her husband? You might be inclined to say no, given how he treated Eliza. He was not a faithful husband and was often an absent father. He was involved in the first sex scandal in American political history due to his two-year affair with Maria Reynolds and corresponding cover-up. Also, he had survived almost a dozen duels before he was shot dead by

Burr. His violent hobby and hot temper left Eliza to live fifty years without her husband. But despite these many faults, Eliza wanted people's memories to be of all his hard work and accomplishments.

In a selfish sense, it was in her interest to have a positive legacy for her husband. Her life was intertwined with his. When he looked good, she looked good. Also, she loved him. Love is caring for others as much as we care for ourselves. Her desire to help her husband's legacy showed how much she still loved him. We should not fault her for her love and determination. We certainly can care about our loved ones too much and do something wrong like cover up a crime. But Eliza's desire to spin her husband's legacy in a positive light isn't so egregious. She didn't desire to cover up the circumstances of his death. Yet, she wanted the world to focus on the positive triumphs of his life. This love is honorable.

Should Hamilton himself have been more concerned about his legacy? Should he have heard the voices saying that "History has its eyes on you?" If he was more concerned about his legacy maybe he would not have dueled, and he might have paid more attention to his family. On the other hand, his son Philip died in a duel trying to protect his father's legacy. Hamilton even tells Philip not to shoot George Eacker. In the song "Blow Us Away," he says to shoot in the air: "You don't want this young man's blood on your conscience." Hamilton's subsequent shot in the air when he dueled with Burr was incredibly courageous, and he didn't want blood on his hands as Burr did. A legacy may not be tarnished by participating in a duel. Killing tarnishes instantly.

The ancient philosopher Socrates had great concern for how he would be thought of after he was gone. He was sentenced to death by the court of Athens for corrupting the youth and arguing against the gods, and was given poison to drink. His friends said that they could easily break him out of jail and take him to a place where he would never be caught. But Socrates decided to stay and end his life. He thought breaking out of jail would be morally wrong as it would send the message to those who followed him that he was above the law. As we saw with the Hamiltons, dignity is as important in death as it is when living.

Tending Our Garden

Another group of ancient philosophers, the Stoics, took a different approach to concern about legacy. Stoics, such as Epictetus, thought that we must distinguish between what we can and cannot control. Fame and reputation are largely beyond our control. As Hamilton says about legacy "It's planting seeds in a garden you never get to see." We should not be frustrated by something that is out of our control and that we will not witness. Our attitude improves if we don't want more than our fate. Nonetheless, our actions do affect our future biographies. Hamilton and Socrates are right that we do sow the seeds of our legacy in our lifetime, and we should make sure they are well planted.

The English philosopher Jeremy Bentham was also strangely obsessed with how he would be remembered. Bentham was the modern founder of Utilitarianism, the moral theory that says we should always try to produce the best consequences for everyone, and he was a strong social reformer. As with Hamilton, he wanted to protect freedom and have government work for the overall welfare of its citizens, and consequently he was for abolishing slavery. One of Bentham's last achievements was helping to found the College of London. His utilitarian ideas are embedded in its charter. The college was the first such institution that accepted the poor, the non-religious, and people of all races, creeds, and political beliefs. It was a college that someone with Hamilton's background and talents could have attended.

Bentham thought carefully about his legacy to benefit his future prestige and maybe even society's future. Attached to his will were instructions on what to do with his body that he called *Auto-Icon: Farther Uses of the Dead to the Living*. In addition to donating his body to science to be dissected, he somewhat eccentrically instructed that it be mummified and his head shrunken (His head was later replaced by a wax head). He is still on display today at the College of London in a study room. They even still roll him out on occasion for the Board of Trustees meetings as a non-voting member. His auto-icon is a creepy bodily legacy for all to observe, and his remembrance does seem to be promoted by his auto-iconic existence. Maybe Eliza should have mummified Hamilton?

Bentham's auto-icon also exposes one of the main problems of his utilitarian view. The utilitarian does not take moral intentions into account. It is the outcome that matters and not the reasons for it. If Hamilton had killed his nemesis Aaron Burr in the duel, he might have created more overall good in the world while improving his own legacy. But he knew it would be wrong to kill to achieve this good end. The ends don't justify the means. Bentham's auto-icon may have been done to further this own fame rather than promote more good in the world. Was he right to have these selfish intentions to improve his legacy?

This criticism also makes us feel uncomfortable when someone joins a civic organization simply to improve her resume, even if she ends up helping society in the process. Hamilton might have been just such a person. There is evidence that he lied about his age in order to allow him to apprentice at a local import-export firm. He knew he would be good at the job if he got the chance. Once in America, he befriended wealthy individuals that he knew could help him rise up. A selfish interest or a little lie isn't as bad as killing, yet there seems some moral discomfort about these cases.

Intention over Consequences

Immanuel Kant's moral theory attempts to overcome this problem with utilitarianism. Kant believed that your intentions determine the morality of your action rather than the consequences. We are rational creatures who act freely and have reasons and intentions that prompt those actions. Good intentions for Kant are "unconditional commands" that he called categorical imperatives. Hamilton was wrong to lie, even though it facilitated his amazing life. You have to tell the truth because it's the right thing to do. As has often been said, lying may have been in Washington's interest after cutting down the cherry tree, but he could not tell a lie. Washington says in the musical, we shouldn't be concerned about our legacy after our death. We should be concerned about our intentions while living.

Kant had two versions of the categorical imperative. The first version says that we should only act on moral rules which we would be willing for everyone to follow. We've all heard the question: "What if everyone did that?" Similar idea. Kant uses an example of borrowing money on a false promise to pay it back. We would not be willing for everyone to follow the rule, because the only way we can borrow money on a false promise is if other people tell the truth and pay it back. If everyone lied, the system would break down. Therefore, lying is always wrong, because lying only works if other people tell the truth. Hamilton's lie about his age was wrong because if everyone lied about their age, then communication about age wouldn't be possible.

The second version of the categorical imperative says that we should treat people as ends and never as mere means. Kant believed that we all have intrinsic worth due to our rationality and so everyone should be treated with respect. People should not be used. Borrowing money on a false promise would be using the lender who is being lied to. Lying is always wrong for Kant because it is disrespecting the person. Killing is the clearest form of using someone as a mere means and Hamilton seemed to know this when he refused to shoot at Burr. Killing would clearly be wrong, even if the world would have been better off without Burr.

Kant's position does have its own problems. First, there do seem to be exceptions to Kant's categorical imperatives. Killing is generally wrong, but there are exceptions such as self-defense. Lying is generally wrong, but lying to save someone's life seems acceptable or lying to your mother that her new dress looks nice. Was Hamilton's little lie about his age acceptable as well? Maybe it was, given it was a small lie that did little harm and helped produce great success.

This criticism leads us to the central problem with the second version of the categorical imperative. It's tough to know when you're treating someone as a mere means. We treat people as means all the time. Servers, retail clerks, car wash attendants, and even teachers are all used as means. The moral problem is when they are treated as *mere* means such as when someone doesn't pay the bill. A person who gives money for naming rights of a building is not usually doing it solely for a better legacy. The person also cares deeply about the organization. Similarly, Hamilton may have lied, but he did intend to do good work and help the company succeed. He may have befriended people to selfishly improve his future, but he also liked them and they wanted to help him and the country.

Finally, just because you would not be willing for everyone to follow the rule you are acting on does not seem to make an action wrong. The philosopher Fred Feldman points out that it seems morally okay to sell all of your stock when the Dow Jones Index hits 20,000. But you wouldn't be willing for everyone to sell at that number for there would be no one to buy the stock. Similarly Bentham likely did not want everyone to become an auto-icon, but that does not seem to make Bentham's mummification wrong. Not everyone could have become Secretary of the Treasury as Hamilton was. But just because everyone could not have done all of the incredible things that Hamilton did, does not make his doing them wrong. He rightly created a lot of good in the world

Hamilton was right to be concerned about his legacy. He was right to be concerned about the consequences of his actions in his lifetime and after it. He knew that he had to balance his intentions and the long-term consequences of his actions, unlike Burr who seemed to have unbalanced selfish intentions and only considered short-term results. Hamilton was right to be concerned with but not obsessed with his legacy. Hamilton had setbacks and faults, but he was driven by how he would look in the future.

Alexander Hamilton and Eliza were right to be concerned about how Hamilton would look in the future, because he was a generally moral person. He had good intentions, had an incredible work ethic, sacrificed his life in battle, developed and promoted the most enduring constitution in the world, and established the foundation of the US economy. They were right to want him be a role model for children from disadvantaged backgrounds and anyone who has a dream to change the world.

How Should Hamilton Be Remembered?

How should we remember people after they have died? Whatever our memories are of others, they are always going to be caricatures of a person's life. Chernow's book on Hamilton is over seven hundred pages of detail and yet it is far from a complete record of his life. Even an avid fan of Hamilton cannot know all of his short life. Thus, we have to make choices on what we remember of someone, no matter how important or famous that person is. We must summarize. But what is a moral summary?

May we make the person whatever we like? Do we need to consider Hamilton in his totality, or should we pick out his best ideas and achievements? There must be some restrictions based on the truth. King George should not be made out to have been a benevolent, humble, and sane leader. He certainly wasn't these things. Is it permissible to selectively improve a person in retrospect? Most everyone has been to a funeral where the deceased is memorialized in a way that is far from factual. The crowd may feel good momentarily, but know deep down that the depiction is inaccurate. Generally this is accepted given the understandable vulnerability of the bereaved after the loss of a loved one. The utilitarian value of good consequences seems to override the Kantian requirement of the truth for memorials. As we saw above, a little beneficial lying is acceptable.

Biographers such as Chernow and even Miranda, seem to have a greater obligation to accurately depict their subject. They have written, respectively, a book and musical that are sketching a biography of the man as a whole. They didn't write the *National Enquirer* version called "The Sordid Life of Alexander Hamilton." Nonetheless, sex does sell and Hamilton's affair with Maria Reynolds is front and center. It is part of understanding this biographical tragedy and why "He's never gon' be President Now." A general biography of President Bill Clinton that avoided mentioning Monica Lewinsky would be a poor portrayal and an immoral deception.

The intended audience is also a factor in deciding on a proper biographical depiction. Hamilton's legacy presented to a first-grade class might be different than that represented in a Broadway musical. But it seems wrong to give even children a wholly inaccurate impression of a person's life. Consider common perceptions about George Washington. Washington is well known and well respected with many streets, schools, cities, the capital, and even a state named after him. He's remembered as an honest, humble, and moral first president who could not tell a lie and brandished a fine pair of wooden teeth.

Washington was in many ways an admirable man. He often humbly worked behind the scenes making sure important work, such as writing and passing the Constitution, got done, and he humbly refused a third term as president—amazing the megalomaniac King George. In truth, Washington never cut down a cherry tree as a child. This was a fabrication by an early biographer of Washington to improve his image. Also, Washington did have fake teeth that caused him much trouble, but they were not wooden. They were made of ivory (from a hippopotamus), and various metals. Dentures stained easily at the time and may have looked wooden to witnesses. Washington was also a slave owner from the age of eleven. Throughout his life he bought and sold slaves, owned over one hundred, and oversaw more than three hundred. Like Hamilton, the measure of his life is a complicated one.

Here again we see a tension between Bentham and Kant on what to do. Bentham's utilitarianism holds that good role models can have positive effects on children and adults. We need good people to be promoted to produce good people. Cynicism can ensue when revered role models are found to have feet of clay. Kant, on the other hand, prized the truth. We have a duty to provide honest memorials even if our role models will be tarnished. Hamilton's adultery and Washington's slaves need to be on the record. False teeth and false apple tree stories do not. Critical minds need to know. Kant's moral theory and Bentham's utilitarianism need to be balanced. There is a duty to tell positive stories of achievement, and of failure too. Character flaws are an integral part of any honest biography and are instructional as well. The storyteller determines the appropriate balance.

Alexander Hamilton's popularity as a hero is fairly recent. Hamilton's Federalist Party no longer exists, and the Democrats held office for nearly forty years after his death. His frank talks and disagreements with Jefferson, Madison, and Burr led to him being vilified long after his death. Eliza Schuyler Hamilton knew that a better story could and should be told, and today Hamilton's hard work and brilliant ideas have endured on stage, in our minds, and in our way of life. Alexander Hamilton helped to start America and he exemplifies America. His political and economic ideas endure as centerpieces of modern America. He paved the way for a strong central government based on liberty, commerce, and manufacturing that set the structure for the United States to be the economic and political superpower that it is today. Hamilton's ideas won.

Hamilton never got mummified, but a century after his death Hamilton did get his face on the ten-dollar bill. We see

him much more often than if he was only on display in a
Columbia University study room. Recently, there was some
movement to have his face removed from the currency in favor
of Harriet Tubman. After all, he wasn't president. In the end
though, Hamilton's treasury decided to remove President
Andrew Jackson's face from the $20 bill, due to Jackson's
immoral acts and Hamilton's rise to Broadway fame.
Hamilton's affair prevented him from becoming president, but
we are now rightly deploring Jackson's bigger moral faults
such as murder, land theft from Native Americans, and owning
slaves.

Hamilton the musical has solidified Hamilton's legacy as a
flawed American hero whose monument is enshrined on our
paper ten-spots, on the Broadway marquee, and in our twenty-
first century experience.

IV

Under Eastern Eyes

11
The Dao of *Hamilton*

AARON RABINOWITZ

Who's the hero of *Hamilton: An American Musical?* If you had to choose? You picked Hamilton? Right? Of course you did! His name's in bright lights on the Marquee. Or maybe you're the suspicious type, so now you're expecting that Burr is secretly the hero and Hamilton's the villain. Burr does provide Hamilton the key to getting his debt plan through congress.

Neither man is really a villain, though. Hamilton and Burr are both the heroes of *Hamilton*, because both of their philosophies play a key role in our nation's founding. Our society has an easy time valorizing Hamilton's aggressive bootstrapping, while Burr's subtler virtues garner faint praise. We can remedy this imbalance with a healthy dose of Daoism, a Chinese philosophy that values a sage like Aaron Burr.

Daoist Sage, at Your Service, Sir

Daoism is a philosophy and religion that arose around the fourth century in China. Daoist philosophy, along with similar Buddhist ideas, provide the basis for much of the modern mindfulness movement.

Daoism emphasizes living in harmony and going with the flow of the Dao. "Dao" means "the way of things." It is the energy that sustains the world, like the force in *Star Wars*. The Dao is also the substance that the world is made of, like the energetic fields of quantum physics. Often the Daoists use similes to talk about the Dao. My favorite compares the Dao to a giant river. Each of us and every piece of the universe is bobbing along in its current as we're pulled downstream. You can try to fight the current, and maybe you'll succeed and push against the current for a time, but you'll get exhausted and eventually the current will take you.

In Daoism, someone who can always go with the flow is called a sage. The *Daodejing*, Daoism's central text, describes the sage as patient and thoughtful. The Dao says "Weapons are instruments of fear; they are not a wise man's tools. He uses them only when he has no choice." The sage knows the right moment for action, and knows that waiting is often the better course. She acts in ways that create no resistance or friction with the Dao, floating along in the river without struggle. According to the *Daodejing*, "After a bitter quarrel, some resentment must remain . . . Therefore the sage keeps her half of the bargain, but does not exact her due". The sage does not try to force fairness or satisfaction. Burr and Hamilton desperately needed that insight.

The sage keeps in flow with the Dao by maintaining a balance of the two fundamental forces of the universe: Yin and Yang. You're probably familiar with the Yin-Yang symbol, and may know that it signifies some sort of energetic duality. Yang is the active, aggressive energy that drives everything forward. Yin is the passive, accepting energy that creates the space for Yang to flow into. Neither force is good or evil, they're both essential for a functional sage, and a functional universe.

It is only when Yin and Yang are out of balance that things go wrong. Human beings are, by nature, overly Yang. We tend to aggressively assert our wills and desires over the situations forcing our existence and our beliefs and our energy on those around us. Therefore, the Daoist sage gives extra attention to cultivating their Yin energy, and so maintains a balance between the active and the passive. The sage is then able to be still when stillness is called for, and to act when action is required.

You can see where this is going, right? Burr is the calming Yin to Hamilton's raging Yang. Burr begins the show on the path to Daoist sagehood. He is cultivating his yin energy, waiting for the moment of action. Hamilton invades that world of passivity with his passionate Yang. He sees every moment as a moment for action. The conflict of *Hamilton* is the meeting of Burr's passivity and Hamilton's aggressiveness. The two men circle each other throughout the show, just as the primal forces do in the yin-yang symbol. Burr's Yin seeps into Hamilton and Hamilton's Yang infects Burr. In the end, Burr gives Hamilton the Yin he needs to succeed, while Burr tragically succumbs to the excess Yang that Hamilton exudes.

The Journey to Balance Begins Under Your Feet

When Hamilton and Burr first meet, they are at opposite ends of the energetic spectrum. Hamilton is pure Yang, charging into situations and beating up bursars. He means well, like a giant puppy smashing around a tiny apartment. Burr, meanwhile, is the epitome of Yin, full of caution and passivity. He waits to even share his name until he understands the situation. Burr advises Hamilton to "Talk less, smile more," just as the central Daoist text, the *Daodejing*, tells us that "The man who knows does not talk, the man who talks does not know". In that first meeting, Burr plants in Hamilton a seed of Yin energy, centered on the insight that the best results arise when consideration precedes action. The message then gets buried under the onslaught of Laurens's band of brash, Yang revolutionaries, but it does not disappear entirely. It lies dormant until Washington, another candidate for Daoist sagehood, breathes life into Burr's advice.

It's odd that Washington and Burr don't hit it off better, given their shared love of caution. It's not clear in the musical why Burr screws up when he meets Washington, but he does. Burr's love for strategic patience should have made it easy for him to understand the wisdom of Washington's guerrilla tactics. Yet he comes at Washington with his aggressive critique, arguing for a strategy that would have cost them the war. Perhaps Burr is nervous at meeting such an important figure, or he mistakenly expected Washington to harbor aggressive desires as well, but Burr's Daoist temperament leaves him in that scene with Washington, allowing Hamilton to secure the coveted position of the general's right hand man.

Burr recovers his sage-like perspective, though. Even as he watches Hamilton secure a position and a happy marriage, Burr achieves true equanimity. Burr's show-stopping soliloquy "Wait for It" is an anthem for Daoists everywhere. The song acknowledges that the universe is unjust and apathetic, caring no more for the good person than the bad. However, instead of demanding action to force the universe to be just, Burr's philosophy is to wait and watch and try to understand the nature of the universe, unfairness and all. The *Daodejing* asks, "Do you believe you can take the universe into your hand and improve it?" and answers that "It cannot be done. The universe is sacred, if you try to change it, you will destroy it."

The sage recognizes that the human desire for a fair world is one of the desires that leads to an excesses of Yang, causing the individual a life of suffering as they career about, seeking to force the world to align with their conception of how things ought to be. Those who are impatient for change and do not follow the Dao are like men trying to straighten out a river. Their efforts are unsustainable, and the river ends up just as curvy as before. Action without understanding often makes the problem worse, and understanding requires that you wait for it.

That's not to say that waiting is easy. Burr, like a proper sage, does not ignore the harshness of reality. He waits despite the vicissitudes of fate, not out of fear of them. Knowing that he cannot just force the universe to be perfect, he waits patiently for the chance to help things just a little. He does what he can, like keeping a bed warm and keeping a promise to his parents, but he does not try to balance all of the good and evil of the universe at once.

The first act ends with our two protagonists set in perfect contrast. Hamilton always pushing to say more, to monologue and extemporize and command the room. Burr always tending towards brevity and even hesitancy. The result is that Hamilton pushes past Burr in the world of achievement, as aggressive individuals often do. There is no doubt that an aggressive individual can achieve and progress in the world, but it comes at a cost, as Hamilton learns. We do not achieve true progress and flourishing until Yang is balanced with Yin. That is why Hamilton, for all his advancement, keeps coming back to Burr for help. Hamilton needs Burr's Yin to balance him out.

He that Strives Is Not Steady

Act Two of *Hamilton* begins with the introduction of Hamilton's proper nemesis, Thomas Jefferson. Jefferson combines Hamilton's ambitious intellect with enough of Burr's strategic caution to provide the perfect foil for the untempered Hamilton. Jefferson hands Hamilton his first major intellectual defeat in their ferocious cabinet rap battle. Jefferson is able to goad the brash young upstart into embarrassing himself in front of Washington. It takes Washington threatening Hamilton's job, and the economic dream he holds for America, for Hamilton to finally see the value of Burr's philosophy.

In "The Room Where It Happens," the energetic shift in both Hamilton and Burr occurs simultaneously. We see the influence that the two protagonists have on each other. In Hamilton's case, Burr's advice finally takes root, giving Hamilton the Yin he needs to deal with some very Yang Virginians. With less talking and more smiling, Hamilton can finally get his debt plan through.

For Burr, the relationship with Hamilton seems to produce a change for the worse. Hamilton's Yang overwhelms Burr's calm Yin, producing in him a powerful need to also hold a position of power. While Burr may have sought advancement in the past, he seemed in control of his ambition; allowing himself time to wait and see how things worked out. By the end of "The Room Where It Happens," Burr is a changed man. He pushes for public office full force, without concern for who he harms. He campaigns the way Hamilton writes, like he's running out of time.

Hamilton's turn towards Yin influences his advice to Philip on his first duel. A younger Hamilton would have encouraged Philip to draw blood for honor, but now he cautions Philip to take the less aggressive path and fire into the sky. Hamilton cannot go so far as to encourage Philip to skip the duel entirely, which would have been the sagely thing to do. We see in Hamilton's response to the Reynold's scandal and to Philip's duel that he still hasn't fully incorporated the importance of passivity in a balanced approach to life. He believes he can use his intelligence and his strength to make things go the right way, and it costs him dearly.

The Dao of Uptown

After Philip's death, Hamilton finally embraces Yin. Before that, Hamilton saw the practical value of being less aggressive, but still couldn't understand how to lead a happy life.

Tragically, it took Philip's death for Hamilton to begin to appreciate life. He responds to tragedy like a Daoist sage, finding the value in the quiet of uptown and peaceful contemplation. He learns that days spent walking the streets in silence can have just as much value as days spent furiously writing. Just because a day spent walking the streets leaves no record behind, it doesn't make it less valuable to a life well lived. In this state of peacefulness, Hamilton and Eliza are able to truly and fully connect for the first time in the play.

Like all things, that peace does not last forever. The pull of the Yang world is strong, and politics demands involvement. Burr has become the Yang monster that Hamilton might have been, had things gone differently. Burr is nakedly chasing what he wants, and he credits Hamilton as his inspiration. The Yang life is not without its costs though. In the same breath that Burr boasts to Hamilton about his aggressiveness, he also laments how draining the Yang way of life really is. Burr's caught in the world of caring too much now, and part of him knows it, but it isn't the part that's in control, and so he pushes on towards the inevitable confrontation that both men can feel approaching.

The Inevitable Return to the Dao

As Burr foretold, it is Hamilton's hubris, his Yang nature, that brings us to the final act. Hamilton sides with the more traditionally aggressive Thomas Jefferson, a man who's not afraid to declare the hell out of something. Hamilton remains unable to embrace Burr's passive philosophy as anything other than a morally suspect strategy. The election's outcome might not have proven fatal, if Hamilton hadn't already infected Burr with his Yang-filled hubris. Burr is unable to balance his ambition with patience, having fallen too far into the world of legacies and accomplishments. He experiences the loss of face and Hamilton's perceived slights as matters worthy of life and death. A man who denounced the foolishness of duels early in his life has come to see it as the only option. This is what it looks like when a Daoist sage falls.

That brings us to Weekhawken, dawn. Hamilton, the man who was born to fight, wants no part of fighting any more, but the Yang in him can't see how to walk away. Burr, the man who never wanted to fight, now driven to madness by a lifetime of perceived slights, can think only of survival and the survival of his kin. He can no longer take the long view, or see the value of non-action, as Hamilton does when he aims at the sky. In the end, Hamilton finally embraces Yin, as Burr succumbs to Yang.

Of course, in reality, Burr and Hamilton likely weren't that different. Both were intelligent, hard-working individuals who cared a great deal about raising America's fortunes, as well as their own. In Miranda's world they serve as personifications of Yin and Yang, and the play provides a parable of warning against the excesses of Yang in one's life. Burr's thoughtful passivity tempers Hamilton's brash aggression enough to build a country, but not enough to save either man. In the end, Burr succumbs to Hamilton's Yang way of doing things, and Hamilton is unable to embody Yin enough to balance Burr. When Burr commits the Hamiltonian act of defending his honor through a duel, Hamilton is incapable of playing the role of Burr and walking away. The result is the destruction of two good lives.

The loss of heroes like Burr and Hamilton is an avoidable tragedy. We, as a society can learn to value Yin and Yang in equal balance. The world is full of would-be Hamiltons. What it needs is more Aaron Burrs, more Elizas, and more Washingtons. Following Washington's example, we can say goodbye with some words on how to live a life of balance, one that ends peacefully under a beautiful tree. A reading from The Dao of Hamilton:

A president who cares only about winning cannot govern.
A lawyer who can't sit down leaves the jury no room to decide.
A politician who stands for nothing achieves nothing.
A founder can only hope for what they leave behind.

Therefore, the sage retains Yang, but embraces Yin.
She keeps her gun unloaded and her shot in hand.
She holds to what is right, but accommodates what is necessary.
First she waits.
Then she acts.
Then she accepts.
Such is the way of the Dao.

12
Eliza Hamilton, Buddhist Master

BENJAMIN ROSS

What is a question you want answered? Is it buried deep or right on the tip of your tongue? Like the characters in *Hamilton*, we are defined by the questions whose answers seem just out of reach.

For the Buddha-like Eliza, her defining question is about suffering. Why does her beloved Alexander suffer from constant dissatisfaction, while she is always satisfied? Eliza desperately wants to grant Alexander her own peace of mind and help him to say, "That would be enough." This kind of equanimity in the midst of suffering exemplifies Buddhist philosophy. It was also a question of suffering that drove the historical Buddha, Siddartha Gautama, on his philosophical quest to find serenity amidst chaotic times. He encountered the realities of life and death first-hand, and was inspired to find an answer to his question, to discover a sense of peace despite adversity, just like Alexander and Eliza.

However, Alexander stands in stark contrast to Eliza's equanimity. He suffers constantly from his desire to somehow set himself apart from the world, and "build something that's gonna outlive me." After all, his name is Alexander Hamilton and there's a million things he hasn't done. His primary question, then, can be put like this: How can I ensure that I do not throw away my shot? How can I ensure that my ego, my name, A-L-E-X-A-N-D-E-R, becomes a legacy that lives beyond me?

The Suffering of a Dissatisfied Self

The Buddha started his teaching career with a sermon that simply suggested all life is suffering. Rather than running away from our suffering as we typically do, he pointed out that confronting why we are suffering is the first step toward finding a way to stop it forever. When we examine the Buddha's word for suffering, *dukkha*, it actually means something closer to "dissatisfaction."

In that first sermon, the Buddha was saying that life is characterized by having what we don't want, and wanting what we don't have. In other words, life is characterized by constantly creating the idea of a self that is somehow separate from our circumstances. The path to inner peace is a matter of finding satisfaction and contentment in the circumstances of our lives, and not looking for those things somewhere beyond where we find ourselves. Alexander hints at this as he confesses to Angelica, "You're like me, I'm never satisfied."

From the Buddhist perspective, Alexander can never be satisfied because he remains attached to an idea of a self that could be made into something eternal and everlasting. The reality is that there is nothing like that. Everything is subject to change, or, as Buddha liked to say, everything is on fire. Attaching to some idea of who we are or what we could be blinds us to the reality of the here and now, which is always slipping away from us. Unable to see that life is characterized by constant change, or impermanence, we are condemned to suffer. The Buddha put a strong emphasis on realizing this truth of impermanence, and taught that liberation from suffering only comes from realizing firsthand that nothing lasts forever.

It may seem like a strange strategy to attack the idea of a self. Nothing could be closer to us and more self-evident, right? But whatt Buddhist philosophy is not saying is that our unique individualities, personalities, and histories don't exist. That's nihilism, and Buddhism is not nihilism. People and things exist. Alexander had his own personal wax seal just like you and I have social security numbers. Alexander and Eliza could remember the events of their lives just like you and I can recall our own.

What the Buddha urges us to see is that there is no characteristic that we possess or thing that we have that could be considered the one, single, unchanging aspect that makes us who we are. Instead, the self just exists moment to moment. We suffer because we constantly attach to things and then say, "That's me," and try to hold on to that momentary identity forever. Today you're a husband, but tomorrow you want a divorce. Yesterday you were a police officer, but today you just can't carry a gun anymore. Buddhists believe that it's a mistake to hold on to an idea of the self as something that is separate from changing circumstances and the parts of us that are always in flux.

Alexander's dream of a legacy is exactly this sort of mistaken view. He has based all of his perceptions, goals, and desires on an idea of an immortal self. Ironically, the legacy that he believes will free him from the prison of his suffering is actually his jailor. He is trapped in *samsara*, the cyclic existence of ceaselessly repeating the same patterns and acting on the same conditioning over and over again, due to the fact that he remains bound by his attachment to a self.

As the circumstances of Alexander's life change, his idea of the self, his idea of a shot, of a legacy should change too. But they don't. And because they don't, he suffers. Suffering exists because we run from this truth that the only thing constant in this world is change. And what's worse is that we tend to respond not by relaxing our grip, but by clinging tighter and tighter to an idea of a self that identifies as me, you, Alexander, or the ten-dollar Founding Father without a father.

What the Buddha realized, after six years of questioning why we suffer, was the truth that Eliza was awakened to upon stepping out of her carriage in New York: we don't have to suffer at all. All we need to do is just live in the moment and accept what comes, dealing with circumstances as they arise, and let go of an idealized version of how we think events and our self ought to be. That would be enough. In finding the composure to do so, we naturally loosen our grip on the notion of a self that must be protected at all costs. Eliza wants to share that truth with Alexander, imploring him to "look around, look around at how lucky you are to be alive right now" ("Non-Stop"). Stopping to appreciate the now is how we break down the illusion of the self.

Check Your "Self"

In Buddhist philosophy, the most important teaching is that there is no such thing as a permanent self. The Buddhist name for these teachings on "no-self" is *anatman*. "Atman" is an Indian idea similar to the Christian idea of the soul. Buddhists claim that the atman is an illusion.

The evidence of a soul is taken to be the feeling of "I am-ness" that supposedly remains stable throughout a lifetime of experiences. The Buddha found that to be as absurd as a tri-angle with four sides. Our personalities and body composition change constantly throughout our lives, and the feeling of "who we are inside" is subject to wild swings as we encounter vari-ous life experiences. Though we might often say "I," and though we mean to refer to the same person, every time that "I" is uttered it is actually different. "I" is spoken each time with dif-ferent air, different sensory information, different knowledge, and different intentions. Who am I? Who are you?

The idea of no-self is challenging to understand, so let's get con-crete—literally—and make an example out of an often overlooked character from *Hamilton*: New York City. What is meant by no-self is that the self as we usually imagine it doesn't truly exist like we think it does. It is exactly the same with the city of New York. Because there is a place we can point to on a map, there must be one thing that we can say makes New York, New York.

It's true that the city has conventional existence as the set-ting of the musical, and it is just as true that it has a unique identity like Alexander or Eliza or you or me, having a name given to it by people who built the buildings from imported materials and assembled the streets and constructed the land-marks. But those landmarks could easily have been different ones, and the city of New York could have its name changed back to New Amsterdam at any minute. The fact that every-thing about New York City could change at any time also means that there is no single thing we can point to in New York that will always be New York. If you were standing on the street when the Schuyler sisters burst onto the scene and someone said, "Yes, I see the bank and the river and the car-riages and the sidewalks, but where is New York City? Tell me, please, where is New York?!" How would you answer? You might gesture wildly and shout, "It's right here!" And you would not be totally wrong, but you would also not be com-pletely right.

The self in Buddhist philosophy is just like New York. Our self is simply what we call the coming-together of certain elements that only *seem* static and unchanging. What are these elements? The Buddha claimed that our "I," our self, is a composite of five things: form, sensation, thought, impulse, and consciousness. We are a human collage of various parts that interact with the world and create the idea of a solid, lasting self. We suffer because we go about our lives thinking that there's such a thing as a self and doing everything we can to grasp onto it, to protect it, to defend our ego from attack, when in reality, what we consider to be the self is just these five elements arising and passing away continuously. The way out of suffering is the same as realizing that the self is actually no-self, just a convenient fiction like New York City.

Some contemporary philosophers suggest that the commitment to a belief in a real self is not rationally justified, echoing Buddhist philosophy. Our sense of self is said to have no independent reality since its existence depends on everything else. Science, too, seems to be on the side of Buddhist philosophy when we consider atomic theory. When vast numbers of atoms assemble to make a table or a hamburger, we experience these things as solid, yet the atoms that make up these things are in constant motion: emerging, attracting, repelling, fluctuating. Further down at the subatomic level, at the core, these things demonstrate none of the comforting density we take for granted. When we examine the self for a single thing that does not change, or a single thing that isn't dependent on other things for its existence, that single thing is nowhere to be found.

Look for Eliza, You Won't Find Her

Eliza realizes that her self is just a fiction of convenience, that there is no Eliza as such, there is only a life lived according to circumstances, whether it's walking around New York, finding a husband, giving birth, receiving word of infidelity, grieving over the loss of a son, forgiving a man's misdeeds, or continuing to live on after him.

Eliza's Buddha-esque philosophy of acceptance is summed up perfectly in one short line in the song "Schuyler Defeated" where she sings, "Sometimes that's how it goes." Eliza escapes the suffering of Alexander by recognizing that everything changes, and that we should enjoy what time we have here, and take what comes without striving to keep everything from changing. For Alexander, both his story and Eliza's story are one narrative dealing with the same triumphs and tragedies. The difference is that Alexander's story is carried out with the I/Me/Mine, his ego, his name, his legacy, foremost in mind. The difference in how they conceive of the self is the reason they respond to the same events in opposite ways.

Alexander was inspired to shape and control his life by bolstering his ego, establishing a strong sense of self, and defining who he is in terms of what he has done and has yet to do. The revolutionary times put Eliza on a different course. Rather than attaching to her name and doing everything she could to vigorously sustain and enhance her ego, Eliza was inspired to subsume her sense of self in a sense of wonder and satisfaction at merely being alive to bear witness and partake of events as they unfolded. She is free to take things as they come simply because she realizes there ultimately is no Eliza.

She realizes that happiness does not occur when one ceaselessly tries to control the world and leave a mark. Yet, she also realizes that the world we inhabit is not mere illusion either. After all, she grieves when her son dies. But she does fully accept that the self we rely on to stumble around in this world does not have any ultimate reality. Rather than spend a life trying to ensure a legacy, Eliza implores Alexander to share her contentment simply by looking around at how lucky he is to be alive right now, echoing one of Buddha's earliest instructions, *shamatha, vipassana*: stop and see.

Buddhist philosophy suggests that many people prefer to seek a way out of suffering in a lifestyle like Alexander's. Thrown into the world as a orphan, he becomes a self-made man and puts all of his resources into the one thing he feels he can control: the person he becomes as he takes his shot. Rather than pausing to think about why he remains dissatisfied, despite his best efforts to the contrary, he clings to an idealized version of life that might exist if he could just get a lot farther by workin' a lot harder, bein' a lot smarter, and a self-starter. Then, all the recognition, wealth, and honor could be his. Then, that would be enough.

The Duality of the Duelist

Though Alexander is finally able to look around, to say "That would be enough," to stop and see after Philip's death in the quiet of uptown, this equanimity is short-lived. Alexander is able to reflect on the past, and has seen firsthand the destructiveness inherent in a life lived for a legacy, rather than the here and now. Though he asks for Eliza's forgiveness and eventually receives it, still he cannot escape the pull of politics. Enraged that Burr can so easily change his ideals to suit any situation, Alexander feels that Burr and the world should conform to him, to his idea of honor, to his idea of a self.

Aaron Burr represents a direct threat to Alexander's sense of self, and so they agree to duel. The duel represents the extreme of what can happen when a person is attached to their concept of a self, so identified with their words, their legacy, their sentences, their paranoia, and the perception of others' that one is willing to kill or die for honor. Yet, this dualism, the sense of separation between a static ego-self in here and a changing world out there, is only one way of experiencing the world. Eliza knows no such duality. She knows that there is no separating the self and the world—there can be no Eliza apart from the world.

Eliza's life is a continuous flow of events in the world without interruption. She retains her individuality, but does not set it apart from the world. There is a oneness to her worldview— a oneness that is lost on Alexander. She implores Alexander throughout the musical that, "We don't need a legacy, we don't need money, If I could grant you peace of mind, if you could let me inside your heart . . ." If only she could have added, "You don't need the idea of a self set against the world!"

Alexander is said to have written Eliza a letter before going to meet Burr on that fateful day, suggesting that they would one day meet again in a better world. Alexander consoles both himself and Eliza with this idea of a future time and a future place, where, finally, that would be enough. We can only imagine Eliza shaking her head as she read these words, knowing that the better world is always right here, right now.

But as long as we believe in an unchanging self and defend it to the death, nothing will ever be enough.

V

The Existential Challenge

13
Redemptive Rapping

Jennifer L. McMahon
and Jacqueline McMahon Smith

Both Lin-Manuel Miranda and the famous French philosopher, Jean-Paul Sartre, use art to examine the challenge of living and telling history.

Both artists created works designed to inform the viewer
that art, particularly music, can encompass and transcend history. In Sartre's masterwork of twentieth-century philosophical
literature, *Nausea*, the protagonist grapples with the dilemmas
of human existence. Written in the form of journal entries, the
book follows Antoine Roquentin, a historical biographer, as he
struggles with the feeling for which the book is named.

Roquentin has been working on the biography of a prominent historical figure, the Marquis de Rollebon, but has become
bored and stymied, unable to relate history in a way he finds
valid or meaningful. After years of struggling to complete the
work, Roquentin abandons his project upon realizing that he
has been using his research as a diversion to avoid confronting
unsettling truths regarding existence. Instead, he finds that it
is music that provides him with the solace and clarity he
desires.

Legions of *Hamilton* fans might think that Miranda has the
answer to Roquentin's dilemma. Had Roquentin had the pleasure (and sheer luck) of seeing *Hamilton,* it would have cured
his nausea, at least for three hours. Unfortunately, his nausea
would surely have been replaced by the equally unpleasant
sensation of envy. While Roquentin failed at his historical project, Miranda has created a masterful work that tells history
through musical theatre.

Unlike poor Roquentin, who searches for a voice to tell existential truths without lying or distracting from the messy business of life, Miranda has found a voice, spoken through the character of Alexander Hamilton. In Miranda's creation, there is a vibrant synthesis of history and art in the musical telling of the storied life of an American forefather. This telling appeals to our most visceral emotions and speaks to the masses.

At first glance, it might seem as if the words and music of *Hamilton* and the fictional work of the existentialist Sartre couldn't be further apart. Likewise, it might appear as if the charismatic Miranda and the brooding French philosopher have little or nothing in common. However, as Sarah Bakewell notes in her recent bestseller, *At the Existentialist Café*, Sartre was a celebrity in post-war France and his fame continued after his death in 1980.

Both great works shed light on the relationship between life and art, fact and fiction, and living and telling, particularly historical telling. Both authors assign music a crucial role in the narrative. Finally, in both *Hamilton* and *Nausea*, the author bears a unique relation to the protagonist. Miranda is not only the creator of *Hamilton*, he also performs the lead role. Likewise, Sartre's main character, Roquentin, offers a look into the life and mind of the renowned philosopher.

Though audiences should never assume that a character represents the experiences or ideas of its author, Sartre asserts in his autobiography, *Les Mots*: "I was Roquentin." While he explains that *Nausea* is a novel, not an autobiography, he admits that his own experiences and insights are the basis for those attributed to his main character. Sartre also contends that literature can be a mirror to life, one that helps us understand life better by virtue of the fact that it offers existential truths in sharper relief, and in a form that makes those truths more tolerable.

Shedding light on the nature of existence was one of Sartre's goals in authoring *Nausea*. Though art reveals reality, Sartre also notes that art can offer an escape from reality, particularly a reprieve from the anguish we experience at the absurdity of existence and the burden of choice that we bear in its wake. Sartre follows in the tradition of philosophers who believe art provides a healing balm that makes living easier. Similarly, in

Hamilton, the musical telling of history is both the means and the message that has generated an artistic phenomenon. The characters in *Hamilton* experienced both victory and tragedy in the creation of a new nation, and Miranda presents the highs and lows of their existence in a production that invokes wonder and acclaim.

Live or Tell: Living Is Harder

In *Nausea*, Sartre introduces his main character, Roquentin, as he confronts the absurdity of life and the realization that "the significance of things and their methods of use . . . are feeble points of reference which men have traced . . . on life's surface." It takes virtually the whole novel for Roquentin to admit that life is absurd. Initially, he only feels that something is amiss. A vague feeling of dissatisfaction, similar to what Hamilton felt about the injustices of his time, disturbs Roquentin and causes him to experience nausea.

One of the things that compels Roquentin's nausea, and ultimately compels his recognition of absurdity, is a change in his relationship to his work: his inability to finish the biography of Rollebon. Roquentin's interest in Rollebon fades at the same time as he begins to question the legitimacy of the historical enterprise in which he is engaged. It dawns on Roquentin that instead of disclosing the unequivocal truth about Rollebon, he is merely producing a story, namely, *his*-story of Rollebon, not the *history* of Rollebon.

Roquentin concludes that Rollebon was just a fiction he created and needed in order to escape thinking about existence itself. He admits, "I had loaned Rollebon my life" in exchange for "the justification for my existence." No longer confident that he can provide a true history, Roquentin abandons his research. His nausea returns full force and he concludes that he must "live or tell."

Showing that Roquentin's dilemma is false, Miranda lives and tells through his work. His *Hamilton* is a dynamic exchange between the author and the subject that intensifies the musical production, creating a resounding message for the audience.

Although Roquentin thinks he wasted ten years of his life writing the story of Rollebon, his assertion that one must live or tell doesn't discourage him from writing or enjoying other art forms. He states, "I can't put down the pen: I think I'm going to have the Nausea and I feel as though I am delaying it while writing." Music provides even more immediate relief for Roquentin's nausea than writing. Again and again, Roquentin returns to his favorite bar to listen to music, particularly a jazz song titled, "Some of These Days." Listening to this song temporarily cures his nausea and makes him feel a "strange happiness." Roquentin believes that music alleviates his nausea because it has things life lacks, like necessity and order. Whereas Roquentin contends that life is absurd, it is as if music is from another world.

Initially, Roquentin maintains that there is a firm distinction between art and life, or at least between music and ordinary existence. We see Miranda challenge that split, bringing art and history to a glorious union. However, as Roquentin listens to the music in the bar, it seems to him that the music is above existence. It is dazzling, instead of nauseating. This distinction between music and life is what allows music to relieve Roquentin's nausea. His nausea is a response to life's absurdity, and music seems to provide a remedy, one that adds the appearance of order and necessity to a world in which they are lacking.

Interestingly, Roquentin asserts that order and necessity are found in several other things that also contribute to *Hamilton's* success: adventure and perfect moments. Adventure and perfect moments are like music. Each possesses order, completeness, and *sense*. In *Hamilton*, we see an adventure-filled musical that tells the life of a founding father through a series of perfectly staged moments. As Roquentin explains, "I wanted the moments of my life to follow and order themselves like those of a life remembered." Miranda gives that gift to Hamilton.

While Roquentin gives up writing the historical biography of Rollebon, he never abandons music. Confronting the absurdity of life and the obscurity of his own existence, Roquentin returns to the bar at the end of the novel and listens once again to "Some of These Days." Rather than reasserting the hard dichotomy between music and life that he had maintained before, Roquentin concludes that the creator of the song justified his existence by creating music. He speculates that he too might justify his own existence through writing, but not by writing history. He could write a novel, one that would be *like* music and with enough truth to motivate people to make more of their lives.

Though Sartre doesn't tell us what happens to Roquentin, he presents us with a character who recognizes the possibility implicit in music and story, who realizes that music can save and stories can redeem. *Nausea* can be seen as Sartre's self-justifying novel. With it, Sartre tells truths differently and more powerfully than with any of the historical biographies he *did* complete. With *Hamilton*, however, we see a synthesis of history and art. A new way of transmitting history that uses music in addition to narrative tools, creating the opportunity for Miranda to recount history and also motivate existential change.

One History for All

Staged with a modern focus that includes a multi-ethnic cast, high-energy choreography and a musical score influenced by hip hop, Hamilton appeals to audience members of all ages, genders, and tastes. Part of its widespread appeal is the way Miranda portrays his characters with great insight and empathy, their flaws and vulnerabilities viewed with an understanding eye. The characters that circle around Hamilton—and they literally do circle around him, the Broadway production has an amazing revolving stage—are authentic, compelling, and fully realized. Aaron Burr, George Washington, Eliza Hamilton and more—the viewer knows them intimately.

Miranda is attuned not just to Hamilton's place in history, but his own as the creator of an artistic work of great influence. Just as Sartre's main character, Roquentin, offered a vision into the mind of the renowned philosopher, a similar link exists between Miranda and Hamilton. Miranda is not only the creative mind behind *Hamilton*; he also performed the lead role through July of 2016. Both Sartre and Miranda created works that speak to the audience precisely because their creators invested themselves in telling their particular story and endeavored to be candid about the subject and themselves in the process.

Miranda's Hamilton—a bastard, orphan, and immigrant with outsider status—appeals to audiences because he started life at the bottom, working his way up through poverty and adversity to become an esteemed figure in American history. Hamilton's journey exemplifies the American Dream and in doing so reminds the audience of their responsibilities as American citizens to strive to determine themselves and to fight against the ills of society. Miranda's investment in his endeavor has led to more than record-breaking ticket sales and awards; his achievement has created a reinvigorated interest in history and social change.

In a 2016 *Rolling Stone* interview, Miranda explained how he personally related to Hamilton's character:

> I'm very aware that an asteroid could kill us all tomorrow. But I create works of art that take years and years to finish. So it's an enormous act of faith to start a project . . . in that way, I'm very Hamilton-esque, in that I'm aware of both time and of the incredible opportunity that I'm lucky to have, and not wanting to squander either.

Like the character, Alexander Hamilton, Miranda does not want to miss his shot.

The Dilemma of Personal History

Roquentin abandoned his pursuit of historical telling, stuck as he was on the impossibility of accurately telling historical truths about Rollebon. His determination that one must "live or tell" was his downfall as a historical biographer. In his telling of the life of Alexander Hamilton, Miranda succeeds where Roquentin fails. Miranda accepts that we cannot control history, our legacy can ultimately lie in the hands of others, and when writing history, we conceal as well as we reveal.

Miranda accepts history as story. The *Hamilton* libretto is replete with references to the notion of surrendering yourself to history. In Act One, George Washington reminds Hamilton and the audience that we cannot control our legacy. Pure truths are rarely told, and our story is crafted not only by our actions, but also by others through the lens of their perceptions, their biases, their memories and emotions.

The existential dilemma, that as much as we try to create our own story, history can still judge us unfairly, runs throughout *Hamilton*. Burr initially comes across as a cautious young man, circumspect in the midst of revolutionary fervor, but in the wake of Hamilton's successes and his own political missteps, he becomes increasingly bitter. Hamilton and Burr, both men riddled with pride, eventually engage in their fateful duel. In the song, "The World Was Wide Enough," Burr articulates his regret that, by surviving the duel, he has ended up on the wrong side of history. He characterizes history as an artist, a vast creative power that elevates or destroys.

Despite the fact that we can never have complete control of our story, both Sartre and Miranda understand the redemptive power of writing. They believe that writing can help us understand life better, by distilling essential truths from the complex mix of everyday life and rendering those truths in a more palatable form. For Miranda, writing is a way to save your soul and to right or write your own history. Miranda devised and performed the character of Alexander Hamilton as a man preternaturally aware of his own demise, a man determined to stay one step ahead of fate. He depicts Hamilton's prodigious writing as both a way to survive difficult circumstances and a way to demarcate his future, however short it might be. Hamilton sings in "Hurricane" about how writing was his salvation, stating that "when my words were met with indifference, I picked up a pen, I wrote my own deliverance." He accomplished what Roquentin hoped he might do.

Music Is the Answer, but Why Hip Hop?

Although Roquentin thought history was wasted effort, he knew about the redemptive power of music. Music cured his nausea. He wanted nothing more than his life to be the subject of a melody. How he would have envied *Hamilton*.

How appropriate that Miranda chose hip-hop music, the voice of urban revolution, as the genre for his musical about America's first revolutionaries. Miranda's choice of hip hop succeeds for the same reason that rap is now part of our literary tradition—it's art that communicates with imminence. Sartre noted that good music offers a sort of perfection, and what rap offers is immediacy. Hip hop deals with life's existential dilemmas in its discussion of present-tense problems like racism, poverty, crime, addiction, and inequality.

Miranda has an insider's knowledge of hip-hop music and pays his respects to the old school rappers. References to

Grandmaster Flash and the Furious Five, the Notorious B.I.G. and Tupac Shakur can all be found in *Hamilton*. In her article, *All About The Hamiltons*, Rebecca Mead wrote "Miranda saw Hamilton's relentless brilliance, linguistic dexterity, and self-destructive stubbornness through his own idiosyncratic lens. It was, he thought, a hip-hop story, an immigrant's story." The genius of Miranda's choice of vernacular is particularly apparent in certain songs like "Cabinet Battle #1," "Cabinet Battle #2," and "The Ten Duel Commandments" that pay homage to the rhythms and rifts of iconic rap songs like "The Message" and "The Ten Crack Commandments."

In "Cabinet Battle #1," Miranda references rap battles that originated between MCs in the 1970s and became part of hip-hop culture in performance, recording, and film. Miranda turns the practice on its head in a fast-paced battle of braggadocio between Jefferson and Hamilton over whether the newly-formed Federal Government should assume states' debts from the Revolutionary War.

In his typical provocative fashion, Hamilton rejects "a civics lesson from a slaver, hey neighbor, your debts are paid cuz you don't pay for labor . . . yeah, keep ranting, we know who's really doing the planting." Miranda successfully mixes a history lesson with a musical genre much of his audience grew up listening to, while simultaneously converting many who never liked rap.

Live and Tell

In his biography, Ron Chernow wrote that Hamilton "was a messenger from a future we now inhabit." The same is true for Miranda. Roquentin thought that we must "live or tell," but Miranda has shown us that we can do both.

In *Nausea*, Sartre wrote of Roquentin as slowly moving towards the realization that art and real life can co-exist, but still unconvinced that art and history can also go together. However, Miranda sees history not as a static telling of the past, but as a means to live and improve life through inspiration and interpretation.

His work unites history and music to inspire us toward the ideals of fairness and equality embodied in the dreams of our forefathers.

14
To Throw Away Your Shot or Not?

TIM JUNG AND MINVERVA AHUMADA

Hamilton shows us two distinct attitudes: Hamilton, who will "not throw away his shot" in the Revolutionary War, and Aaron Burr's more cautious approach, "You spit. I'm 'a sit. We'll see where we land."

Is there a better attitude to take towards life and your own death? Martin Heidegger might provide us with the answer. Heidegger is well-known for his work *Being and Time*, which philosophically re-imagines humanity as meaning-making creatures, using a branch of philosophy known as *phenomenology*. *Phenomenology* is different from past philosophical systems, because phenomenology believes that we interact with the "things themselves"—a past philosopher like Immanuel Kant (1724–1804) believed that we have nothing more than access to our processed senses of the external world instead of direct access to the external world. For Heidegger, we have access to the "things themselves," as they provide us with information about how humans interact with the world.

While his work may have aimed to get to a better understanding of "Being," a term whose meaning he thought was never adequately understood in the history of philosophy, Heidegger aims to understand Being by looking at human "beings," whom he calls Dasein—a German term which translates to something like "being there." Heidegger's analysis of Dasein addresses questions of death, authenticity or an "owned" existence, and how moods may affect our perception of the world.

What's Your Name, Man?

The beginning of *Hamilton* provides us with a hurricane of an autobiography of Alexander: he is a "bastard, orphan, son of a whore, and a Scotsman." Alexander Hamilton is "dropped" into an obscure Caribbean island—*thrown* into his existence, you might say. According to Heidegger, *thrownness* is the idea that we are thrown into our personal, historical, and cultural contexts—we find ourselves in a *world*.

Perhaps Lin-Manuel Miranda is a secret scholar of Heidegger, as the circumstances of anyone's birth—being "dropped" "by Providence"—is very important to Heidegger's philosophical understanding of the person. The accidents of our existence can seem very surprising, as we find ourselves in very specific conditions.

Though Hamilton's circumstances are quite unfortunate, *thrownness* does not have to have negative connotations. The Schuyler sisters: Angelica and Eliza (but not Peggy—more on her anxieties later), express astonishment at their own existence: "Look around, look around at how lucky we are to be alive right now!" While this is a point of celebration for someone like Angelica, who has been reading Thomas, Peggy is much more cautious.

Violence on the Shore

Sometimes we can marvel at the world and at how lucky we are to be alive at this given time and feel at home, but other times, the world feels uncanny, or, if we are literally translating from the German *unheimlich*, un-homelike or unsettling. Peggy, in the midst of the hubbub of Manhattan, is worried because "Daddy said to be home by sundown," in addition to the fact that he said, "not to go downtown." While this might look like a fear of consequences to disobeying her father's wishes, Peggy expresses an anxious disposition when she mentions, "It's bad enough there'll be violence on the shore". Heidegger explained that existence is not easy—issues come up for Dasein.

Anxiety shows us that we take the world around us for granted. In Heidegger's words, this means that the "world has the character of completely lacking significance"—or, in Lin-Manuel Miranda's words, "the world turns upside down." What happens with anxiety, according to Heidegger, is that we lose two basic and meaningful ways of interacting with the world and the objects in it: *readiness-to-hand* and *presence-at-hand*. *Readiness-to-hand* describes how we may use tools, and the meaningful relationship that tool has in a broader, worldly, context.

While Heidegger explains readiness-to-hand through the example of a hammer, perhaps something more relevant to *Hamilton* would be a dueling pistol. In order to examine how we take tools for granted, we must analyze them as though they are *present-at-hand*, or objectively. The dueling pistol reveals itself to be an object that is in a broader context: 1. it is to be used during a specific time and place; 2. it has the purpose of killing someone who has taken umbrage with what you have claimed about their character, or for defending your honor against a person who has sullied your good name; and 3. the dueling pistol reveals itself to have meaningful relationships with other kinds of weapons.

However, if we are struck by angst or anxiety in our own existence, and holding something like a dueling pistol in our hands we may forget its meaning. We may start questioning the choices we could possibly make in our situation or even question the past that led to this point in the duel. Anxiety turns our world upside-down, as we are reminded that nothing is certain. We are forced into the possibilities of our existence—all of the potential choices we must make—and, in Heidegger's words, we must choose to "win ourselves" or "lose ourselves."

Though Heidegger was clear that he was not writing about ethics in *Being and Time*, or providing us with virtues we ought to adopt, the question still arises: How do we win ourselves? Heidegger's answer: By being authentic, or having an owned existence. However, we can't always act authentically, or own our existence, for Dasein is always composed of two components: inauthenticity (the *they*self) and authenticity (or *oneself*).

Idle Talk

To explain an authentic or owned existence, it may be easier to show what an inauthentic or disowned existence looks like. Heidegger believed that Being-with-Others can lead to *falling*. *Falling* occurs living day-to-day, where it is easy to get caught up in the *They*, and to lose oneself. Heidegger's example of where we may lose ourselves is in something he calls "idle talk." In idle talk, you are "passing the word along," or gossiping. Everything you need to know is already there, and you don't really need to think about what you are gossiping about. Here, it's easy to think of celebrity news and all the minutiae of celebrities' lives. You don't need to think: you only need to pass the word along.

Aaron Burr, James Madison, and Thomas Jefferson best demonstrate inauthenticity when they read of Hamilton's affair. Madison, with glee, announces his request for "Highlights!" The three conclude that the Reynolds pamphlet shows someone destroying their own life. Idle talk, for Heidegger, is always a "closing-off"—there's no possibility for further individual development, because the Dasein in question is not looking towards their own possibility or potential.

There is no ambiguity about the issue at hand to allow for an individual Dasein to make up their own mind about a topic. Similarly, we may consider the weather as a topic of idle talk: the conversation is already done for us—we know what to say, and passively take up a role in the conversation instead of actively creating a conversation.

Burr's Inauthenticity

Aaron Burr seems to be very concerned with the talk of others, and never seems to take a stand for himself. Burr's advice to Hamilton is to talk less and smile more—"Don't let them know what you're against or what you're for." Hamilton is rough around the edges. He did, after all, punch the bursar—because the bursar thought Hamilton was stupid (he's not stupid). It seems that Burr is encouraging Hamilton to engage in nothing but idle talk. To be fair, Burr is justified in thinking that "Fools who run their mouths wind up dead"—but what does Burr actually want?

Hamilton wants to build something that will outlive him, while Burr just wants to "be in the room where it happens." Jefferson and Madison entered into negotiations with Hamilton aiming to actively participate. Does Burr simply want to be witness to these historical events? Does he wish to show up to talk less and smile more? Burr, at least according to Hamilton, has no personal beliefs, or doesn't make them known. In this way, Burr is living inauthentically, or is not owning his own existence. After Burr defeats Philip Schuyler in the New York senate race, Hamilton asks, "Since when are you a Democratic-Republican?" Burr responds, "Since being one put me on the up and up again." Burr always engages with the *they*, and perhaps all politicians do, but Burr always plays it safe: his existence seems to be *idle talk*.

Consider even how seriously Burr takes the idle talk of Hamilton declaring publicly, "Jefferson has beliefs. Burr has none." Burr finds no alternative but to engage in a duel, and to participate in the duel as an average person would—by shooting Hamilton. Burr's participation differs from Hamilton's, and Burr shows how excruciatingly difficult it would be not to shoot Hamilton: Hamilton looks seriously intent, and his wearing his glasses, presumably to make his shot more deadly accurate. Burr thought that there was no choice but to take aim and shoot—from the moment the bullet leaves the gun, Burr seems to show signs of authenticity.

The World Was Wide Enough

According to Heidegger, when our conscience calls to us, the self we present to the *they* disappears; in his words: "Conscience summons Dasein's Self from its lostness in the 'they'." A conscience is a very strange thing, it exists within us and comes from us, and in some ways, makes us *anxious* and turns our world upside down, giving us a moment to reconsider our possibilities by making us feel guilty. Burr reflects that when Hamilton aimed at the sky, his death follows, but Burr paid for it. Burr owns his mistake, recognizing that he ought to have known the world was "wide enough" for both of them. This is what Heidegger calls *resoluteness*: this is an authentic moment for any Dasein, whereupon you take responsibility for your own existence.

My Dearest, Angelica

Angelica shows authenticity, or an owned existence. As she is toasting her sister, the musical pauses, and we are rewound to Angelica meeting Hamilton. The past is something that none of us can change, and Angelica is aware of this. Actually, Angelica is aware of three truths.

Number one! Angelica knows that as a woman her "only job is to marry rich." Angelica, already distinct from Jefferson, Madison, and Burr, separates herself from the gossip or idle talk in New York. She understands her thrownness—that society makes certain demands of her—and yet she makes her own decisions. Angelica could marry Hamilton, despite his being penniless. She contemplates this decision, making it her own, leading us to . . .

Number two! Angelica is not so sure as to why she introduces Hamilton to Eliza, but shows obvious signs of regret. Maybe, she thinks, she did this because Hamilton was pursuing Angelica because marriage to a Schuyler sister would give him social status.

Number three! Angelica knows she must let her sister marry Hamilton, and, tragically, find a way to keep Hamilton's eyes in her life.

Despite these reflections, Angelica is resolute in her decision. She's truly standing by her decision to be by Eliza's side, as she owns her decision, though she may never be satisfied. Emotions affect and color our perception—for Heidegger, there is no pure abstract reason, free of emotion; everything has an emotional background that affects our outlook. Perhaps this is best shown in mourning.

The Unimaginable

When the Hamiltons move uptown after Philip's death, they are still coping with their loss. Angelica and the company sing that he is "working through the unimaginable." While Heidegger did not go in depth and provide an analysis of a specific emotional process like grief, he did emphasize that moods and feelings—or what he calls *attunements*—can allow us to recognize our thrownness. In other words, our moods show us where we are in our world and how we're interacting with it. If we are walking "the lengths of the city" due to depression, we may have a moment of recognizing our thrownness.

Dealing with a death is one thing, but understanding your own death—this is the unimaginable. Let's begin with the experience of a death of another person. The one who has died, according to Heidegger, is distinct from the dead body, for the one who has died has been, in Heidegger's words, "torn away" from those who are left behind. The body is present, but the *person* is not, and the dead body is an object of concern in the way the body is to be dealt with via funeral rites, internment, or incineration. You act differently around a dead body; the one lost is no longer a Dasein, and their body is a strange reminder of that.

But in addition to this reminder, Heidegger explains that no one can die for us—our death is ours alone, and this can boggle the mind. Death is unlike other possibilities for our existence: it is, in Heidegger's words, the "possibility of the impossibility of any existence at all." This is not to say that you can't die for the sake of another person—but it is saying that dying is something that each and every Dasein must take upon themselves. Death is a personal and intimate affair for Dasein, and you can have (you guessed it) two relationships to it: an authentic relationship with death, and an inauthentic relationship with death.

Death and Authenticity

Hamilton shows an authentic relationship with death. Hamilton, engaging in a duel, raises his pistol and *throws away his shot*. This seems to be a strange choice—and doesn't seem to be a "fleeing from" death, which Heidegger characterizes as inauthentic or disowned. Hamilton seems to engage in an authentic choice regarding his own death.

Hamilton does not reconsider his choice to raise his pistol, following the same advice that he gave his son Philip. Hamilton walks to his death, though he could have chosen either to shoot Burr first or to avoid the duel altogether. This is not to say that Hamilton would have acted inauthentically by not embracing his death in this situation—but it is through thinking about our death and feeling anxiety about it that we may come to have an authentic relationship with death. Hamilton admits that he "imagines death so much" and goes on to prove it, providing imagery of what his last moments might be, acknowledging death, with anxiety, while not turning away.

Who Tells Your Story?

Hamilton seems to suggest that we should follow Heidegger's analysis in *Being and Time* by having an owned or authentic existence. But Heidegger wasn't necessarily *prescribing* the authentic existence—even though the examples of Hamilton and Burr make it pretty clear which kind of existence we should prefer.

Hamilton has authentically owned the decision of throwing away and not throwing away his shot. Someone like Burr, on the other hand, needs to make a few mistakes before having an owned existence. Regardless, we should take care to ensure that we are authentically engaging in our lives—by experiencing everydayness and avoiding *falling* into the *they*, and by acknowledging that our own death may be near us.

15
Action against the Chaos

LISA MAXINE MELINN AND ADAM MELINN

Action is an integral theme in Lin-Manuel Miranda's *Hamilton*. The Broadway game-changer features set pieces which move and transform, a chorus of dancers who never seem to sit still and a non-stop eponymous lead who is shaped by his commitment to realizing his goals.

The liberated person relies on their actions to define who they are, to illuminate their being and to rationalize the very freedom that would otherwise become a curse. Action is the word applied to the existentialist's approach to managing reality, taking action against the chaos of the world. True freedom can only result from action, from acting, from human actors, *act4act*.

Hamilton celebrates a fearless dedication to action through both the portrayal of America's first Secretary of the Treasury as well as "America's favorite fighting Frenchman," Marquis de Lafayette. Like the lightning-speed rapping Lafayette ("Yorktown"), French existential philosopher Jean-Paul Sartre relied on his own "tactical brilliance", using his skills to spread philosophical views of action, situation, and freedom through theatrical works.

Sartre argued that the most meaningful dramatic action is political action, not acting out or acting up, not action toward love or action toward wealth, not the selfish act or the zealous act; it's only through political aims that consciousness and community come together and form a union. Portraying the complex freedoms of the individual on stage is a way to place philosophical ideas into a political action.

Situation is a core element of Jean-Paul Sartre's plays. Existentialism holds that humans ought to deal with their situation, with the task at hand, rather than concerning themselves with matters of ultimate meaning. Our human situation is set by the pain of choice. When faced with the labyrinth of doors open to us; choice becomes a strain. This is situation; it's the juxtaposition of decision and vision.

Sartre instructs the audience to place the political over the psychological. You don't tackle the universal conflict of human rights from the perspective of a player's psychology, but from the unifying human struggle which is centered on questions of power, justice, privilege, and choice. Sartrean theater utilizes the absurd to increase distance between art and audience. His dramatic vision includes the spectator in a new ritual, one which celebrates artificiality rather than attempting to hide it, one that avoids the illusions of cinema while establishing a shared visceral experience.

Absurdities exhibited on stage, which *Hamilton* has plenty of, are no more illogical than daily human routines. Sartre wanted to show beings formed by their choices, right before the eyes of the viewer, not altered by edits and effects, but in the flesh and "in the room where it happens" ("The Room Where It Happens"). Like Lin-Manuel Miranda, Sartre shows that when individuals make personal choices for themselves, they're also choosing for all society. Every revolution is comprised of individual revolutionaries who opt to act upon their dream.

Another consistent ingredient for a piece of Sartrean theater is playing with time, showing characters with knowledge of their past as well as their future, including their mortality. *Hamilton* demonstrates this beautifully in the frozen action during the duel itself. Historical records remain unclear as to whether or not Alexander Hamilton actually fired his shot up into the air, firing at the gods above, visually establishing an altruistic act, accepting personal moral responsibility and sparing his enemy in the name of superior morality. On Miranda's stage, the levity of this choice is paused and examined. Should he run or fire his gun . . . or should he let it be? That choice is Hamilton's alone.

We Rise and We Fall and We Make Our Mistakes

Choice is a tough thing to write into historical depictions when outcomes have already been recorded as non-fiction. Facts become myths for the public domain. The audience can control the way *they* choose to see their heroes. Americans have rewritten and diversified tales of our nation's forefathers, their quotations and their faces, their morals and their crimes, their vision for the country as well as their fears for humankind. This is the difference between historical figures and mythological ones. As inheritors of both myth and nation, we can cast our founders into newly drawn caricatures to suit our needs.

Alexander Hamilton is both patriot and folktale. Lin-Manuel Miranda, as well as his fans, can recast Hamilton (cast in bronze or cast on stage) in any way which has practical value for our modern needs. We need a Founder who works for today's America, for a traumatized yet free society; we can see these traits and hear their rhythms in the traumatized yet free actions of a new man in New York, looking to write his own legacy.

For Sartre's existentialism, free choice is always present in every moment. It's only human aversion to the responsibility of choice which pushes us to find scapegoats for our situation. People may claim to be controlled by government, by bosses or shareholders, by familial duties or religious mandates, playing victim in the face of indecision. We blame heredity. We shake fists at the heavens. We curse silent deities.

Sartre sees such behaviors as absurd reactions. People are embarrassed to admit that the reason they chose what they chose was based on nothing more than personal desire. The man shackled to his bunk in the prison camp still has the power to choose. The girl with a gun to her head still has power to choose. The orphan, the duelist, the writer, the politician, the traitor, idealist or treasurer ought never to forget that they alone make the choices and changes which shape what they're becoming.

Lin-Manuel Miranda was free to pronounce himself an avatar for Alexander Hamilton. He's free to make rhymes about the *Reynolds Pamphlet* and freestyles out of congressional debates. Even his actors, following a script that he wrote for them to follow as if it were an untwistable destiny; they still act within each spot-lit moment as unpredictable embodiments of possible outcomes. The actor's dilemma is a confused state between pre-determined movements and the illusion of spontaneity. This conundrum is one faced by actors performing the same roles, night after night. When handled correctly, viewers remain unaware of the actor's dilemma, instead marveling at the vitality that *Hamilton* exudes.

Actors remain free to actuate cadence and timing, free to smile or stumble, free to enunciate a lyric they opt to highlight. The player chooses to follow a script which was written for their character, but at the same time they recreate that character as an agent of immediacy. They present it live, for it's only in this real-time live setting that freedom, chance and situation can not only be experienced, but palpably felt across audiences.

Yes, Exit.

Sartre's most famous work for the stage is *No Exit*. Even people who've never seen a live production are familiar with its famous conclusion that "Hell is other people." Perhaps Hamilton would express his own purgatory as "Hell is governing with Southern-mother-fucking-Democratic-Republicans," and Aaron Burr would certainly relate to the complicity of Sartre's characters.

In *No Exit*, Garcin, Inez, and Estelle find every opportunity to fall back on self-pity and inaction. They create the confines of their own purgatory. Inez is hysterical at her inability to act when given the chance. When the locked door at last flies open, nobody moves towards the exit. Inez laughs at this absurdity, saying, "The barrier's down, why are we waiting? . . . But what a situation! It's a scream! We're—inseparables!" Like the characters in *No Exit*, most people stand frozen before open doors. But patrons should never leave *Hamilton* wanting to be frozen like Aaron Burr, "waiting to see which way the wind will blow" ("Non-Stop"). They should want action.

Alexander Hamilton never waits for doors to open for him. He kicks them down, jumping through the shards in Lycra pants and leather boots. Born a bastard orphan, Hamilton fights off disease, rises above the loneliness of having no parents to lean on, and ignores his young age and lack of traditional educational background. Penniless and homeless, Hamilton will not submit to being defined by circumstance. He responds to his situation with the action of writing.

Sartre was able to overcome the scars of a lonely childhood through writing his autobiography, Miranda continues to take action through writing, and Hamilton himself combines existential despair with the power of the quill when he sings, "When my prayers to God were met with indifference, I picked up a pen, I wrote my own deliverance" ("Hurricane").

Empowered by the written word, Alexander Hamilton creates a life that transcends its precedent by never acting reticent. Freedom is a fever, burning with possibility. Freedom can also be about restraint, requiring self-command, self-government, and self-mastery. It all depends on how each individual chooses to act when faced with an open door.

Who Tells Your Story?

The real Alexander Hamilton died before the existentialists reshaped our views of art and philosophy. With hindsight, it's possible to reflect on the words and deeds of this Founding Father as containing key elements of Sartrean libertarianism. Primarily, Hamilton's life as a self-made man without parental support or monetary patronage, without Gods to thank or scapegoats to blame, clearly shows his life was one which carried the pains and rewards of an individual who owned up to personal responsibilities and the outcomes of his free choices.

Alexander Hamilton saw liberty as a natural certainty which couldn't be infringed upon by any other person, power or ethos. He saw freedom as the core quality of human existence, and one we ought to praise when he declared, "there is a certain enthusiasm in liberty that makes human nature rise above itself in acts of bravery and heroism." He was a man of actions, of trying and climbing, a person who believed that to exist is to act.

What about Lin-Manuel Miranda? When he's off the stage and out of the puffy shirt, is he a man of existential action? Does his life embody these traits of responsibility, absurdity and liberty? Like the historical figure he portrays, Miranda is a self-made man who thrives without patrons or scapegoats to rationalize his successes and stumbles. Only an individual can create success or failure, glory or disaster, not the legacy of the stage and not the rules of fate. It's a brazen violation rather than complacent supposition, as is hip hop in the Richard Rogers Theater. Hip hop is the music of action, rhythm of the masses, beats of modern situations, poetry for the *next* American Revolution. Then there's this existentialist anecdote Miranda posted to Facebook:

> I never had a crib. Instead I had child-sized futon, and I'd drag it all around the house and sleep wherever . . . My father's reasoning: "I hated being in a crib. I hated being cooped up. I decided you were going to be free." It sounds crazy, and sometimes the floor was cold, but it worked. I have always been free."

Another action which stands out in the context of this question is Miranda's *Ham4Ham* performances and ticket lotteries, keeping his feet in the street, proletarian rooted, looking fans in the face and creating spontaneous dramatic moments rather than theorizing a world where such theatrics should be exhibited. As Sartre suggested; we ought to always have a project which aims to amend the status quo. Sartre always wanted to see his audiences riled up and taking his plays' messages out into the streets. *Hamilton* accomplishes that goal.

Existential liberation can be as simple as redefining one's purpose, because we define objects and entities by how they're used. A washcloth being used to prop open the bathroom door is not really a washcloth at all. It's a doorstop. By changing context or association, a thing takes on new meaning and frees itself from any prior classifications.

George Washington, not wishing to be misconstrued as a despot or pseudo-monarch, steps down from the office of president after his second term, abolishing the confines of that label. Jean-Paul Sartre never became complacent in one role, constantly shifting between philosopher, novelist, screenwriter, biographer, and political commentator. He even declined the Nobel Prize for literature because he didn't want to be labeled as a Nobel laureate. In much the same way, Lin-Manuel Miranda needed to step down from the role of Hamilton in order to avoid being trapped in the image of that particular icon, epitomizing this main theme of freedom through personal choice.

He'll move on to new projects, reshaping his dynamic existence from moment to moment without conceding to media pressures, public preference, or anyone's will but his own.

VI

The Hideous
Blot

16
Daveed Diggs's Doubling

MARLENE CLARK

"What'd I miss?" When MC Daveed Diggs first struts his Jeffersonian stuff across the stage in the jazzy, Gil Scott-Heron-ish opening number of Act II in *Hamilton*, audience members should be forgiven if they fail to realize they've been watching Diggs perform throughout Act I. During the first half of the show, Diggs plays the Marquis de Lafayette, a man who is both Jefferson's dear friend and in some respects his nemesis. Diggs is "doubling."

And he doubles in more ways than one. As any MC worth her salt knows, rap is filled with doubling, or "ad-libs," the background music that fills in, echoes, and emphasizes the main rap; *Hamilton* is full of it. The ensemble, acting as a Greek chorus of sorts, ad-libs like crazy throughout, syncopated *oomph* and *whoa wha?* alternating the gas pedal and the brakes to the MC's ride.

The double doubling of this musical is no accident. *Hamilton* is a story of conflict. In Act I, it's military, and in Act II, it's political. Rap doubling enables a musical point-counterpoint syncopation that emphasizes those quarrels. Performance doubling highlights the interplay of outsized personalities coming up against each other. The most significant of the doubled roles in *Hamilton* are played by Diggs and Okieriete Onaodowan ("Oak"), who takes turns as the larger-than-life, bombastic, almost thuggish Hercules Mulligan in Act I and the diminutive but determined policy wonk James Madison in Act II. Lin-Manuel Miranda has said that he enjoyed playing with the optics of having Hamilton's best buddies in Act I transform into his archenemies in Act II. And it works.

It works because the musical traces a familiar dramatic arc. In Miranda's design, Act I follows Hamilton through his rise in the midst of the tumult of the Revolution. During this time, his brother-in-arms Lafayette never strayed far from his side. Act II, by contrast, concerns Hamilton's fall, from hero to embattled politician, struggling to keep his vision for the new country alive. Enter Jefferson, the consummate operative, ready to butt heads to have it his way.

Through the lens of *Hamilton*, the man *and* the musical, Lafayette would seem to be everything Jefferson was not; one a hero, the other an anti-hero. But a look at their lives offers a different view. The pair got to know each other well in Paris during the late 1780s and established a fast friendship—one that would endure until the final year of Jefferson's long life. And in fact, though separated in age by fourteen years, in many respects Jefferson and Lafayette could have been philosophical twins of different mothers.

Both men appear to favor the English philosopher John Locke's views on Natural Law and human rights. Lafayette put his money where his mouth was, and fought beside Washington and Hamilton in support of their quest for human freedom. Jefferson cribbed the opening of the Declaration of Independence from Locke, as did Lafayette for France's Declaration of the Rights of Man and of the Citizen. But there was one important area of disagreement between the two men, and it concerned just two words in Locke's thought: "slavery" and "property."

The words "all men are created equal" meant just that to Lafayette, all men. They meant the same to the Northerners of Act I, such as Hamilton. Act II's slave-holding Virginia planters such as Jefferson and Madison, however, added a silent quali-fier: "all (white) men are created equal." That hedge put Jefferson at odds with both Hamilton and Lafayette, and, most importantly, with John Locke. Was Jefferson's reading of Locke, as Lafayette seemed to think, missing something? Even Jefferson seems to wonder. As he swaggers in from France at the opening of Act II, he leads off with a loaded ques-tion that would have made the real Hamilton and his crew laugh.

Locking Down Locke

Both Lafayette and Jefferson owned plenty of property, though Lafayette's holdings generated what was at that time astronomical wealth, while Jefferson's Monticello generally left him in the red. Despite that common ground, their educations could not have been more different. Lafayette, a member of France's "sword class," was schooled early in life primarily in Latin and Republican Rome, as well as the martial arts. At thirteen he was transferred to the Collège du Plessis Acadamie in Versailles, where he tried and mainly failed to learn the social graces appropriate to a courtier/warrior of the period.

By contrast, Jefferson's education was much more academic. At age seventeen, he left home for the College of William and Mary, where for two years he immersed himself for up to fifteen hours a day in the Enlightenment philosophy of Locke, Bacon, Newton, and Adam Smith, and for five years after that studied law. And yet, at the time of the American Revolution, the political philosophy each had inherited and internalized was, in many ways, all of a piece.

How could that be? Lafayette remained martial Roman to his core, always looking for an excuse to saddle up and charge. Jefferson, on the other hand, by training and inclination, considered himself a peace-loving, bookish gentleman farmer. Nevertheless, a strong belief in the core principles of Locke's philosophy united the two. We know where Jefferson acquired his understanding of Locke, though he had to adjust it a bit to accommodate that qualification of "all men."

Lafayette, as far as we know, never read Locke. At the time of the American Revolution Lafayette had studied only classical Rome. Locke was also obsessed with Rome, though, which made Lafayette's understanding of Locke's principles closer to Locke's understanding of his own philosophy. As a result, though Jefferson and Lafayette's political philosophies share many points of agreement, one point of disagreement ripped a lasting rift between them—slavery.

To get the gist of Jefferson and Lafayette's disagreement about slavery, it helps to look at Locke's *Second Treatise of Government*, especially Chapters IV ("Of Slavery"), XVI ("Of Conquest"), and V ("Of Property"). While there is still disagreement on the finer points, the *Second Treatise* was written primarily as a justification for England's 1688 Glorious Revolution and as an appeal for a representative government as opposed to an absolute monarchy.

In "Of Slavery" and "Of Conquest," Locke agrees with classical Roman thought with regard to slavery. He allows for slavery, but only as found in antiquity. Locke accepted and acknowledged the Roman practice of enslaving prisoners of war (with the possibility of ransom) as part of "the spoils of war." The practice of taking slaves as spoils of war actually continued well into the eighteenth century. For decades, the Barbary pirates waged war against England, France, and the United States on the high seas, taking many a to-be-ransomed "slave" from their ships as trophies of these contests. These attacks remained a bone of contention throughout Jefferson's Presidency.

Locke is loath to accept this practice as latter-day Roman business as usual, let alone "natural." He notes that slavery itself constitutes a "state of war" between even a "lawful conqueror and a captive." He delegitimizes any claim that a "sedate and settled" agreement between slave and master is possible. Instead, he firmly concludes that "a man, not having power over his own life, cannot, by compact, or his own consent, enslave himself to anyone." No matter what the apparent "agreement" and terms of a "peaceful" co-existence between slave and master may be, no matter how "benevolent" and "paternal" the master, and no matter how "submissive" and "well fed" the slave, between them, daily life never ceases to be anything but a state of unrelenting war.

The slaves of Virginia were not captured in a war. Instead, they were rounded up by enterprising mercenaries mostly in Central and Eastern Africa and sold on auction blocks throughout the South after their disastrous Middle Passage. The plantation gentry, including Jefferson, considered them "property"—and valuable property at that. Slaves were bought when a family prospered (George Washington actually "leased" slaves from a neighbor), were sold when a plantation's fortunes floundered (or, when Georgetown University nearly failed), and were routinely inherited as a crucial element of an estate. Sometimes inherited slaves were even more important to family fortunes than the land itself. Washington's holdings included 153 "dower" slaves. Jefferson inherited the Hemings-family slaves from his father-in-law, including Sally Hemings, Jefferson's future "concubine" and mother of six of his children.

Slavery of this sort ran counter not only to Locke's position on slavery but also to his thoughts as to what constituted personal "property." Locke says in "Of Property," that "The labor of our body and hands properly belong to us." The logic of Locke's argument here seems to run as follows: You can amass property through labor, by working the land, but the investment of labor belongs to the laboring body itself and not to the land. The slavers of the South wished to argue that they owned their slaves by virtue of their slaves' labor on their plantations. This interpretation mocks Locke's own words in a way well illustrated by a more recent experience. During the urban blight of the 1970s, many New York City landlords abandoned their buildings, unable to turn a profit. "Squatters" moved in, taking over these properties, and investing "sweat equity" to convert these buildings into habitable apartments, which they then occupied. Decades later, when New York City property again became valuable, the landlords re-asserted their claims to ownership. The squatters pushed back. They insisted that they owned these buildings by virtue of their invested labor and years of residence. The courts generally sided with the squatters. Locke probably would have agreed with the courts. But imagine if the landlords had gone to court claiming that by virtue of the squatters' labor investment in their properties, they "owned" not just the buildings they had abandoned but also the squatters themselves! That claim would have made Locke sputter in disgust, but it's the claim many slavers tried to stake.

Modern readings of Locke's view on slavery and property seem to fall into two groups. Some claim that Locke's argument supports slavery. They argue that the Africans of the Gambia lived their lives primarily as nomadic hunter-gatherers and so failed to live as God intended in an "industrious and rational" world. Moreover, they claim that by neglecting to enclose and cultivate their holdings they laid it to "waste" and entered a State of War with nature. Therefore, they deserve to have their property taken from them and become the enslaved captives of those who do God's industrious and rational work. That the slaves then invest their labor in the slaver's land just seals the deal.

This reading offers slavers a rationale for their ownership. Others read this interpretation of Locke as nothing more than self-serving hogwash. They hold that Locke's argument proves all slavery "unnatural" by virtue of its "unlawful conquer." These readers then interpret Locke to say that due to legalized slavery, the South was already tangled up in an infinite war, slave against master, always and everywhere. By these lights, the North did nothing more than join a civil war, already well underway, on the side of the slaves.

The first reading of Locke's thoughts may well have offered Jefferson a dubious defense for his slaveholding, yet in his own writing he wisely never made use of it. Rather, he thought "property" a "misnaming" of slaves and welcomed slavery's "cessation." Other plantation owners heartily disagreed, and so Jefferson kept the peace and saved his political skin by hedging. The second reading opens an intellectual path to Jefferson's bob and weave. He insisted he supported emancipation, so long as a place to relocate the American slaves could be found—in Africa perhaps, or the Caribbean.

"As it is," he wrote, "we have the wolf by the ear, and we can neither hold him, nor safely let him go." Why? Because "justice is in one scale and self-preservation in the other." It may be just to free the slaves, Jefferson admits, but Locke's Natural Law requires us first to preserve ourselves. He well knew that the slaves of the Southern planters experienced life as Locke envisioned: an infinite state of Hobbesian war, nasty, brutish, and short. Set the slaves free in their midst? Not on their lives! The patriarchs' devotion to Locke was not strong enough to overcome their fears should the slaves be emancipated and remain on American soil. Given the reality of even the most "benevolent" slavery, they knew their very lives depended upon holding the wolf by the ear. And self-preservation came first.

So, Does Jefferson Get a Bad Rap?

When the curtain first rises on *Hamilton: An American Musical*, Daveed Diggs is doublin' every way possible. In the first song, Diggs raps as both Lafayette and Jefferson. But he is dressed as Lafayette, in cream, white, and navy military attire, his hair pulled tightly back in some semblance of an eighteenth-century pigtail. Lafayette's opposition to his dear buddy Jefferson on the question of slavery comes up with the lights.

As Hamilton puts it, Lafayette is a member of their "revolutionary manumission abolitionists" club, "poppin' a squat on conventional wisdom." And by the end of the first act, Lafayette and Hamilton are high-fiving on the battlefield of Yorktown. Their shared purpose of freedom for all men makes for harmony in the midst of the discord of Act I's war.

That mood starkly changes when Act II opens with a house-rocking Diggs performance, all Jefferson, just rolling in from France. Despite his avid Republicanism, Jefferson is dressed in "royal purple," his hair freed in a huge Afro emphasizing his size. When Diggs finally comes down to earth and walks, he either struts across the stage or sort of moonwalks, backwards, all the while never missing a jazzy finger-snapping rapid beat. Diggs is known for both the speed and precision of his rap, and his Jeffersonian staccato pace and booming voice add additional *oomph* to Jefferson's reported charisma.

It's impossible to take your eyes off this fast-talking whirlwind, even for a second. But *whoa wha?* Are slaves pushing the (airline) stairs Diggs rides in on and descends as he raps his opening lines? Are slaves scrubbing the floor on hands and knees to mark his homecoming and portering his bags? "Sir, you've been off to Paris for so long!" So what'd I miss? What'd I miss?

Diggs's Jefferson comes off as brash, arrogant, exuberant, entitled, and clueless. Jefferson's most powerful words, taken straight from Locke, first read, "We hold these truths to be self-evident, that all men are created equal and are endowed by their Creator with certain inalienable Rights, that among these are the rights to Life, Liberty, and Property."

Years later in France, where Jefferson "helped Lafayette draft a declaration" those words remained as such; in the United States, the hedge on "all men," required a duck-and-cover change of "Property" to "the Pursuit of Happiness." Deprived of both their right to property and the pursuit of happiness because they were themselves property—at least to the Southern gentry—the slaves bustling around Jefferson during the opening of *Hamilton*'s Act II underscore the ways in which the political philosophy of the Enlightenment struggled when trying to rationalize slavery.

17
Founding Fathers, Founding Slavers

Andrew T. Vink

Most of the portraits that we see of the founding fathers are scrubbed clean. The likenesses of these men are generally accurate, but the flaws are usually hidden. We never see Washington's wooden teeth, nor the scars from years on the battlefield.

The stories we are taught in our US History classes are the same. We document the great triumphs of genius rebels who shrugged off British rule and put the American Experiment into motion while rarely discussing their failings. We are told the tales of gods, forgetting that they were mere men, flawed just like the rest of the human race.

The great flaw we overlook in the retelling of United States History is the relationship between the Founding Fathers and slavery. Washington owned over three hundred slaves who worked the tobacco fields of Mount Vernon. James Madison, the mind behind the compromise in the US Constitution counting slaves as three fifths of a man, owned over a hundred slaves upon his death. Thomas Jefferson, who was romantically involved with a slave, wrote in his *Notes on the State of Virginia* about the intellectual and emotional inferiority of men and women of color, comparing them to animals.

This leads to an important question: can we celebrate these men for their great accomplishments in the realm of politics and nationalism, even though they partook in a dehumanizing practice?

The Nature of Good and Evil

Before we can talk about history and the complicated lives of Hamilton and Jefferson, we need to address the question that lies at the heart of this conversation: do good acts and evil acts balance one another out in the grand scheme of history, or must these acts stand independent of one another? This question is central to the study of ethics since it affects how we are to judge and understand people.

Two of the traditional ways of talking about this problem emphasize different aspects of the action. Some philosophers, like Immanuel Kant, focus on the act itself, without considering the consequences. Owning slaves is evil, and therefore slave owners are committing inherently evil acts. Other thinkers, like John Stuart Mill, look at the consequences when judging the act. Owning slaves allowed men like Washington, Jefferson, and Madison to do a great deal of good for the American colonies and United States, therefore slave-owners aren't necessarily evil if they also produce good consequences. Neither of these approaches gives a satisfactory answer to the complexity of the situation, so what should we do?

Distinguishing between judging acts and judging people can help us address these complex moral problems. It can be difficult sometimes to judge whether an act is right or wrong. The morality of an action can depend on context, such as Hamilton's payments to James Reynolds. On the other hand, acts like murder or rape are clearly wrong, regardless of circumstance. So there are times where we can develop a clear moral judgments about particular actions.

Individuals are far more complex than a single action, making it difficult to judge a person as completely good or completely evil. We see Alexander Hamilton as a good man: he speaks up for truth, writes against the abuses of slavery, and deeply loves his family and his country. Yet, at the same time, he cheats on Eliza with Maria Reynolds and then publishes the details. Does this act of adultery make Hamilton a bad person? We don't see him that way. We still cheer him on as our hero until his death at the hands of Aaron Burr. This shows that our moral judgments about a person's character are not determined by a single act. Rather, moral character is shown by a history of actions.

So, we have a new question: does a repeated immoral action outweigh many good actions? Do Jefferson's intellectual endeavors, diplomatic service, and major role in the founding of the United States outweigh his racist comments and involvement with the slave trade? To answer that question, we need to look at a philosophy of history.

Historical Mindedness

Bernard Lonergan (1904–1984) was a Jesuit philosopher who worked to revitalize the philosophy and theology of St. Thomas Aquinas by introducing concepts from modern psychology and historical study to strengthen Aquinas's metaphysics. For our purposes, we can push most of the metaphysics and psychology to the side and focus on certain elements of his theory of history. Lonergan focused on historical mindedness, collective responsibility, and the importance of creativity and healing in history.

Historical mindedness is a two-pronged introspection that involves reflection upon yourself as well as the object of your thoughts. First, it's a recognition that you, as a person, are born into a particular point in history with a cultural and societal background that affects the way you see the world. You will always carry those backgrounds with you, no matter what you do. The second prong is the recognition that the object of your thoughts is conditioned in a similar way. For example, Jefferson, born in the midst of the eighteenth century, can't help but think like a man born in such a circumstance. According to Lonergan, historical mindedness is essential to understanding and making judgments about the past.

Lonergan's second major concept is collective responsibility. This concept is based on a fairly simple argument: since an individual is responsible for the life she chooses to lead, a society as a whole must be collectively responsible for the state society is in. Imagine if Hamilton and his revolutionary compatriots have more than that third pint of Sam Adams, create a ruckus, and ruin the bar. While Hamilton may not be at fault for all the destruction in the ruckus, he and his friends have a shared responsibility to help make repairs. The idea of collective responsibility forces a shift from a mindset focused on the individual to a mindset that focuses on the community and the common good.

The last concept, creativity and healing in history, is intimately connected with collective responsibility. We need creativity when facing events or institutions that harm members of the community. Creative solutions to these harmful elements allow the community to heal and move forward towards a brighter future. Members of a society have a collective responsibility to recognize the things in society that harm members of the community, and to come up with creative responses. This is how we achieve social progress.

The Founders and the Hideous Blot of Slavery

When we look at the Founding Fathers and their responses to slavery, we should judge them in context. Anti-slavery movements were active in the colonies and early United States, with abolitionist groups forming in various cities, such as New York. Both Hamilton and Aaron Burr were members of an abolitionist group. So, when we judge the Founding Fathers for their role in slavery, we're looking to judge these men by a standard that existed in their own time, and not by a sensibility unique to the twenty-first century.

Alexander Hamilton, Fervent Abolitionist

Hamilton, just as he is portrayed in the musical, was a firm believer in the equality of all people, regardless of color. He wrote several essays against slavery, protesting the immorality of the practice, regardless of the economic benefits. Even though Philip Schuyler owned several slaves, Hamilton and Eliza never brought slaves into their home. Given his writings and personal convictions, shared by Laurens and Lafayette, it would seem as though Hamilton is untouched by the stain of slavery.

Unfortunately, Hamilton was involved with the slave trade. According to research done by Ron Chernow, Hamilton had two major involvements with the slave trade. First, as a clerk in the Caribbean, besides trading rum and sugar cane, Alexander did occasionally buy and sell slaves for his patron. Later in his life, Alexander bought slaves for his brother-in-law and sister-in-law, John Baker Church and Angelica Church, while setting up their estate in preparation of their return to New York from Europe. Hamilton even went as far as to rent slaves for use on his property, which was a common alternative to owning slaves.

At this point, you might be thinking, "Wait a minute, that wasn't in the show!" You'd be right. While Miranda was inspired by Chernow's biography, it isn't a strict adaptation. In fact, Hamilton's hands were far dirtier than the version of we see on stage. Why leave this out, when we see Hamilton's other flaws on display? Maybe it was a dynamic way to distinguish Hamilton from Jefferson. Regardless of Miranda's reasoning, the fact is that Hamilton's hands were not as clean of slavery as the musical suggests.

George Washington: Tobacco and Slavery

Washington, besides leading the Continental Army and United States Executive Branch, was a tobacco farmer in northern Virginia. Slavery was an essential factor in how farms were able to maintain profitability. Washington's estate had over three thousand acres of land that were cultivated, primarily by the over-three hundred slaves he owned. With over fifty years of farming tobacco, among other crops, it is clear that Washington engaged with slavery regularly for most of his life.

The positive element to note of Washington's history of slavery is that he's the only figure of the four we are discussing that had instructions for emancipating his slaves in his will. The directions were for the slaves to be freed upon his wife Martha's death. While she ended up freeing the slaves earlier than instructed, it still speaks to Washington's views on servitude.

Thomas Jefferson's Contradictions

Jefferson's relationship with the issue of slavery is complicated. While owning about 130 slaves at Monticello, he arguably worked the hardest of these men to end slavery in the United States. Jefferson famously referred to slavery as a "hideous blot," and worked to end the practice. He introduced a law in Virginia in 1778 that outlawed the importation of slaves from Africa. In 1807, he used his presidential authority to outlaw the importation of slaves into ports under the jurisdiction of the United States. From these facts, you might think

Jefferson was a leader of the anti-slavery movement in the United States.

The other side of Jefferson's checkered history was his statements on the inferiority of black men and women to whites. His "solution" to slavery was to eventually deport the emancipated slaves back to Africa, since he believed that whites and blacks could not live together in a peaceful society. Add this to his alleged fathering of multiple children with his slave Sally Hemming, who he never freed, and the words "All men are created equal" begin to seem a little less sincere.

James Madison's Religious Case against Slavery

Madison's personal position on slavery and the question of what to do with freed slaves was very similar to that of his friend Jefferson. Madison believed in relocating freed slaves back to Africa, keeping American citizens of European ancestry. He owned slaves throughout his life, bringing a slave with him to Philadelphia while serving in Congress. Upon his death, as mentioned above, Madison owned over a hundred slaves, and made no provision for their freedom.

Madison's opposition to slavery came from his Christian convictions. In a letter to Harriet Martineau, Madison claims that the enslavement of black people was contrary to the teachings of the Bible, yet the clergy will not preach that from the pulpit. By noting the complicity of the clergy in the practice of slavery, Madison questions whether or not the clergy were protecting their own interests. This challenges the popular notion that slavery was supported by the Christian scriptures.

How Do We Tell Their Stories?

As we see from the above discussions, the history of the Founding Fathers and slavery is complicated to say the least. The slaveholding Jefferson arguably did the most of the four men to end the institution of slavery in the United States, while still holding deplorable views on black people. The abolitionist Hamilton bought and sold slaves for others.

So what should we do? We don't want to call any of these men villains, nor do we want to give them a free pass. They all served the United States with passion, duty, and distinction. They all have done great things and terrible things. Based on the intuitions mentioned earlier, it would seem unfair to completely condemn or absolve any of these men. Given their historical situation, the Founding Fathers had to engage in a world that was shaped by slavery as an institution. It would be unjust to blame these men for engaging in a world and culture that they did not create. On the other hand, there were anti-slavery movements calling for freedom and equality for people of color, so it's not like these egalitarian ideas were not already in the air.

The best answer comes from making use of collective responsibility and creative solutions. We have a responsibility as a society to tell our national history in the most complete fashion possible. We also want to prevent unfair demonization or whitewashing of terrible events. With creative works like *Hamilton: An American Musical*, we open a door that allows us to see both the good and the bad in our historical figures, reminding us that they were complicated, flawed human beings just like you and me. When we get to see the whole picture of our national history, we can begin to understand the consequences of slavery for our society. Once we recognize these consequences, we can rise up together, face the harm, and creatively move our society forward. Could our Founding Fathers ask for a better legacy?

VII

The Excluded
Speak

18
Young, Scrappy and Hungry

MINERVA AHUMADA AND TIM JUNG

Lin-Manuel Miranda's *Hamilton* is not only an original and fun musical, it's also a statement about the making of Alexander Hamilton and of the United States. It starts by posing the question: How does a "bastard, orphan, son of a whore," dropped on an obscure Caribbean island, develop into a "hero and a scholar"?

The question is rephrased in several occasions throughout the musical. As the question that moves the narrative forward, it allows us to become more acquainted with Hamilton and the problems an immigrant of simple origins faced in the 1700s. Miranda seems to be telling us that Hamilton advances because he has the grit to succeed, but also because he embeds himself in the fight for independence. In this way, he is just the same as George Washington or Hercules Mulligan. They are colonial subjects fighting for independence from an oppressive regime. Miranda's decision to cast a diverse ensemble raises the further question: would someone like Hamilton have the opportunity to advance to the same extent today?

Sugar, Rum, and All the Things He Can't Afford

As we know, Hamilton is a bastard, orphan, son of a whore. He is also a Scotsman from the island of St. Croix in the Caribbean. On that island, Hamilton suffered extreme poverty and several tragedies (his mom died, his cousin committed suicide); he also clerked for his mother's landlord. Commerce in the island includes trading sugar cane and rum (and all the things he can't afford!).

We also learn that while this is happening, "slaves were being slaughtered and carted away" while Hamilton struggled and kept his guard up. If one is no fan of history, maybe these lyrics aren't very good at helping us identify who Hamilton is, but the beginning of the second song should put all these phrases into perspective: "1776." The United States did not exist yet. The colonies did. And if colonies existed, then there was a colonizer: the *center* (as personified by King George).

King George's songs are always funny. When he sings to the colonies that they should "not change the subject, Cuz you're my favorite subject," he is also giving us a history lesson: the colonizer is the one who has the power to dictate the way in which those living in the colonies act. Those in the colonies are known as "the colonial subject." Their lives revolve around the wishes, desires, and spending sprees of the monarch. Someone like Enrique Dussel would say that King George is the *center* in this relationship, while the colonial subjects are the *peripheral* subjects. Think about King George as the sun and the colonies as the planets.

This subjection the colonies faced was not only in terms of taxes and legal representation, but also in terms of knowledge. The view of the world, according to Mexican philosopher Enrique Dussel, is focalized through the center. Dussel asserts that Europe became the center in the fourteenth century with the expansion of Portugal and Spain (towards the North Atlantic). The expansion of the Brits follows suit, and with these expansions, Europe begins to consider itself the archetypal culture, the place that can produce definitions and explanations for the places which it is now occupying.

The center reigns over the *periphery* or, in other words, Europe assigns itself the role of the sun and now everyone else must bow down to them. In the case of the Thirteen Colonies, King George rules, defines, and determines life in the Americas. The periphery, then, is a subject that is considered other, not the same as the center. Distinct, and not equal. The colonial subject in the periphery is unlike the subject in the center.

The Thirteen Colonies are just one example of the many colonies that existed across the globe prior to 1776. Hamilton's story presents to us some of the conditions in which poor people existed in the colonies. It must be mentioned that Hamilton was of Scottish descent, which should make us think that however hard his upbringing was, there were other individuals, like the slaves being carted away, who did not have his privileges. Yet, Hamilton should still be understood as a peripheral subject, as the King defines and determines Hamilton's fate from a distance.

As we hear in "You'll Be Back," King George's love comes with a steep price. King George reminds his colonies, "Remember we made an arrangement when you went away." Being a colony meant that the subjects living there were under the colonizer's rules. In the case of the thirteen Colonies, they had to pay taxes on products they exported to Britain (there were taxes on hats, sugar, molasses, and clothes); the colonies had no representation in Britain, yet the newly formed United Kingdom profited from the colonies and denied settlers the right to oversee their own trade and other activities. The UK continued its expansionist efforts and was perceived to be increasing taxes and control over the colonies in order to finance these new settlements.

According to Dussel, the way in which the center thinks of itself ends up alienating the periphery, because colonial subjects are thought of as less deserving and less intelligent, which allows the center to impose on them heavy financial and ideological burdens. One can think here of the way in which the natives of different lands were judged as savages, barbarians, less-than-human, based on the understanding the center developed of them. Or, as King George puts it: "You say our love is draining and you can't go on." Being *loved* by the center means being restricted, becoming a possession. When King George sings "I will send a fully armed battalion to remind you of my love!" he expresses both the alienation that subjects like Hamilton are exposed to, as well as his dangerous and obsessive way of "loving" the colonial subject.

When You're Living on Your Knees, You Rise Up

Imagine King George as a handsome yet stalker-ish lover who does not let you live your life how you think best. The center often made the colonial subjects feel this way, as if they did not have their own ideas and needs. When Hamilton debates (Bishop!) Samuel A. Seabury, Lin-Manuel Miranda demonstrates the different factions that arose in the colonies. While there are some loyalists who are happy to be a part of the Empire, the Sons of Liberty oppose the many ways in which they are not allowed to be free. As Hamilton says in "My Shot," the colonies run independently, yet Britain taxes and regulates them, while the King spends lavishly, and will never set the colonists free. This can only lead to revolution.

This song explains the process of emancipation that began in 1776. The peripheral subjects had very little to lose. As every oppressed people knows, freedom is worth the risk of dying for your liberation. For the periphery, it's always worth taking a shot.

That tavern where Hamilton, Lafayette, Mulligan, and Laurens sing happily about their shot can be seen as the starting point of the movement for emancipation. Breaking up with King George wasn't easy, but it allowed the colonial subjects to disentangle themselves from the identities that the center had imposed on them. They become free not just from political and financial control, they become free from the King's expectations. King George can no longer say you are "mine to subdue." The world turns upside down as the oppressed take control of their own lives.

Socially Advance Instead of Sewing Pants

Lani Guinier and Gerald Torres's book *The Miner's Canary* explores how race impacts life in the US. Guinier and Torres discuss the obvious topics for blacks and Mexican Americans, like the ways in which these minorities continue to be marginalized, the lack of opportunities to advance, and the many places where race seems to be used to enact a distinction of who belongs and who doesn't. But Guinier and Torres also analyze the way in which these conditions give rise to a sense of community, pride, and belonging. People can be forced by circumstances to identify with a group of people, and it's this identification that brings the singular person out of isolation and alienation. For the marginalized individual, this identification with others is a blessing.

Hamilton had been struggling to survive, both in that forgotten island in the Caribbean and as an immigrant in New

York. The people he is talking to are not immigrants like him. Lafayette is the closest, but he is just a visitor and not someone who is planning on making the Colonies his new address. Still, as peripheral subjects, they are marginalized by the British Crown—or, in Hamilton's words, "Britain keeps shittin' on us endlessly." It is as part of the Sons of Liberty that Laurens, Mulligan, Lafayette, and Hamilton find each other. This group is ardent to fight against the different oppressive measures that the King has imposed on the colonies.

According to Guinier and Torres, people who identify as members of a subordinate group develop an oppositional conscience. This conscience is usually the product of bonding over the injustices the individuals in the group have suffered— whether this be personal indignities or a feeling of anger caused by the social conditions in which they exist. This oppositional consciousness can be seen in the participants of "My Shot," as they all unite against the rule of the King and identify with the nascent United States by singing, "I'm just like my country . . . young, scrappy and hungry." For Lafayette, "I dream of life without a monarchy/The unrest in France will lead to 'onarchy?", the idea of life without a monarchy is key. Mulligan's revolutionary hopes are linked to a future where individuals have social mobility. And, as Laurens reminds the group, this is not only about them and their chances: they will never be truly free until those in bondage enjoy the same rights.

Oppositional conscience is seen as an empowering mental state, as it unites the group in brotherhood. It is through this brotherhood and identification that the Sons of Liberty develop strategies to overthrow the power that oppresses them. *Political race* is, then, not only about identifying as a marginalized group, but about the ways that group provides the oppressed with a path towards a better future. This is why political race "is not a moment, it's the movement, where all the hungriest brothers with something to prove went."

Political Race as a Lens

In *The Miner's Canary,* Guinier and Torres present political race as a process that is in constant evolution, because it engages both with past injustices and with the creative paths that open up once one recognizes that others are also similarly oppressed. Guinier and Torres look at political race as a "lens" that helps identify injustices and the way in which they are not only felt by a single group. The metaphor of the miner's canary is a clear way to understand this. When mining, a canary was sent in with the miners, the canary's frail system would act as an alert system if there were dangerous gasses in the mine. These gasses would kill the canary and provide the miners with a clear signal: the environment isn't safe for them either.

Guinier and Torres look at the injustices suffered by people of color as a canary: if the environment is not safe for these people, will there be anyone else affected by it? The Sons of Liberty show us the way in which their oppressions intersected; while they recognize that these forms of oppression were dangerous, they also came up with new plans to make sure that people in the colonies (the mine if you wish to follow up with the metaphor) were safe.

Guinier and Torres identify three steps that would allow us to use political race as a lens. The first step involves working towards solidarity and connection between those who have been impacted by race, or, in the case of the founding fathers, marginalized as peripheral subjects. The second step involves articulating an agenda that guarantees social justice, not just for the miners, but also for the canary. This idea of social justice should be broad and inclusive. As a logical result of the first two steps, the third step necessitates a willingness to engage and experiment with new democratic practices.

The bond between the Sons of Liberty exemplifies step one. The first act in *Hamilton* offers many examples of the ways in which these shared experiences create the bonds of solidarity and brotherhood that Guinier and Torres deem relevant.

This unity and solidarity can't be denied in "Yorktown (The World Turned Upside Down)." The mere existence of a revolutionary army highlights the unity felt by those fighting for freedom. When Hamilton comes up with his plan to "Take the bullets out your gun!", the army, surprised, also decides to trust their leader. Hamilton's "We cannot let a stray gunshot give us away" allows us to highlight the second step in the use of political race as a lens: the unity that has been forged will be used to produce a measure that will provide the army with a win. "The code word is Rochambeau, dig me?" asks people to follow, but also to trust that this measure is a way to seize the moment and protect those who are taking "the bullets out their guns." We see the quartet combining their assets to make sure this plan succeeds.

The third step in the project of political race makes it into stage as part of the Battle of Yorktown: the battle is wrapped in parenthesis between "And so the American experiment begins" and "The world turned upside down." The monarchy has been defeated and a new experiment gets started in this newborn nation.

The group's resiliency and understanding of how the fate of the many is being affected by the monarchy allows people to come up with plans that make one question: "How does a rag-tag volunteer army in need of a shower somehow defeat a global superpower?" Those who have been marginalized, treated as other, could leave victorious from the quagmire if they unite forces, resources, and have a shared outcome. As Guinier and Torres write, "Like race itself, solidarity in the form of community is not just one thing. It has the potential to free its members from externally imposed stigma." What we celebrate in *Hamilton* is the triumph of solidarity, the creation of the American Experiment, and the ways in which the Founding Fathers created a better future for centuries to come.

Not Yet . . .

Although the Founding Fathers were white, the fact that they were colonial subjects marked them as inferior: they were mar-ginalized and did not enjoy the same rights British citizens had. They might have been superior to Native Americans and slaves, but they still occupied a position that marked them as different from the pure British officers. As colonial subjects, this marginalization might have produced similar experiences to those described by Guinier and Torres in their book. Political race allows us to see that any subject from the periphery—any-one who has been categorized as inferior—shares a wealth of experiences that can be used to connect to others and, more importantly, to resist and overcome the oppression. Unity and solidarity are key in undoing oppression.

In his 2009 appearance in the White House, Miranda says, "Alexander Hamilton embodies the world's ability to make the difference." Miranda sees Hamilton—and the founding fathers—as the people who were able to turn their fate upside down. In 1776 *they* were the underdogs. In order to clearly represent how much of an underdog they were, Miranda's ensemble of *Hamilton* visually brings forth what the underdogs look like in 2016. A clearer understanding of what a colonial subject is and what can be achieved through political race can also lead us to *see* that the experiment with democracy began in 1776, but it is not over. Not yet.

19
To the Revelation!

Alison A. Dobrick

With every repeated listen, *Hamilton* fans hope in vain that the young, promisingly talented Philip Hamilton and his illustrious, "non-stop" father will come to their senses, maybe even realize "how lucky they are to be alive right now" ("Non-Stop").

Part of us must silently hope that *this* time they'll avoid their clearly misguided choices to engage in the duels that end their lives. Instead, the hopes, excitements, choices, and tragedies unfold as always, bringing elation, regret, and death. Though we know that "the die is cast," the dramatic power and moral significance of Philip's and Alexander's deaths are freshly felt with each new listen.

Hamilton portrays critical differences between moral systems that can be considered masculinist and feminist. Alexander and his cohorts represent a masculinist ethical philosophy based on honor, justice, and legacy. Eliza and Angelica epitomize a feminist ethical philosophy grounded in care and interconnectedness. *Hamilton* follows these co-existing, contradictory ethical systems as they influence the Founding Fathers and their families. The revelation that all people are created equal is an essential feature of *Hamilton*, but the show is ultimately a celebration of the masculinist ideal with only a nod to its feminist counterpart.

Mars and Venus

John Gray's popular 1992 book, provocatively titled *Men Are from Mars, Women Are from Venus*, returned to philosophical and biologically-based notions of male- and female-oriented moral approaches. Feminist ethical theorist Sarah Hoagland has said that the wide adoption of a feminist "ethic of care" would signify a "revolution" in moral thought and action.

But is there really a distinct male or female, masculine or feminine, way of looking at life? How would we define these distinct philosophies? How does the existence of so-called masculinist and feminist descriptions of ethics add to, rather than hold back, society's understanding of women's contributions, outlooks, and approaches? How does *Hamilton,* a fast-paced, celebratory explosion of patriotism, nationalism, and other "masculinist" ideals, portray these co-existing, contradictory ethical systems?

Philosophers in today's supposedly equal society examine masculinism and feminism in dynamic, multi-layered ways. Some see feminist philosophy as more sociological and era-bound than other branches of philosophy. It's true that in order to fully grasp the notion of "feminism" or "masculinism" as ethical philosophies, we cannot separate these notions from changing social norms. The emergence of gender-queer and gender-fluid identities is just one example of a social change that affects our understanding of feminism and feminist ethics.

While social changes continue to affect how philosophers consider masculinist and feminist characteristics, more universal notions of rights and equality between genders have existed for centuries. In her feminist classic, *A Vindication of the Rights of Women* (1792), Mary Wollstonecraft made feminist "declarations" just a few years after Angelica Schuyler's declaration of her desire for true equality. Wollstonecraft described male and female ways of experiencing the world, and how these orientations to life are mediated by damaging social norms like "reputation" and "modesty." Her thinking is clearly relevant among today's feminist philosophers, and to females in society in general.

At its root, any feminist strand of philosophy holds that the oppression of women is unjust. With this essential premise, feminist philosophy takes a clear ethical stand from the beginning. Feminist ethical philosophy examines traditionally "feminine" tendencies. It does not lose sight of the fact that oppression has characterized women's experiences in history and continues to affect their experiences today. Wollstonecraft and her successors believe that because female agency in general has been suppressed, we can only imagine how feminist ethical theories could influence society at large. Meanwhile, "masculinist" ethical systems have been writ large in history and remain dominant in contemporary public and private life, despite the many advances women have made in their movement to achieve equal treatment.

Masculinism and the Revolution

Many ethicists, sociologists, and psychologists working from a feminist orientation have defined a traditionally masculinist ethical system as strongly focused on competition, with violence, sex, money, and status serving as totems to exert power over women and other men. Sociologist Gordon Fellman refers to the traditionally masculine ideal as the "adversarial" approach to life. Dr. Fellman has documented the fact that the violent, competitive, masculinist system is infused throughout popular culture, from violent *Tom and Jerry* cartoons for children, to *Rambo* films, to public monuments (almost all monuments are for wars, displaying society's values in literally concrete ways).

Philosopher and psychologist Carol Gilligan explored what she called the "ethic of care" and the "ethic of justice," distinct outlooks that she emphasized could not be aligned or used together, but were also not opposites. To Gilligan, the impossibility of reconciling the ethic of care and the ethic of justice suggested the need for further exploration into how the two sets of morals might ideally function, either in tandem or on their own. In the well-known, authoritative words of civil rights activist and writer Audre Lorde, "the master's tools will never dismantle the master's house." Many feminist ethical philosophers believe that an ethical system based on care, interconnectedness, and other traditionally female traits must be employed if humanity is to successfully address society's many problems. Many describe a revolution of sorts as the only way to envision such a feminist ethical system's implementation on a societal scale.

I'm (Legally) Helpless

Hamilton takes place, in the words of Angelica Schuyler, "in a time in which my only job is to marry rich." Howard Zinn evocatively termed women of the Revolutionary era "the intimately oppressed": living intimately alongside men, but unable to own property or vote, or even to engage freely in public or private life. Strictly defined roles as daughters, wives, and mothers dominate the Schuyler sisters' and most other women's lives. *Hamilton* radiantly depicts female characters who, though legally "helpless" on their own, show more intelligence and accomplish more legacy-building on behalf of men than many of the men who work on their legacy full time.

Eliza's love and support, her devotion to sharing Alexander's story, and the avoidable tragedy and aftermath of Philip's death, all provide glimpses of what Gilligan called the "ethic of care." An ethic of care—one informed by relationships, interconnectedness, and love—is represented not by "helpless" waifs but by Angelica and Eliza. These strong, intelligent, interested women choose to elevate Alexander's status via marriage. They also work for decades after his death to preserve his legacy. *Hamilton* ends with Eliza and other characters describing her many efforts to promote the legacies of her husband, George Washington, and all of the soldiers who fought with them. It is worth asking: Without Eliza's dedication to living out the ethic of care, where would Alexander's devotion to the masculinist ethic of justice have left his precious legacy?

Deeds, Duels, and Destruction

Hamilton excitingly portrays the traditionally valued masculinist ethic of honor, prestige, and battle. On its surface, the musical is a brightly lit, fun, patriotic pageant celebrating accomplishments like changing history, creating and solidifying an empire, and shaping men's legacies. But *Hamilton* also puts on clear display the inherent problems in a masculinist ethic of empire, violence, and competition.

There are accidental duel deaths, descriptions of war wounds, ruinous infidelity, and hints at the horrors and ubiquity of slavery. Lives dedicated to this masculinist ethical ideal are presented alongside those adhering to the feminist ethic of care, nurturing, and making sure one's family members stay alive. Alexander's doomed marital affair and its aftermath, in which he proclaims that sharing the affair's lurid details "is the only way to protect my legacy," represents effectively the destructive, violent, legacy-obsessed impulse that can convince someone to disregard their loved ones' humanity ("Hurricane").

Defining ethical approaches as masculinist and feminist bring to mind Gilligan's notion that "justice" and "care" centered moralities are contradictory, but not opposite. Masculinist and feminist ethical systems exist uneasily and imperfectly alongside each other, complementing and contradicting each other, as they do with great dramatic effect in *Hamilton*. Overall, the show's celebration of masculinist themes of competition, legacy, and empire overshadows its nod to more caring-centered alternative value systems.

Masculinist and Feminist Ethics in *Hamilton*

Alexander and Eliza are the clearest representatives of masculinist and feminist ethical philosophy in *Hamilton*. The two versions of "Stay Alive" best embody these moral systems. Act I's "Stay Alive" represents a masculinist ideal, and Act II's "Stay Alive (Reprise)" expresses feminist ethics.

In the first act's "Stay Alive,' Angelica, Eliza, and other women sing "Stay alive!" in the background, praying that the men live through the grueling, perilous experience of war. Alexander describes the low morale of his boss, George Washington. He complains of harsh, winter conditions and an almost total lack of food, ammunition, and other critical resources.

"Stay Alive" in Act I focuses on the life-or-death importance of honor, personal excellence, ambition, and achievement. Hamilton, Laurens, Mulligan, and Lafayette describe their valiant efforts to support the Revolution. The righteous "camaraderie and bravery" that Laurens describes fills the entire group of revolutionaries. The song begins with Washington's military brilliance, but ends with the seeds of the show's first of three misguided and petty duels (note: all duels are petty and should not have occurred).

In the heartbreaking Act II reprise of "Stay Alive," Alexander and Eliza experience personal tragedy when their son Philip dies in a duel. Philip used Alexander's guns in the duel, attempting to follow his father's advice in "Blow Us All

Away": "Come back home when you're done. Take my guns. Be smart. Make me proud, son." Act II's "Stay Alive" vividly highlights the differences in Alexander's and Eliza's moral philosophies, two lives devoted to masculinist and feminist ethical systems.

Their beloved son Philip's last words are heartbreaking. With his weak, dying breath, he says "I did exactly as you said, Pa. I held my head up high." The fact is that while Alexander obviously loved his son, his actions—lending him his pistols and giving him dueling advice—belied his fatherly feelings. Alexander advises Philip to aim at the sky, thus not losing his honor or his life, simultaneously trying to protect him from the masculinist value system while also feeling the need to embrace it by engaging in a duel. This sad family situation reminds us of the contradictions found within as well as between ethical systems.

Moments later, Philip cries out, referring to his childhood piano lessons and to Eliza's advice in general, "Mom, I'm so sorry for forgetting what you taught me." Eliza strives mightily throughout the show to convince Alexander to "take a break" and enjoy some of his life, to "look around at how lucky we are to be alive right now" ("Non-Stop"). Recall Gilligan's intriguing thesis that the two sets of ethics, represented here by Alexander and Eliza, can live uneasily together, but are not opposites. Alexander never takes his break with Eliza, never enjoys his dip into a familiar world infused with the "ethic of care," until he is forced into mourning by Philip's death. The consequences of Alexander's refusal to live a balanced life and embrace spending time with his family are immediately apparent as the ominous first notes of "Say No to This" are heard.

Eliza's ethic of care was truly tested. She faced her son's death because of a botched attempt to defend Alexander's manly honor. This happened after Alexander did his best to destroy his honor with Maria Reynolds. Eliza eventually forgives, and then steadfastly supports, her husband. We learn of Eliza's lifelong dedication to Alexander's story after his untimely death in yet another masculinist, violent duel. Her description of the orphanage she builds in Hamilton's memory brings listeners to tears. Founding the orphanage brings the ethic of care to its logical conclusion: Eliza gives of herself for the sake of orphans, for no other reason than to have meaningful relationships and to help these children in unfortunate circumstances. The tears that the words "The Orphanage" elicit are testaments to the emotional appreciation and human connection we often feel toward philanthropists and social activists who practice real-life applications of the ethic of care.

Feminism: Still a Revelation

Angelica's proclamation, "You want a revolution? I want a revelation! So listen to *my* declaration," immediately presents her as passionate about feminist ethical ideals ("The Schuyler Sisters"). The Schuyler Sisters belt out the legendary words of the Declaration of Independence, meant for a highly patriarchal society: "We hold these truths to be self-evident, that all men are created equal." Angelica's iconic line then rings out with the flourish of a record scratch to stop the action: "And when I meet Thomas Jefferson—I'ma compel him to include *women* in the sequel!" Renee Goldsberry's distinct delivery of the word "women" exudes how she feels about the first Declaration mentioning only men's rights. She plans to compel, not to mildly suggest.

At the root of feminism and feminist ethics is the belief that people should be treated with dignity, regardless of their gender. Extended to its natural conclusions, feminism must connect and overlap with anti-racist efforts, as noted by Kimberlé Crenshaw. For *all* people to be treated equally, revolutions must occur at both personal and societal levels. These kinds of revolutions are not fought with "guns and ships," but forged through individual and social "revelations." We must address diverse social issues facing women—income inequality; unequal pay; restricted health services; street, school, and workplace harassment; violence; double standards; and a persistent lack of women in positions of power in all realms of society. We remain in continual need of Angelica's feminist revelation.

20
History's Icons

KATELYN BOTSFORD TUCKER

When the students I teach flip through their decrepit text-books, they undoubtedly come across tiny vignettes of person-ages and presidents and fail to see themselves in any of them.

Teaching history is at times a challenge, not simply because of class time lost due to assemblies or standardized testing, or the sheer depth and breadth of content covered, but also because students find it difficult to buy into learning a story whose cast of characters is impossible to relate to. Moreover, students are quick to do the math and note that with so many people in the world and so few studied in History class, the chance of them being one of those whose story gets told is slim to none.

While History may be a great and intricate tapestry, its fab-ric has the look of fluid silk, but feels more like stone. Hard. Unbending. Unmoving. The tapestry of History is tightly woven, but with the passing of time, threads seem to be coming undone in places and are in need of re-weaving. With this re-weaving comes repairing and re-imagining old images of the past, and gives us the chance to rewrite History with a new design. But it is not just for my students. Everyone wants to see themselves reflected in the story. History itself is shared, but it is also owned by everyone in it. Everyone wants to be able to stake a claim in the narrative.

Changing the Master Die

It isn't hard to recognize that one of the reasons students can't see themselves in the story is because that story has so little diversity. Women and people of color are often after-thoughts. This stems from a longstanding tradition of exclusion. History is written by the winners; the winners own the narrative. Follow the money and see where it goes.

On April 20th 2016, an historic day that will no doubt go down in the archives of many a Twitter and Facebook feed, Treasury Secretary Jack Lew announced that after ten months of searching, the new icons of American currency had been chosen. In just four short years, the faces we see on the fronts and backs of the five-dollar, ten-dollar, and twenty-dollar bill will look a bit different. A bit more like women and people of color, actually.

Honest Abe is safe on the front of the five-dollar bill, but the back will feature Eleanor Roosevelt, Marian Anderson, and Martin Luther King, Jr. The new twenty-dollar bill caused the most uproar; the genocidal maniac with fantastic hair and a Napoleon complex, Andrew Jackson, has been replaced by free-dom fighter and suffragette, Harriet Tubman. Never fear, AJ will still appear on the back of the note.

The Founding Father without a father made famous by Ron Chernow's extensive yet readable biography, *Alexander Hamilton*, and by Lin-Manuel Miranda's epic rap-opera, *Hamilton: An American Musical*, is also safe on the front of the ten-dollar bill. That's probably thanks to the Benjamins Broadway is currently raking in due to the popularity of the show. But the back will feature suffrage leaders Lucretia Mott, Sojourner Truth, Susan B. Anthony, Elizabeth Cady Stanton, and Alice Paul; fitting seeing as how reliable with the ladies Alexander was. Going from zero to eight women is a huge feat. Even women and men of color have, it seems, been given a refreshing spotlight. Look around, look around at how lucky we are to be alive right now!

Unfortunately, throughout history and into the present, women and people of color have been relegated to the background. They serve as supporting characters, if that, rather than the lead roles throughout history. This can be seen everywhere, from history textbooks, to CEOs of major companies, to the currency we exchange every day. No wonder students can't find a place for themselves in the narrative.

A New Narrative

Not only is history written by men—read *white* men—but many, regardless of how deserving of the spotlight they might be, often find themselves outside the narrative itself. In *Hamilton*, the Schuyler Sisters are very much present in the narrative of the production, offering a glimpse into the women in Alexander's circle.

However you won't find Angelica, Eliza, or Peggy on any bills anytime soon, despite their importance to the story of one of America's oft-forgotten Founding Fathers. The show only makes brief mention of Angelica's political influence on Alexander and does not have time to delve deeper into her political and social ambitions or her correspondence with a lusty Thomas Jefferson. It also glosses over the deep personal connection shared between Eliza and the Washingtons. The unfortunate reality is that women and people of color get shortchanged in history.

This isn't a problem taking place two hundred years ago. It's happening now after the first African American man was elected to serve as President of the United States. Barack Obama, who came after two hundred and twenty-seven years of wealthy, middle-aged, white Christian men at the helm, was met with criticism and resistance for eight years largely due to his race. The birther movement alone served as a not-so-veiled attempt at demeaning and discrediting his presidency.

Women, too, have typically been marginalized throughout history; their insignificance spans both space and time. Palaces are built out of paragraphs to men yet mere sentences are dedicated to the works of women in textbooks. Perhaps you'll find a brief mention of Christine de Pizan in a study of the Renaissance, or a nod to Rosalind Franklin in a biographical work on Watson and Crick; perchance a footnote with the name Diane Nash in a chapter on the Civil Rights Movement.

Men have also been denied access to the main stage if they are not white, or at least mainstream. The Reverend Dr. Martin Luther King, Jr. is often a focal point of the Civil Rights Movement over individuals like Bayard Rustin, Rosa Parks over Claudette Colvin. Even internationally recognized figures like Cesar Chavez and Nelson Mandela get little more than a sentence or two in history textbooks across the country. While it is certainly not feasible to expect that teachers like myself discuss every single important figure, surely many of those names belong among the main ideas and not brought in as afterthoughts. But the problem comes not just from History itself, but also from the gatekeepers of History.

The venerated Virginian veteran, our first President, tells us in *Hamilton*, "You have no control who lives, who dies, who tells your story." If your story gets told at all. History itself is partly to blame. Women were not afforded the same rights as men and therefore have been kept out of social, political, and economic roles beyond that of the household, for the most part. People of color have experienced a similar plight. Both groups are still experiencing some resistance as they make their way to the forefront of History. Things are changing, albeit at a glacial pace. One of the ways doors are being opened to history s outsiders is through art forms like music, literature, and theater.

Hamilton has created a unique production that utilizes specifically non-white actors to portray hugely important, and historically white, roles, not only changing the color of Broadway, but making a statement about history as well. And in part, *Hamilton* pays homage to this in writing strong female leads who tell the story of the titular character. It is, after all, Eliza who brings her Hamilton's story to light after he dies in a duel with Aaron Burr. She helps to reconstruct the narrative of Hamilton's life. She tells his story, although few know hers.

Who Owns History?

Eric Foner's collection of essays, "Who Owns History?", addresses the question of the direction in which history seems to be going. Foner cites James Baldwin who said, "The great force of history comes from the fact that we carry it within us, are unconsciously controlled by it in many ways, and history is literally *present* in all that we do."

Foner says that we are still in the midst of the "heritage industry," in which books, TV, and movies capitalize on people's love of the past. This is evident with shows like *Pawn Stars* and *American Pickers*, although perhaps not so conspicuous through programs like *Ice Road Truckers* and *Counting Cars*, all of which can be found on The History Channel.

But even The History Channel is not immune; a 2012 mini-series entitled *The Men Who Built America* illustrates the point. This partly isn't fair. White men like Henry Ford and John D. Rockefeller were integral to America becoming the nation it is today (dependent on cars and oil), but the show could have capitalized on the fact that there were a lot more than just a handful of white men who "built" America. A quick search will shoot back names like Stephanie Kwoleck, the inventor of Kevlar, or Margaret Knight, the "lady Edison," so prolific were her patents. African Americans like Granville T. Woods, who essentially eliminated train collisions with his multiplex telegraph invention, basically air-traffic control for the rails, Elijah McCoy, inventor of "the real McCoy" automatic oil cup, or Lewis Latimer, who first used carbon filament in light bulbs, also appear to prove that it's not just white men who are responsible for building a nation.

Foner writes that:

> the past thirty years have witnessed a remarkable expansion of the cast of characters included in historical narratives . . . Groups neglected by earlier scholars—African-Americans, women, working people, and others—have moved to center stage in accounts of the past, and the professoriate itself has changed so that it more fully reflects the composition of American society.

For the first time, groups that have received essentially zero focus from historians are actually being researched. What's more is that information is now being presented in a way that gives these groups the credit they deserve. But these changes are slow to come. While Foner's assessment about the historical narrative may be true as it is in fact shifting to groups of others over time, history itself remains a commodity owned and operated by white men.

For our part, and Foner would agree, we are a culture obsessed with even the most loosely based, historical shows and movies; 2015 alone saw the release of such box office successes as *Bridge of Spies, The Big Short, The Revenant, Hidden Figures*, and *Straight Outta Compton,* each of which delves into niche topics in history, like the housing crash of 2008 and the rise of gangsta rap.

Even the Great White Way knows what the people want; in 1969 with *1776* and in 2010 with *Bloody Bloody Andrew*

Jackson and *The Scottsboro Boys*, which popularized the captivating and never dry history of John Adams and the
Constitutional Convention, brief glimpses into the life of the
man on the twenty-dollar bill, and the heartbreaking story of
the accused by the same name. Foner tells us that "Each generation rewrites history to suit its own needs." This couldn't be
more true than in the case of *Hamilton*.

A Staged Revolution

With a continued excitement and vigor for the heritage industry, *Hamilton* has been able to breathe new life into the history
of the Founding Fathers and the early Republic. One of the
ways Miranda did this was through what has become a fiercely
criticized casting call which stated that the show was seeking
"non-white" actors. For some, this may seem potentially problematic for two reasons. Firstly, weren't all of the Founding
Fathers white? Some might have raised an eyebrow at the
notion that Alexander Hamilton or Aaron Burr, let alone
George Washington or Thomas Jefferson, could be portrayed
with a full racial reversal.

Chernow does make mention of the possibility that
Alexander himself may have been of mixed race. There is currently an ongoing National Genealogical Study, although results
are not yet conclusive regarding Alexander's heritage. For the
most part, the average person understands the Founding
Fathers to be White Anglo-Saxon Protestant. Secondly, some who
are unfamiliar with theatrical customs see this race-specific
casting as discriminatory. The answer to the latter is easier to
address than the former: although there are limits on whom a
casting director has a right to cast, many casting directors have
a right to specify who they're looking for to portray certain roles
in their productions. This is usually circumvented by creating a
character description which specifies race.

Certain productions require certain ethnicities, and in the
case of *Hamilton*, the cast was expected to be largely non-
white. However, this choice to create a production about the
short-tempered, protean creator of the Coast Guard, founder of
the *New York Post*, that consisted largely of a non-white cast
was deliberate. After criticism from Actors' Equity, producers
altered the casting call from "nonwhite men and women" to "all

ethnicities," but clarified that the "principal roles, which were written for nonwhite characters (excepting King George), be performed by nonwhite actors" and that they would "continue to cast the show with the same multicultural diversity . . . employed thus far." Because part of the show's appeal is the diversity it brings, and the other part is the way it is challenging the narrative of History itself.

Hamilton is about who gets to write history. Because so many women and people of color have been excluded from history and the narrative itself, Miranda's *Hamilton* gives them their shot. The cast of racially re-imagined men and women who helped shape America bring the story to life so well that it is hard to retain the stuffy images of John Trumbull. The casting was not lost on President Obama who, in March of 2016, spoke at the White House before a guest performance of *Hamilton*:

> We feel the fierce, youthful energy that animated the men and women of Hamilton's generation. And with a cast as diverse as America itself, including the outstandingly talented women—the show reminds us that this nation was built by more than just a few great men—and that it is an inheritance that belongs to all of us. Because Hamilton is . . . a story for all of us, and about all of us.

The diverse cast allows the audience to find themselves in the story and thereby find themselves in the history regardless of their race or ethnicity. *Hamilton* says very clearly to audiences that our founding belongs to all of us. Even to those who were excluded. It is our history. Our story.

Despite overwhelmingly positive reviews, some have criticized the casting itself as glossing over a period in American history in which slavery existed and few people of color were given their shot. Lyra Monteiro writes that the abundance of Black actors blinds audiences to the fact that there are a scant few Black actors who receive credit among the Founding Fathers. Annette Gordon-Reed supposes that were the actors white, the "rosy view of the founding era" might "grate" on the audience. And critic Ishmael Reed has gone so far as to liken *Hamilton* to blackface.

Look, even Christopher Jackson, who played George Washington, has acknowledged the Founding Fathers' part in the institution of slavery and said that he'll "never make peace" with the fact that GW "owned people." While it is certainly a valid argument to call to the carpet historical inaccuracies or modifications, of which there are a few in Miranda's production, it may be wise to consider that one of the purposes behind the casting may have been to create not only images that audience members can see themselves in, but also to raise serious questions about the founding of our nation, including how the Founders viewed slavery, money, and power.

Furthermore, the passions, ideas, and daily occurrences of the main characters, regardless of what the actors who play them look like, transcend time, place, gender, and race. Perhaps this is why the current Broadway cast, as well as the touring casts, have retained the traditional diversity of the original production and why Miranda himself has not ruled out a female Alexander in the future.

But it's not simply the race of the actors that makes *Hamilton* revolutionary. It's also the revelation of the women behind Alexander. Due to their high socioeconomic status and family's political prominence, the Schuyler Sisters are as enveloped in the nation's founding as Jefferson and Madison, yet because of their sex they are unable to rise above their station and receive little recognition in a retelling of the period. Angelica, as in Chernow's biography, serves as Hamilton's intellectual counterpart, while Eliza's noble and heroic work revolves around gaining recognition for her late husband. Through that work, she creates a history for herself that is entirely about her. It is Eliza who pleads mid-way through Act I, "Let me be a part of the narrative in the story they will write someday." Although she changes her mind in Act II, erasing herself from the narrative by burning the memories, burning the letters, she ends the show by serving as one of the most important voices.

Despite its revolutionary nature, even *Hamilton* fails to be a perfect representation of history for all of us. We're only given a tiny glimpse into Eliza's achievements as a postscript at the end of the musical. While it does open doors for women and people of color, they're still a long way away from achieving a central role in history. Eventually, at least we hope, everyone will get the chance to have their story told.

The circumstances which already exist in our historical narrative have excluded women and people of color. These involuntary pariahs of history established a void which continues to plague us today. Though historians now are looking through a broader but also more critical lens in order to complete the historical narrative, much work remains. Hamilton has helped to bring a new sense of understanding about the Founding Fathers. The musical style has established a new standard for Broadway. And the actors themselves have made it impossible for us to view these men and women from centuries passed in the same way ever again.

VIII

Rewriting
the Past

21

History Has Its Eyes on You

CHAD WILLIAM TIMM

"Who lives, who dies, who tells your story?" is an intensely philosophical question. What's considered history and who gets to write it are questions that require philosophical thinking.

What we know of Alexander Hamilton's life depends on the stories historians tell us, and they often disagree on the best way to represent the past. Whether Hamilton's a "bastard, orphan, son of a whore," "the smartest in the room," or "doesn't get enough credit for the credit he gave us" depends on the philosophy of the historian doing the writing.

Some historians claim the job of the historian is to tell the truth about the past, recounting history as it actually happened. Other historians claim this is both impossible and undesirable because not only is the truth of the past uncertain but the historian has a greater obligation to write histories that change the present.

The historian Howard Zinn (1922–2010), for example, sought to use historical writing to call out past injustices for the purpose of confronting similar injustices in the present. Zinn's histories emphasized the role that women and people of color played in challenging authority and promoting social justice, leading his critics to accuse him of revising the past for his activist agenda. Does Lin-Manuel Miranda's musical, *Hamilton,* which depicts a cast comprised almost entirely of people of color and highlighting the story of an immigrant "comin' up from the bottom" represent the true history of Hamilton's life, or is it a revising of the past?

Who Tells Your Story

History as an academic discipline and profession in the United States is just a baby at over a hundred years old. In the late nineteenth and early twentieth centuries, American historians sought to solidify their street cred by demonstrating the ability to recount the objective truth of the past. If these "young, scrappy and hungry" historians tell the truth of what happened in the past, the academic community would certainly give them their shot and the respect they deserved! Historians adopting this approach claimed the truth of the past existed, as it happened, and their job was to be objective and let the facts speak for themselves.

The George Washington depicted in *Hamilton* epitomizes this philosophy of history, especially in "History Has Its Eyes on You" when George exclaims, "I made every mistake, I felt the shame rise in me, and even now I lie awake, knowing history has its eyes on me." It's as if history, for George, is a drone with a camera flying high above the action, watching and recording his successes and failures as they happened. George trusts this idea of history as truth-teller so much he even refuses to challenge the smack-talking comments Charles Lee made against him in "Stay Alive," when he states "Don't do a thing. History will prove him wrong." George's response reflects his trust that as long as the historian remains objective and neutral, the truth of the past can speak. Thus the historical drone flying high in the sky records the truth of history as it happens.

After the devastation of the Second World War, historians from the "We tell the truth of the past club" worked to create a new framework for understanding American History, one which de-emphasized our differences and sought to highlight our similarities. After all, with the Cold War heating up we needed to come together to defeat the red commies. Relying on the idea of "Consensus," these early pioneers of the historical profession sought to tell the whole truth of American history by emphasizing what they thought made us the same. Unfortunately, widespread racial and gender discrimination meant these historians were overwhelmingly white and male. So, their histories emphasized the perspective of white men in positions of power and largely ignored the roles of women, people of color, and the poor.

Zinn the Zany

The social and political activism of the late 1950s and 1960s opened the doors of the historical profession to women and people of color for the first time. Understandably, their interests differed from the political history of white men often highlighted by Consensus historians. Their research interests centered on the ways America's history has oppressed and marginalized, in essence revising previous historical interpretations by looking at the past through a different lens.

One of these new "Revisionist" historians, Howard Zinn, proclaimed, "I didn't pretend to an objectivity that was neither possible nor desirable." Zinn claimed "Historical writing always has some effect on us. It may reinforce our passivity; it may activate us. In any case, the historian cannot choose to be neutral; he writes on a moving train." Because the world is already moving in certain dangerous directions, if the historian claims to be objective and neutral they run the risk of contributing to those dangers by ignoring them.

In Zinn's case he sought to engage historians in the social issues of the 1960s to 2000s, challenging historians to use their work to participate in the conversations surrounding the rights of African Americans, women, students, the LGBTQ community, and American soldiers fighting and dying in wars overseas. Although certainly not the only Revisionist historian, Zinn became a spokesperson for historical activism because he sought to make history accessible to a large audience by emphasizing what he called "a people's history," leading him to being one of the most widely read historians around.

In many ways *Hamilton* reflects Zinn's revisionist approach because it represents a similar desire to challenge current social and political conditions. Lin-Manuel Miranda's *Hamilton* throws neutrality and objectivity out the window. The musical highlights the significant role that immigrants played in the forming of our nation, in the midst of a political climate where then presidential candidate Trump characterized some immigrants as rapists and murderers. Hamilton is "another immigrant, comin' up from the bottom" and he reminds us that those seeking refuge and opportunity helped build this country. The musical, therefore, emphasizes a historical example where "Immigrants . . . get the job done" and create "a system that he can shape however he wants." In the musical immigrants like Hamilton and the Marquis de Lafayette are not seen as a menace but rather as integral to the development of an American nation.

By challenging the idea of objectivity Zinn didn't say historians should just make things up. Instead, in *The Politics of History* he asserted "If to be objective is to be scrupulously careful about reporting accurately what one sees, then of course this is laudable." But accuracy is only part of the process of writing history. The historian must also choose the stories and the perspectives they represent in their histories, and this is where Zinn challenged the Consensus goal of objectivity. It isn't an accident that these predominantly white and financially secure Consensus historians focused their histories on affluent white America, it's who they identified with most. Zinn's point is that historians are human beings, and as human beings we are influenced by our lived experiences. These experiences shape the way we see the world in addition to the histories we write.

It is insincere, therefore, for a historian to claim they are objective and neutral when they do historical research. Of course historians should seek objectivity if that means looking at all the facts and reporting them accurately, like including Alexander Hamilton's infidelity in the musical. If being objective, however, means pretending to not have an opinion or to not engage in the meaningful issues of the day, then objectivity is to be avoided. For the historian, Zinn writes, "Our values should determine the *questions* we ask in scholarly inquiry, but not the answers." Instead of claiming neutrality and unrealistically presenting the objective truth of the past, Zinn claims historians should support an activist history and seek to engage in conversations aimed at eliminating injustice and inequality.

Howard Zinn's most popular book, *A People's History of the United States*, sold two million copies and was published in 1980, tells the history of the United States from the perspective of those whose voices were largely ignored by previous Consensus historians. Emphasizing the role that women, people of color, immigrants, and working class Americans played in United States History, *A People's History* reflected a radical revising of American history by exposing "the limitations of governmental reform, the connections of government to wealth and privilege, the tendencies of government toward war and xenophobia, and the play of money and power behind the presumed neutrality of law."

The Consensus historians' emphasis on the voices of those in positions of power to tell the history of the United States gives the impression that nothing ever changes. The powerful stay powerful and the influential remain influential, often at the expense of the rest of us. Zinn's Revisionist philosophy of history challenges the status quo and demonstrates, in his words, "the uncertainty of history, of the possibility of surprise, of the importance of human action in changing what looks unchangeable." Zinn's approach to history is that of an activist as much as that of an historian.

Revolutionary Revisionism

Hamilton reflects Zinn's perspective in many ways and is something of a Revisionist history of the founding of America, because Miranda gives significant roles to people not typically emphasized in histories of the period. The perspectives of the rich and affluent during the revolutionary period are already known well known and documented in numerous historical accounts but, as historian Ray Raphael writes in *A People's History of the American Revolution*, "Real people, not paper heroes, made and endured the American Revolution."

The real people Raphael refers to are the women, people of color, immigrants, and ordinary working people who built this country. Howard Zinn referred to the philosophy of writing history from the perspective of those often ignored for the purposes of eliminating injustice in the present "radical history." What makes this history radical is that it seeks to point out the ways our social, political, and economic institutions have historically oppressed and marginalized women, the poor and people of color.

According to Zinn, a traditional and supposedly objective approach to history is oppressive because "it can destroy compassion by showing us the world through the eyes of the comfortable" like "the slaves are happy, just listen to them"—leading to "the poor are content, just look at them." This neutral approach reinforces the status quo, making us comfortable in our apathy because we think this is how things have always been. After all, it's in our history books!

A radical approach, on the other hand, is liberating because uncovering the histories of the oppressed can show us how average, ordinary people like us can alter the course of history for the better.

Listen to My Declaration

One of the radical perspectives portrayed by *Hamilton* is that of women asserting agency, or the power to make their own decisions and influence history. In the early 1800s women were a long way from equal rights but that didn't deter them from challenging the status quo. Consensus historians often depict women as passive recipients of male domination but in "The Schuyler Sisters" Angelica Schulyer announces "I've been reading *Common Sense* by Thomas Paine . . . You want a revolution? I want a revelation so listen to my declaration:" and Eliza and Peggy join in with "'We hold these truths to be self-evident that all men are created equal,'" and Angelica exclaims "I'm 'a compel him to include women in the sequel!" While Consensus historians emphasized political and diplomatic history, generally from the perspective of white men, Revisionist historians highlight social history which includes the everyday lives of women. Instead of presenting a history of women through the eyes of the men they married, Revisionist historians write the history of women from their own perspectives, using their own voices.

Angelica Schuyler, for example, demonstrates how women have their own ambitions and goals in the exchange where Hamilton says "You're like me. I'm never satisfied." Angelica continues "So this is what it feels like to match wits with someone at your level." Angelica is *as* driven, intelligent, and aspirational as Alexander Hamilton but lacks the freedom to choose.

Angelica's story demonstrates how women's hopes and dreams depended on social norms determined by men. When she sings "I'm a girl in a world in which my only job is to marry rich. My father has no sons so I'm the one who has to social climb for one" we are confronted with her lack of freedom. While Alexander can use his intelligence and motivation to aspire to great political influence Angelica is forced to use her intelligence and motivation to marry a politically influential man. *Hamilton* points out this contradiction and reminds us of the injustices experienced by women while showing us their resilience in the face of inequality.

This influence and resilience is especially evident in *Hamilton's* portrayal of Eliza Hamilton. Her ambition is legendary, as she devoted fifty years to defending Alexander's reputation in order to preserve their family legacy. In "Who Lives, Who Dies, Who Tells Your Story" she informs us "I interview every soldier who fought by your side" and "I try to make sense of your thousands of pages of writing."

Mulligan, Lafayette, and Laurens even remark "She tells our story." In this way the musical reflects Eliza's role in actively preserving not only the history of her own family, but by interviewing the soldiers who served with Alexander she preserves their stories as well.

This is exactly the type of agency that Revisionist historians criticize Consensus historians for ignoring. When Eliza burns her personal letters to Alexander and states "I'm erasing myself from the narrative. Let future historians wonder how Eliza reacted when you broke her heart" she is taking her history into her own hands. The musical's Eliza Hamilton is a complex and sophisticated woman and not a passive, two-dimensional caricature. We see her fall in love, suffer the pain of her husband's adultery, and grieve for the loss of both her child and then her husband. We witness her "speak out against slavery" and establish the first private orphanage for hundreds of children in New York City. In the end we witness Eliza take control to determine the narrative of her family's history. By emphasizing the everyday experiences of women in the late eighteenth and early nineteenth centuries and demonstrating their lack of equal rights, *Hamilton* challenges the viewer to take a closer look at gender equity in the present, at a time when a major political party nominated a woman for president for the first time in United States history.

Revolutionary Manumission Abolitionists

The musical also confronts the issue of race, bringing race literally to the forefront of the history of *Hamilton*. Significant contributions made by black Americans and the outright ownership of slaves by most of the founders takes center stage in *Hamilton*'s history. John Laurens and Alexander Hamilton, two of the musical's main characters, openly support the abolition of slavery. The historical John Laurens even sought congressional approval to put together a regiment of black soldiers to fight in the American Revolution. This is reflected in Laurens's prophecy in "My Shot," where he proclaims "But we'll never truly be free until those in bondage have the same rights as you and me . . ." Later in "Stay Alive" Laurens exclaims "I stay at work with Hamilton, we write essays against slavery." In "My Shot" Hamilton asks "What are the odds the gods put us all in one spot . . . a bunch of revolutionary manumission abolitionists?" and later adds "We'll never be free until we end slavery!" Together, Laurens and Alexander Hamilton represent a growing movement for the abolition of slavery.

Perhaps the best example of *Hamilton* as a Revisionist history of race relations in American is the way the musical points out the contradictions in the Founders' desire for equality and freedom while owning slaves themselves. In "Cabinet Battle #1," Thomas Jefferson and Alexander Hamilton disagree on how to handle the young country's debt crisis.

Hamilton, the first secretary of the treasury, advocates the federal government putting all the states' debt together and then raising taxes on everyone in order to pay it off. Jefferson and other southerners oppose this plan because their states had already paid most of their debts, and would now be taxed to pay the debt of states like Massachusetts. Hamilton's comments go straight to the heart of the slavery issue when he asserts, "A civics lesson from a slaver. Hey neighbor, your debts are paid cuz you don't pay for labor . . . we know who's really doing the planting."

This moment points out a glaring contradiction in American history, where politicians openly called for political and economic freedom while simultaneously denying that freedom to millions of women and people of color. What's even more ironic is that people of color comprised nearly the entire cast of the original Broadway musical, no doubt making a point to give people of color a place at center stage in this story of America's founding.

Black Lives Matter?

Howard Zinn represented a new generation of historians committed to revising the Consensus view of American History.

Instead of an impossible objective truth of the past, one that emphasized unity from the perspective of influential white men, these Revisionist historians sought to point out the injustices, inequalities, and contradictions of America's past in the hopes of eliminating them in the present.

While much of *Hamilton*'s outward appearance reflects this revisionist approach, does it go far enough? Despite a cast comprised almost completely of people of color there are no historical people of color in the musical. Every single historical figure in the musical was in fact white, and nearly every figure was either politically or economically influential or from an influential family.

The basic premise for *Hamilton* is another story of a prominent white Founder, only this time told from the mouths of nonwhite characters. This emphasis on influential Founding Fathers is more in the tradition of Consensus history than it is Revisionist history, as it represents, according to Zinn in *Declarations of Independence,* that "in our culture, the most trivial activities of the presidents are considered of great significance, while the life-and-death struggles of ordinary people are ignored." Is *Hamilton* simply a Consensus history in Revisionist clothing?

Although the musical confronts the viewer with the irony of founding figures played by people of color, historian Lyra Monteiro asks "Is this the history that we most want black and brown youth to connect with—one in which black lives to clearly do not matter?" And historian Annette Gordon-Reed claims that *Hamilton* overstates Alexander Hamilton's support for the abolition of slavery, that he was not pro-immigrant, and that he was an elitist who wanted the president to serve for life. Gordon-Reed asserts that the portrayal of Hamilton in the musical reflects the Alexander Hamilton we would like him to be, not the real historical person.

King of the Crazies

But historian Ron Chernow, whose biography of Alexander Hamilton served as the primary historical reference for Lin-Manuel Miranda's musical, has stated: "This show is the best advertisement for racial diversity in Broadway history and it is sad that it is being attacked on racial grounds."

Perhaps *Hamilton's* critics are just being too critical. Despite the stated shortcomings, the musical makes race a central point of discussion, gives weight to the voices of women, and contributes to a national conversation about important contemporary social issues. As Zinn contends, a Revisionist "people's" approach to history can motivate us to take action for equality in the present "By widening our view to include the silent voices of the past, so that we look behind the silence of the present . . . It can reveal how ideas are stuffed into us by the powers of our time, and so lead us to stretch our minds beyond what is given." This inclusion of the ignored and dismissed voices of the past to stretch our minds has never been more important than today, a time in our nation's history where recent political tensions are perhaps at an all-time high.

Many Americans still cling to the traditional Consensus history of the United States, like Republican Representative Steve King from Iowa. Congressman King, when questioned in a recent interview about the lack of racial diversity in the Republican Party, remarked "I'd like you to go back through history and figure out, where are these contributions that have been made by other categories of people you're talking about, where did any other subgroup of people contribute more to civilization?" King's comments reflect a Consensus understanding of American history, ignorant to the contributions of anyone other than white Europeans. Some Americans long for an end to the recent social and political turmoil and national conversations about race and gender, which might help explain how King's won seven consecutive Congressional elections in Iowa.

History's Eyes on You

Despite these legitimate concerns, isn't it better to have a history of Hamilton that puts women and people of color front and center, especially at a time when race and gender are part of a national conversation about equity? Doesn't it make sense to craft a history of a prominent white man performed with the voices of people of color to show that these narratives can be brought together into one vision for the future? Zinn's work challenges us to be constantly aware of the way power is wielded in crafting the histories we tell and in creating what we know about the past, because we can't escape the effects of power.

In *Declarations of Independence* Zinn reminds us "The pretense of objectivity conceals the fact that all history, while recalling the past, serves some present purpose." The Consensus history of the American Revolution and early Republican period where a unified and predominantly white America overcame insurmountable obstacles to create a new nation still dominates the textbooks used in public schools today. Lin-Manuel Miranda's depiction of *Hamilton* challenges us to look at the past from a different perspective.

The musical blatantly points out the irony of an American history that largely ignores the voices of women and people of color by literally shining the spotlight on women and people of color. The fact that a diverse cast tells a largely white history of *Hamilton* confronts viewers to with that irony. If we view *Hamilton* with an understanding of Howard Zinn's "people's approach," we are compelled to be hopeful even in bad times. Howard Zinn's radical history aimed to highlight the extraordinary struggles of everyday Americans in order to remind us that, as he wrote in *You Can't Be Neutral on a Moving Train*, "We have been surprised before in history. We can be surprised again. Indeed, we can *do* the surprising."

Lin-Manuel Miranda's *Hamilton* inspires us to re-examine our history and consider what we've ignored, namely the perspectives of women and people of color. The musical reminds us that we can't throw away this shot because it hatches a plot blacker than the kettle calling the pot . . .

22
Casting in Living Color

ADAM BARKMAN AND RACHEL WALL

We're sitting in the Richard Rodgers Theatre, a third of the way through the first act, blissfully ignorant of the fact that we paid several thousand dollars to warm this seat.

Aaron Burr introduces one of the most well-known characters in the show: "Here comes the general! *(Spoiler: it's George Washington)* Ladies and Gentlemen, *(You know, the guy on the $100 bill?)* the moment you've been waiting for! *(His face is literally carved on a mountain, if you still don't have a reference.)* The pride of Mount Vernon! *(A perfectly triangular white mop of curls complements his fair skin, tired eyes, and rosy cheeks. Certainly you know the picture. Here he comes!)* GEORGE WASHINGTON!"

Aaaaaaand . . . out walks a burly black man, looking distinctly un-Washington-like.

It may sound like a twisted joke, but this is what takes place at the Richard Rodgers Theatre, eight times a week. America's Founding Fathers, whose porcelain skin glares like a spotlight from every US history book, are played by people who look distinctly unlike their historic counterparts. So, now it's 2016 and Thomas Jefferson has an afro.

Lin-Manuel Miranda has made historic leaps with his choice to employ a racially diverse cast to play historic events against a background of hip-hop music. When America's Founding Fathers are becoming the stuff of Internet memes and dinner discussions, and a teenage girl has a poster of the Marquis de Lafayette on her wall, something monumental has occurred. *Hamilton* is a revolution in musical theater, and like any good revolution, there are people indignant about Miranda's choices and even more people raising a glass to artistic freedom. Yet despite the naysayers, and those ranting about Miranda smashing the integrity and accuracy of the original story, *Hamilton* was literally the most elusive ticket in the world; so some part of this new telling of an old story must be working out.

But can he do that? Can he *rewrite* history? No, we get it. He already did. However, in a show that has consumed America like a true revolution, every choice has consequences. Just because something can be done, doesn't mean that it should be done. And whether or not it was Lin-Manuel Miranda's intent, the "color-blind" casting—ignoring the race of the cast members—speaks philosophical volumes and raises pointed questions. What are the consequences of color-blind casting? Is color-blind casting a moral choice? In the words of King George III, "What comes next?" Philosophers have conflicting opinions on race and whether or not it even exists.

You Can Be the Same Man You Always Were because You Were Born That Way

First, there are philosophers who claim that race is a genetic part of human biology. It's an evolutionary characteristic that separates members of the human species. A person's race is passed on through his or her parents, just as their eye color and risk of certain diseases. Within this category are people in two camps: those who believe that race is an essential, biological feature of humans, and those who believe it is non-essential and non-biological.

For those in the first camp, race is a biological trait that is essential to a person. A person's race tells more about him or her than just the color of their skin. It reveals something about a person's intellectual capabilities or personhood. If race is an essential biological property, then I can know something about who you are solely based on your race.

Biological race theories have often provided a scientific justification for racism, understood as discrimination based on race. If race is an important biological feature that determines personality and abilities, then it could be concluded that one race is better than another. As soon as a hierarchy is formed, people are treated differently based on their race. We take the strong stance that racism is morally wrong, and creating a hierarchy based on apparent intrinsic differences is racism.

If we apply the view that race is an essential part of who we are to Miranda's casting choices, an all "color-blind" or non-traditional casting choices would be unethical. If race is an essential biological feature that defines who a person is, then chaining the race of the characters changes something crucial about them. George Washington of *Hamilton* would lose all identity with history's George Washington, because the casting director had changed something intrinsic to the character.

This view of race has contributed to countless acts of discrimination and racism in the world's history. A biological view of race led to Hitler's Holocaust and justified the North Atlantic slave trade. While it's difficult to tell whether racial differences are caused by genuine biological factors or by culture and the way a person was raised, there is no evidence that there is some intrinsic value attached to a person's race that changes who they are.

Hence those in the second camp, who claim that race is a biological reality but is no more important than any other physical feature. A person's race is just their skin color, and it doesn't influence anything essential about who we are as people. The fact that we have white skin means no more than that we have brown or blonde hair. This view is closer to the way that the twenty-first century society is leaning. Unfortunately, this post-racial view is also flawed, because race does have some influence on who we are.

You Can Maybe Be a New Man if Society Tells You that You Can

Another perspective is that race exists purely as a social concept. It has no biological relevance, but is something that came about through socialization. If the events of history had gone differently, or if we grew up in a different society, race might look entirely different or be completely meaningless. However, because the concept of race has been built into our societal structure, it is something that we deal with every day. Humans define race. The reason that I think of people as different races is far less because of their inherited skin color than because society instructs me to view Latinos as distinctly different from white people.

Defining race from a socially constructed perspective is difficult, because social-constructionism claims that race has no inherent definition other than what a given society defines it to mean. If we accept that race is socially constructed and has no essential features, it becomes more difficult to define race. This problem leads many philosophers to claim that race has no real meaning. It is invented rather than discovered, and can be changed at will.

Think of the way that being overweight has changed meanings. Once a sign of wealth and luxury, it is now interpreted as an indicator of laziness, lack of self-control, and poverty. This has nothing to do with the intrinsic definition of weight or a clinical assessment of a person's health, but society's interpretation. Since the social definition of race has caused so many problems, some theorists reason that it would be best to get rid of the concept entirely. So much of society is attempting to move us to a "post-racial" world, where race doesn't exist. "You should be ashamed of yourself if you so much as think of people as having a race. There is only the human race!" This is mostly a cry heard from white people, but more on that later.

A post-racial world would surely be a world free of racism, because without race, no one can discriminate based on race. Pretending to live in a post-racialist world won't do anything to solve the problems of racism. Again, if this perspective were applied to *Hamilton*, the cast could be all-white or all-black and it wouldn't make a difference in the performance. The race of the performers does seem to matter, though. So, eliminating racism by eliminating race might sound like a valiant goal, but it misses the mark.

Attempting to eliminate race entirely is problematic, because race is not merely an arbitrary term. It cannot be rewritten to mean whatever the person wants because it is loaded with history and pain. Just because something has been defined by humans rather than discovered scientifically does not make it meaningless. Society tells us that we need to wear clothes. We could claim clothes are meaningless and revolt against society's harsh reform. We could burn all our clothing and prance around naked because #FreeTheNipple or whatever. But there will be consequences, because in history, people have worn clothes, despite what I think about them. We will be refused service. We may contract more diseases. We won't be able to attend work or live our lives normally because the influence of clothes is present in society, whether we like it or not. So, before we can denounce the evil powers that envelop the term *race,* we must understand that "socially-constructed" does not mean "arbitrary."

There's a history of pain caused by race, and at the center of that is a power struggle. One group decides that they are more important than another because they are different, and they act on it because they have the social power to do so. To ignore race is to ignore that this power differential has existed for centuries, and it's wrapped up in *whiteness*. Racism does not occur whenever one group of people disagrees with the other. Rather, one group must have the political power to create a hierarchy. This is the role that white people have played.

A white person claiming they experienced racism is similar to a thin person claiming they've been skinny-shamed, or made fun of because of their small size. It is still harmful. It is still something that should be avoided, but because the societal norm is for people to be slender, it cannot be compared to the ridicule and fat-shaming that overweight people receive as an entire group. A white person being mocked because of his or her race is a solitary incident. A black person being discriminated against—something, we should note, that still occurs on Broadway, Off-Broadway and Off-Off Broadway—is a consequence of an entire system of racism. Racism combines social power and a desire for dominance with the belief that race is an essential part of a person. Yes, the world would be better without racism, but that doesn't change the fact that it exists. When theorists applaud a post-racial society, they trivialize the discrimination that has occurred throughout history.

Telling the Story of America

We are stuck in a paradox. We can only speak for the North American mentality, but racial diversity is one of the most celebrated aspects of a social system that at the same time is desperately trying to eliminate race. Diversity has become more a buzzword for surface-level inclusiveness than a recognition that we are all humans and all different. When a push for equality becomes an attempt to glaze over the past, there is a problem. Adam teaches at small, private university, where approximately eighty percent of the student body is white. Yet all of the school's promotional materials seem to feature an endless amount of racial diversity that's not actually representative of the university. The student who was featured on the "International Students" page for several years because of his Asian appearance has lived in Canada his entire life. There is a history behind race that will not be told if we try to move past it. There are stories and hurts and pains and celebrations attached to race.

Miranda's *Hamilton* is not just a parade of racial diversity. It tells a larger story. While the musical claims that "We have no control who lives, who dies, who tells our story," *Hamilton* tries to reclaim the power for anyone to tell the story of America.

Hamilton's casting is the farthest thing from color-blind. If it were truly color-blind, the race of the actors and actresses would be irrelevant, and it would probably feature a cast full of white faces, since that's what the world of Broadway historically prefers. In interviews and in his book, Miranda has expanded on the reasons he chose racially-diverse casting. The first should perhaps be obvious. This is a hip-hop musical. Hip hop is rooted in Latino and black culture. It combines old and new to create something that is teeming with life. Every casting director's goal is to find the people that will best fit the roles, and here's a fun fact: the people who perform best in rap, R+B, and jazz are often not white. Miranda is retelling an old story in a new way, and stories change depending on who's telling them. For this production, that means that the cast looks different too.

We believe that the only reason that his casting is receiving any criticism is because colored people are playing white roles. Heaven forbid that there be something that a white person does not have the option to do or some role a white person can't play. Broadway has been a white man's world for so long. Blackface got its cruel start in the theatre, as even the roles of black characters were given to white people, and race turned into a mockery. Shows have been created and cast for white people, and over the years, with countless more revivals and recasting, that doesn't change.

Although white people can't imagine an opportunity that's not open to them, black, Latino, and Asian people have been excluded from opportunities in movies and theater based on race for generations. What's worse is that this can be justified by a casting director's ability to choose or deny an actor based on his appearance. Ignoring that race exists only perpetuates the white-washing of theater. *Hamilton* should cause us to ask, "Why can't white roles be played by colored people?" More than that, it should bring us to say that we *need* to allow theater to be a space for racially-diverse casting. Allowing white people to continue to dominate casting, just because it's traditionally done that way, perpetuates the racism that has strangled our culture for so many years.

The theater is a place to tell stories. It allows us to recognize ourselves in other characters as the story on stage becomes part of our story. It's a sanctuary for the broken and an escape for the hurting. So why is it also a place where mass groups of people are often barred from roles based on their race?

The morality of racially flexible casting doesn't go both ways. If a role is written for a non-white person, it should certainly be played by a non-white person. This is not discrimination, because no group has ever had the social power to demean white people as a whole. It's a way to stand up to the traditions that have done more harm than good, by allowing every person the chance to have a role in the theatre. There will never be a limit to white roles, but when people of color are limited to token characters and loyal sidekicks, something needs to change.

Back in the Narrative

For everyone concerned with accuracy, maybe musical theater is not a place where you can get comfortable. It's a world that is founded on a collision of fantasy with reality. No one sings every time they face a moral dilemma, although we would love to see a world in which this did happen. The stage allows these things to come to life. Every time a person is cast in a role, whether the show is based on reality or the musings of a playwright, the role changes. Reality is checked with the coats at the door. Even the most traditionalist and accurate production of a show like *Hamilton* would be tainted with the present. Lin-Manuel Miranda just skipped the pretense: "This is a story about America then, told by America now," Miranda states in interviews and in his book.

Hamilton changes things, and the amount of discussion that the casting of *Hamilton* has raised proves that we are nowhere near the post-racial society that many philosophers would like to believe we are approaching. People still notice race. *Hamilton* stands out because of it. Color-blind casting is unethical. But there is nothing blind about *Hamilton*. It makes breakthroughs in the way that the theatre considers casting and race (though not necessarily in its narrative content). It's a reflection of the differences that serve a much stronger purpose if they are celebrated instead of suppressed.

No one is supposed to ignore the various shades of brown dressing the characters on the Richard Rodgers Theatre stage. It's a celebration of where America has come from and hope for where it is going.

23
Dueling Conceptions of History

DAVID LAROCCA

Alexander Hamilton made history, but does his achievement mean that the celebrated Broadway musical—trading on his name—is also history?

Lin-Manuel Miranda's theatrical production revitalized interest in Hamilton as a person, a persona, and a player! It *appears* to follow the facts in telling Hamilton's story, so audiences may be forgiven for assuming that *Hamilton* is history. One common understanding of history tells us its statements must accurately describe the events as they happened. With this familiar account of history, we can ask: What kind of truth does *Hamilton* provide?

In *The Idea of History*, R.G. Collingwood claims that merely checking for "correspondences" between fact and event, or between event and description of event, won't do when trying to identify something as historical. The truth is not "out there." So, what is *Hamilton*? Is it history or is it something else? If we apply Collingwood's controversial views on historical truth to *Hamilton*, we come to the contentious conclusion that *Hamilton* is art, not history.

To be sure, that piece of artwork has already recommended itself as part of history, particularly the history of theatre, of Broadway, and of New York City. Many of us have been startled to find that a musical about the first secretary of the US Treasury could be a serially sold-out cultural touchstone, winning eleven of the sixteen Tonys it was nominated for, just one shy of the record. Yet, despite the show's appeal and acclaim, and the fact that Miranda subsequently received a MacArthur "genius" grant, we should adopt a critical relationship to the musical's status as a work of history.

History as Art, or Something Else?

Some historic figures are steeped in mythic controversy. Did Socrates really say those things, or were they mainly Plato's creation? Can we attest to the historical Jesus? Did William Shakespeare write the plays we associate with his name? Thanks to the proximity of time and ample historical documentation, we can be more confident in the *fact* of Alexander Hamilton's existence: that he was born, lived, and died. We can consult his possessions, his manuscripts, and the testimonies made by others. Hamilton comes to life as a historical reality on account of all these contributions. Yet, when we see and hear the theatrical musical *Hamilton*, what are we to make of the claims it makes about the man?

Hamilton, originally played by Miranda himself, frequently declares "I am not throwing away my shot." By the end of the play, we discover the line is both foreshadowing and a double entendre. "The shot" is Hamilton's desire for a chance at a good life, as well as his actual bullet in the duel with Aaron Burr, which he *does* ultimately throw away. We can then add irony to the line's meaning, since he loses the first shot when he throws away the second.

We also see Hamilton liken himself to his nation, the United States, saying that both entities are "young, scrappy, and hungry." We learn in a confessional mode "I wrote my way out of hell," thus connoting that writing is a form of creation. Lastly, Hamilton claims that America is an "unfinished symphony," which implicates the strivings of Miranda and his company in the pursuit of happiness two centuries after the death of their hero.

Where did Miranda get his facts and ideas about Hamilton? He acknowledges direct inspiration from Ron Chernow's biography, *Alexander Hamilton*. So, if Chernow's book is considered a genuine work of history, and Miranda's musical is based on Chernow's work, then is *Hamilton* also history? Though Miranda's creation has costumes and music that Chernow's book lacks, they are telling the same story, aren't they?

When we watch a sci-fi film, we don't think about its correspondence to reality, or past events, or deceased people, even when such depictions are said to have occurred "a long time ago, in a galaxy far, far away." We never think, even briefly, even accidentally, that *Star Wars* is historical. When a story is based on something, we're naturally encouraged to see it as linked somehow with history. Consider *Selma* or *Malcolm X, The Last Temptation of Christ* or *JFK*. These are what? Sort of history? How does a musical such as *Hamilton* fit into our thinking here?

Provisionally, we might say that all of these examples are mythological, but some feel more real than others because of a presumed sense of connection to real people and actual events. That's why many directors try so hard to find actors that look like the figures they portray, like David Oyelowo as Martin Luther King, Jr. or Denzel Washington as Malcolm X. The likeness makes the link to history more compelling. *Hamilton* has famously deviated from this habit of fiction in casting a Puerto Rican as Hamilton, African-Americans as George Washington and Thomas Jefferson, and, indeed, assembling a cast comprised mainly of non-white actors. The casting call itself created a discrimination controversy.

In the musical, we hear about "the room where it happens," with the reminder that no one—none of us—was in the room where it happened. So, what can be said of historical merit or truth in the play, or beyond it? We can but conjecture. This is history-as-sausage-making: we don't know what goes into it; we merely contend with the result.

The overarching concern here, in our reflections on *Hamilton*, is what we know, or think we know, about past events and people. This study, this preoccupation, is called historiography. But, in a volume dedicated to the philosophy of *Hamilton*, we want to ask about the *epistemology* of historiography. It's not enough to ask how history is generated by means of how it is recounted—we're pressed further to ask what sorts of claims that methodology makes about our relationship to knowledge, defined as true, justified belief. Whenever we discuss the making of history, as a kind of record, we have to consider the relationship between fact and interpretation. Is it a fact that the chambers at the Constitutional Convention were 95 degrees Farenheit, or was the debate just really heated? This distinction haunts any history.

How much of what we call history is conjecture, a picture, a guess, an impression, an invention? "History is happening," exclaims one of the Schuyler sisters with preternatural assurance. Yet, if her claim proved to be true—and Alexander Hamilton ended up being a figure of historical significance at a time when, as people say, "history was made," what do we make of the musical *Hamilton*'s relationship with that history? Can we—or should we—say that in *Hamilton* "history is happening?" There are good reasons to think it is not.

History as Other than Art

There are many contending theories of history—what history is, how it's made, and so on. Let's consider, then, the influential (if also strangely neglected, occasionally unattributed, and arguably underutilized) notions proposed by Robin George Collingwood, the Oxford philosopher, historian, and archeologist (1889–1943). Collingwood made an elegant, if controversial, distinction between the kind of knowledge achievable by natural science and that by history. Simply put: natural scientists can use empirical observation, in the present tense, to substantiate claims and theories, while history, having the past as its object, cannot employ the outward senses to any profitable effect. Rather, history is a form of re-creation or re-thinking based on material evidences.

As Collingwood writes, since "the past is never a given fact which [the historian] can apprehend empirically by perception . . . the historian is not an eyewitness of the facts he desires to know," but rather, "the historian must re-enact the past in his own mind." Collingwood's idea could be distilled this way: "the past is ideal and only the present real."

Still, the proposal that the past is "re-enacted" in the mind may seem odd, as if it were a movie being replayed, and yet, we're told that nothing like direct experience is at issue: historians are not witnesses to history. Since history is an activity of re-enacting the past, for Collingwood, historical knowledge is only possible when an historian "re-thinks for himself the thought of his author." How does this work in practice? Collingwood explains such "re-thinking" by reference to Euclid's claim that "the angles at the base of an isosceles triangle are equal": "if I understand what is meant and recognize that it is true, the truth which I recognize . . . is the same truth which Euclid recognized. . . . But my act of asserting the proposition is not the same act as his."

Collingwood, therefore, divides *acts* of thinking (which take place in time and therefore cannot be shared or identical) from *objects* of thinking (which can be identical, and thus enable us to know the same *truth* that Euclid experienced millennia ago). With thousands of years between them, Collingwood and Euclid share an *object* of thought, not an *act* of thought. With this schematic, it could be said that Collingwood aims to set history upon a scientific foundation, but one all its own—not a *natural* scientific basis. Collingwood unapologetically divides history from what might be called the art of impressions we make about the past.

How does Miranda's musical *Hamilton* fit into Collingwood's theory? First, we can easily glean that Miranda is pushing beyond the historical documents—imagining, inventing, projecting, riffing, often, for dramatic purposes. The goal for Miranda is to achieve exceptional *drama,* not historical *truth.* Accordingly, perhaps especially, we are enlightened and moved by the inventive methods by which Miranda *departs* from history. In this way, Miranda is playfully deconstructing the historical record—challenging us to rethink our relation to accepted, authoritative accounts of the past. Consider this brief exchange between Leslie Odom, Jr., who played Aaron Burr, and Miranda:

> ODOM: In the first two minutes of this show, Lin steps forward and introduces himself as Alexander Hamilton, and Chris steps forward and says he's George Washington, and you never question it again. When I think about what it would mean to me as a thirteen-, fourteen-year-old kid, to get this album or see this show—it can make me very emotional. And I so look forward to the day I get to see an Asian-American Burr.

> MIRANDA: That'll be the note that goes with the school productions: If this show ends up looking like the actual founding fathers, you messed up.

To Odom's point, the show aims to embody *characters*, not for verisimilitude with historical facts. Racial color here stands for a radical reconsideration of inherited narratives, but it is not meant as an alternative history. We know that Alexander Hamilton was not of Puerto Rican descent, so Miranda casting himself in the role is an artistic provocation that prompts us to think, among other things, about Hamilton's status as an immi-grant from the Caribbean. The casting, then, is not a bit of faulty historical research. Miranda's riposte to Odom's observa-tion adds further evidence of anti-historical ambitions, namely, that if some future production did in fact aim for historical verisimilitude, then it has failed to be the kind of creation Miranda intended it to be. *Hamilton* is best understood as par-ticipating in the art of biography, not the practice of history.

According to Collingwood: "a biography . . . , however much history it contains, is constructed on principles that are not only non-historical but anti-historical." Biographies, diaries, memoirs, and the like, he emphasizes, are "a form of literature, . . . but his-tory it can never be." Biography might achieve the level of poetry—one thinks of autobiographies such as Henry Adams's *Education of Henry Adams* or T.E. Lawrence's *Seven Pillars of Wisdom*—but for our historian, biographies are but works of art, however glorious. Achievements, to be sure, but not of history.

With Collingwood's proposals at hand, the various contro-versies and eruptions of discontent about *Hamilton's* devia-tions from the historical record seem misplaced at best, wrong-headed at worst. For instance, Nancy Isenberg, admon-ishes us: "Let's Not Pretend *Hamilton* is History," yet her mode of debunking amounts to a compare-and-contrast of what the musical gets right about the standing historical record and where it strays from that record. Paradoxically, Isenberg has to presume that *Hamilton* is history in order to show the ways in which it is not. Saying that the musical cheats audiences of something like access to history misses the point.

According to Collingwood, *Hamilton* should be understood as a text in contention with history, perhaps even going so far as to announce itself as a joyous form of propaganda, an anti-history as antidote to settled thinking that is itself full of dis-tortions, cheats, and lies. Hamilton is poetry, literature, biography, but also song, dance, and political art-activism. All of these elements address and antagonize history by other modes and means.

Film, History

Is the conflict over *Hamilton's* historical credentials due to its failures to defend them, or is it owing to other reasons, beyond the musical itself? Perhaps because of its popularity and its artistic form, the Broadway musical? In the same season that debates have roiled about what to call *Hamilton*, or how to consider it, Gary Ross's movie *Free State of Jones* was released, also drawing the attention of historians and film critics attuned to the film medium's potential relationship to history.

A.O. Scott remarked that "with blunt authority and unusual respect for historical truth, *Free State of Jones* explores a neglected and fascinating chapter in American history." How did it achieve this? "Mr. Ross," we are told, "consulted some of the leading experts in the era"—as Miranda did Chernow, no?—and "has done a good job of balancing the factual record with the demands of dramatic storytelling"—as Miranda did with his deployment of modes of American hip-hop and Broadway staging, no? Scott concludes that *Free State of Jones* is a "riveting visual history lesson." Like *Hamilton*, though, the film includes sound, and as with most films, sound is a crucial but often overlooked factor in its emotional impact; indeed, the Greek origin of *melos* (as in *melo*drama) means music!

Yet, why is someone as astute as Scott so eager and unconflicted in calling Ross's film history, while Miranda's musical provokes such dissent? When critic Jennifer Schuessler came to write about *Free State of Jones* she said it might "lay claim to a more unusual title: the first Hollywood film to come with footnotes." Again, she points up Ross's use of "historical sources, including many primary documents." Sounding at once defensive of his own work and condescending to other screenwriters, Ross told Schuessler: "this film wasn't the glib work of a screenwriter who was inventing things."

Ross, like so many others, would benefit from taking on Collingwood's distinction between *act* and *object*. Ross's entire screenplay, and the entire movie emerging from it—especially its performances by professional actors—is entirely invented. It is, in a word, all *act*. (The *object* of this work, meanwhile, may be something that can be given credentials as historical.) Ross—and the film critics who praise his movie's status as history, its depictions as historical—would appear to conspire to trick the audience into believing it is seeing something it cannot possibly see: the empirical events as they happened. Who's cheating whom now?

Is this critical legerdemain a function of the film's magical qualities as a medium for representation? Are we fooled—with the encouragement of film critics—into thinking film shows history, is historical, because it, well, looks and sounds like the things it's purporting to show? Film, we could say, gives the impression of being there, as if we're looking through a window onto a living world, while musical theatre and the like gives the impression of being *here*—in this seat, in this theater, and thus, oddly, in the present. "History from theatre" would then be an oxymoron, learning of the past by means of the present.

Theatre is more like a college lecture, despite the costumes and music and acting. And likewise it teaches. But what does it teach? Not history, according to Collingwood. So what about film? Film invites the *impression* of re-enactment, whereas theatre calls attention to "acting!"—the immediacy of the live performance and the presence of the actor on stage. Theatre's novelty *is* its presentness of action, whereas film, again, courts the effect—the insistence—that what we see and hear happening, is or has, in fact, "happened," is past, is history. The critics and directors who see nonfiction film as history assume a pretense for the medium, in contrast with theatrical form. Films project verisimilitude greater than any stage production could supply. Watching a film, we are "there"—by which we mean the past. Hence the trick.

The Real as Imagined

When it comes to events and persons, the figure or actor or character often becomes a cypher for our values and interpretations. Indeed, the thinner the historical record, perhaps the greater the impact: Buddha, Socrates, Jesus have the briefest biographies and yet consider their expansive influence.

Still, a robust documentary record doesn't forestall, much less dissuade, our powers to create myths and compelling symbols. Look to any number of biopics, bio-documentaries, and docudramas. With movies, with theatre, we do not so much tap into a historical record as invent figures and phantasms for our own purposes. As we change, and our need for them changes, so *they* change. A good satire or spoof, too, can further nudge our re-alignment about when "history is happening," as with Gerard Alessandrini's *Spamilton*—since this musical's metacritique-comedy demands awareness of the fabricated nature of Miranda's spectacle. We are, for Collingwood, getting further and further away from an historical account. History is not happening.

Alexander Hamilton, like his other famous contemporaries, has entered what one historian has called the "'Founders Chic' phenomenon." As another historian noted, with praise and worry, "*Hamilton* is an amazing piece of theatre, but it concerns me that people are seeing it as a piece of history." The two sentiments present a unified observation, namely, that re-telling history is not a neutral act, and moreover, does not guarantee that something based on history will itself be history. Miranda doesn't re-enact Hamilton's life story, he invents it anew. Where Mt. Rushmore gives us a myth cut into stone, Miranda gives us his own face as Hamilton's and sings his way to the achievement of art.[1]

---

[1] This chapter is dedicated to my daughter, Ruby. As a Hamiltone—a gifted interpreter of Miranda's lines and rhythms—she is, needless to say, an acute sufferer of Hamilaria. I fear, with pride, that it may be a lifelong affliction. —With love and admiration, Dad

Bibliography

Adams, Henry. 2009 [1906]. *The Education of Henry Adams*. Wilder.

Adams, John. 1961. *The Adams Papers: Papers of John Adams*. Volume 1: September 1755–October 1773. Harvard University Press.

Addison, Joseph. 2004. *Cato: A Tragedy, and Selected Essays*. Liberty Fund.

Aristotle. 1984. *The Complete Works of Aristotle*. Princeton University Press.

———. 1999. *Nicomachean Ethics*. Hackett.

Augustine. 2003. *The City of God*. Penguin.

Auricchio, Laura. 2015. *The Marquis: Lafayette Reconsidered*. Vintage.

Bakewell, Sarah. 2016. *At the Existentialist Café: Freedom, Being, and Apricot Cocktails with Jean-Paul Sartre, Simone de Beauvoir, Albert Camus, Martin Heidegger, Maurice Merleau-Ponty, and Others*. Other Press.

Bauman, Zygmunt. 2006. *Liquid Times: Living in an Age of Uncertainty*. Polity.

———. 2014. The Good Society and the Future of Art. In Joke Brouwer and Sjoerd van Tuinen, eds., *Giving and Taking: Antidotes to a Culture of Greed*. V2 Publishing.

Bentham, Jeremy. 2002. *Jeremy Bentham's Auto Icon and Related Writings*. Thoemmes Continuum.

Brantley, Ben. 2015. Review: Hamilton: Young Rebels Changing History and Theater. *New York Times* <http://www.nytimes.com/2015/08/07/theater/review-hamilton-young-rebels-changing-history-and-theater.html?smid=pl-share>.

Bushnell, Rebecca W. 1990. *Tragedies of Tyrants: Political Thought and Theater in the English Renaissance*. Cornell University Press.

Chernow, Ron. 2004. *Alexander Hamilton*. Penguin.

———. 2011 [2010]. *Washington: A Life*. Penguin.

Crenshaw, Kimberlé W. 1991. Mapping the Margins: Intersectionality, Identity Politics, and Violence against Women of Color. *Stanford Law Review* 43:6.

Danto, Arthur. 2003. *The Abuse of Beauty: Aesthetics and the Concept of Art*. Open Court.

Darwall, Stephen. 1977. Two Kinds of Respect. *Ethics* 88:1.

Dussel, Enrique. 2003 [1985]. *Philosophy of Liberation*. Wipf and Stock.

Ellis, Joseph J. 1996. *American Sphinx: The Character of Thomas Jefferson*. Vintage.

Epictetus. 2000. *Enchiridion*. Dover.

Epicurus. 1994. *The Epicurus Reader*. Hackett.

Fellman, G. 1998. *Rambo and the Dalai Lama: The Compulsion to Win and Its Threat to Human Survival*. State University of New York Press.

Foner, Eric. 2002. *Who Owns History? Rethinking the Past in a Changing World*. Hill and Wang.

Gibbs, Constance. 2015. How the Hero of Hamilton the Musical Is a Woman. *Mary Sue Comments*. <http://www.themarysue.com/how-the-hero-of-hamilton-the-musical-is-a-woman/>.

Gilligan, C. 1982. *In a Different Voice: Psychological Theory and Women's Development*. Harvard University Press.

Gordon-Reed, Annette. 2009. *The Hemingses of Monticello*. Norton.

———. 2015. Hamilton: The Musical: Blacks and the Founding Fathers. *National Council on Public History* <http://ncph.org/history-at-work/hamilton-the-musical-blacks-and-the-founding-fathers/>.

———. 2016. The Intense Debates Surrounding Hamilton Don't Diminish the Musical—They Enrich It. *Vox*. <http://www.vox.com/the-big-idea/2016/9/13/12894934/hamilton-debates-history-race-politics-literature>.

Gordon-Reed, Annette, and Peter S. Onuf. 2016. *"Most Blessed of the Patriarchs": Thomas Jefferson and the Empire of Imagination*. Liveright.

Gray, John. 2012 [1992]. *Men Are from Mars, Women Are from Venus: The Classic Guide to Understanding the Opposite Sex*. Harper.

Guinier, Lani, and Gerald Torres. 2003. *The Miner's Canary: Enlisting Race, Resisting Power, Transforming Democracy*. Harvard University Press.

Habito, Ruben L.F. 2004. *Living Zen, Loving God*. Wisdom.

Haraway, Donna. 1990. *Simians, Cyborgs, and Women: The Reinvention of Nature*. Routledge.

Hitchens, Christopher. 2009. *Thomas Jefferson: Author of America*. Harper.

Hoagland, S. 2008 [2000]. Separating from Heterosexualism. In A. Bailey and C. Cuomo, eds., *A Feminist Philosophy Reader*. McGraw-Hill.

Huang Po. 1958. *The Zen Teaching of Huang Po: On the Transmission of Mind*. Grove Press.

Isenberg, Nancy. 2008. *Fallen Founder: The Life of Aaron Burr*. Penguin.

———. 2015. Nancy Isenberg: This *Hamilton* Is Not History. *Dallas News* <www.dallasnews.com/opinion/commentary/2016/03/22/nancy-isenberg-this-hamilton-is-not-history>.

———. 2016. *White Trash: The 400-Year Untold History of Class in America*. Viking.

Jefferson, Israel. 2014 [1868]. The Memoirs of Israel Jefferson. Frontline <http://www.pbs.org/wgbh/pages/frontline/shows/jefferson/cron/1873israel.html>.

Jefferson, Thomas. 1950. *The Papers of Thomas Jefferson: Volume 1, 1760–1776*. Princeton University Press.

———. 2011. *The Jefferson Bible, Smithsonian Edition: The Life and Morals of Jesus of Nazareth*. Smithsonian.

Kant, Immanuel. 1996. *The Metaphysics of Morals*. Cambridge University Press.

Knott, Stephen. 2002. *Alexander Hamilton and the Persistence of Myth*. University Press of Kansas.

Langer, Suzanne. 1953. *Feeling and Form—A Theory of Art*. Scribner's.

Lao Tsu. 1989. *Tao Te Ching*. Vintage.

Laozi. 2007. *Daodejing: A Complete Translation and Commentary*. Open Court.

Locke, John. 1980. *Second Treatise of Government*. Hackett.

Lorde, A. (1984). *Sister Outsider: Essays and Speeches*. The Crossing Press.

Meacham, Jon. 2013. *Thomas Jefferson: The Art of Power*. Random House.

Mead, Rebecca. 2015. All About the Hamiltons. *The New Yorker* (February 9th).

Mill, John Stuart. 1978. *On Liberty*. Hackett.

Miranda, Lin-Manuel. 2016. *Hamilton* Creator Lin-Manuel Miranda: The Rolling Stone Interview. *Rolling Stone* (June 1st).

Miranda, Lin-Manuel, and Jeremy McCarter. 2016. *Hamilton: The Revolution*. Grand Central.

Montaigne, Michel de. 2003. *The Complete Essays*. Penguin.

Monteiro, L.D. 2016. Review Essay: Race-Conscious Casting and the Erasure of the Black Past in Lin-Manuel Miranda's *Hamilton*. *The Public Historian* 38:1.

Newton, Michael. 2015. *Alexander Hamilton: The Formative Years*. Eleftheria.

Nishitani, Keiji. 1982. *Religion and Nothingness*. University of California Press.

Paulson, Michael. 2016. Hamilton Producers Will Change Job Posting, but Not Commitment to Diverse Casting. *The New York Times* <http://www.nytimes.com/2016/03/31/arts/union-criticizes-hamilton-casting-call-seeking-nonwhite-actors.html?_r=0>.

Piepenburg, Erik. 2015. Why *Hamilton* Has Heat. *New York Times* <http://www.nytimes.com/interactive/2015/08/06/theater/20150806-hamilton-broadway.html>.

Plato. 1991. *The Republic*. Basic Books.

———. 1997. *Republic*. Hackett.

———. 2000. *The Trial and Death of Socrates*. Hackett.

Primus, Richard. 2016. Will Lin-Manuel Miranda Transform the Supreme Court? *The Atlantic* <http://www.theatlantic.com/politics/archive/2016/06/lin-manuel-miranda-and-the-future-of-originalism/485651/>.

Rahula, Walpola. 1974. *What the Buddha Taught*. Grove Press.

Raphael, Ray. 2016 [2001]. *A People's History of the American Revolution: How Common People Shaped the Fight for Independence*. New Press.

Reed, Ishmael. *Hamilton: The Musical*: Black Actors Dress Up Like Slave Traders . . . and It's Not Halloween. <http://www.counterpunch.org/2015/08/21/hamilton-the-musical-black-actors-dress-up-like-slave-tradersand-its-not-halloween/>.

Rousseau, Jean-Jacques. 1968. *Politics and the Arts: Letter to M. D'Alembert on the Theater*. Cornell University Press.

Samuelson, P.L., Matthew J. Jarvinen, Thomas B. Paulus, Ian M. Church, Sam A. Hardy, and Justin L. Barrett. 2015. Implicit Theories of Intellectual Virtues and Vices: A Focus on Intellectual Humility. *Journal of Positive Psychology* 10:5.

Schuessler, Jennifer. 2016. *Hamilton* and History: Are They in Sync? *New York Times* <http://www.nytimes.com/2016/04/11/theater/hamilton-and-history-are-they-in-sync.html?_r=0>.

Schulman, Michael. 2015. The Women of *Hamilton*. *The New Yorker* <http://www.newyorker.com/culture/cultural-comment/the-women-of-hamilton>.

Shakespeare, William. 2000. *Macbeth*. Penguin.

Siderits, Mark. *Buddhism as Philosophy*. Indianapolis: Hackett, 2007.

Sloterdijk, Peter. 2013. *Nietzsche Apostle: The Emancipatory Potential of Self-Praise*. Semiotext(e).

Tocqueville, Alexis de. 2004. *Democracy in America*. The Library of America.

Troyer, John, ed., *The Classical Utilitarians: Bentham and Mill*. Hackett.

Whitcomb, D., H. Battaly, J. Baehr, and D. Howard-Snyder. 2015. Intellectual Humility: Owning Our Limitations. *Philosophy and Phenomenological Research*.

White House Press Office. 2016. Remarks by the President at "Hamilton at the White House." The White House <https://www.whitehouse.gov/the-press-office/2016/03/14/remarks-president-hamilton-white-house>.

Whitehead, Alfred North. 1978. *Process and Reality: An Essay in Cosmology*. The Free Press.

Wilson, Woodrow. 1970. *The Politics of Woodrow Wilson: Selections from His Speeches and Writings*. Harper.

Wollstonecraft, Mary. 2008 [1792]. *A Vindication of the Rights of Woman with Strictures on Political and Moral Subjects*. Norton.

Zinn, H. 1980. *A People's History of the United States*. Harper.

———. 1991. *Declarations of Independence: Cross-Examining American Ideology*. Perennial.

———. 2002. *You Can't Be Neutral on a Moving Train: A Personal History of Our Times*. Beacon Press.

A Well-Regulated Militia

MINERVA AHUMADA is Lecturer in philosophy at Arrupe College, Chicago, and has interests in ethics and social and political philosophy.

Minerva Ahumada teaches at Arrupe College
And here, first and foremost, she'd like to acknowledge
The students of hers for teaching her to reach
For a Hamilton *reference to clarify philosophical speech.*

ROBERT ARP works as a researcher and is the author and editor of numerous books, book chapters, and articles in philosophy and other areas. His innumerable works include *1001 Ideas that Changed the Way We Think* (2013), *What's Good on TV? Teaching Ethics through Television* (2011), and *Scenario Visualization: An Evolutionary Account of Creative Problem Solving* (2008). See <robertarp.com>.

My name is Rob, last name is Arp
My rhyme's are kinda dull, but my pencil's sharp.
I like learnin' history and philosophy too
Yeah, I still use a pencil, so what's it to you?

ADAM BARKMAN is an associate professor of philosophy at Redeemer University College. He is the author and co-editor of ten books, most recently *Making Sense of Islamic Art and Architecture* (2015) and, with Rob Arp, *Downton Abbey and Philosophy* (2015). He is also the author of more than seventy articles and book chapters on philosophy and related themes. While Barkman doesn't know as much about Hamilton the man as he'd like, he does know a lot about Hamilton the city, in which he works.

I'm straight outta Canada, in a town where it ain't too hot.
It's name is also Hamilton, believe it or not.
I likes me some philosophy and also some art
If I had a role in Hamilton, *I'd play the Aaron Burr part.*

CARRIE-ANN BIONDI is Associate Professor of Philosophy and Chair of her department at Marymount Manhattan College in New York City. Her research interests include Aristotle, citizenship, political obligation, patriotism, virtue ethics, children's rights, Socratic pedagogy, and popular culture (including Harry Potter, Sherlock Holmes, and Steve Jobs). She is also Co-Editor-in-Chief (with Shawn Klein) of the philosophy journal *Reason Papers*. Proving the truth in the adage "You've got to be in it to win it," she entered the in-person lottery for Hamilton tickets over two hundred times in 2015, and had the good fortune of seeing the musical ten times that year.

Aristotle, Locke, and a dash of Searle,
Carrie-Ann's most def a philosophy girl.
She also loves Hamilton *and seen it ten times.*
It's fresh, and it's dope, and it's got great rhymes!

KATE BOSSERT is an assistant professor of English at Notre Dame of Maryland University, where she teaches Shakespeare and directs the Drama program. She is grateful to her students for introducing her to *Hamilton*.

The name is Bossert, and I'm an early modernist.
I study how Renaissance philosophies persist.
The Bard's my favorite when I teach English Lit
So I dig Lin-Manuel Miranda's #YayHamlet!

JOE CHAPA is a Major in the US Air Force and a Senior Instructor of Philosophy at the US Air Force Academy, Colorado. He holds an MA in Philosophy from Boston College, an MA in Theological Studies from Liberty Baptist Theological Seminary, and a BA in Philosophy from Boston University. His areas of expertise include the Just War tradition, military ethics, and especially the ethics of remote and autonomous weapons. The views expressed in his chapter are his own and do not necessarily reflect those of the US government, Department of Defense, or Department of the Air Force.

J–O–E C–H–A–P–A, I got philos for the sophiā
Credible pages, mad publications, pat myself on the back for those
    statements.

My reams seem to stream, no ending . . . it's simple seeing empiri-
cal things
The more meaning I come across, the more paper I need.

MARLENE CLARK teaches courses full of literature, film, philosophy, and history offered by the Department of Interdisciplinary Studies at The City College Center for Worker Education, CUNY. Recent and forthcoming publications include Lefebvre-influenced studies of some literary landscapes of Brooklyn, and a new look at the six numbered Woman paintings of Willem de Kooning.

Teachin' and writin' and inspirin' is my gig
In literature, film, philosophy, and history, you dig?
I work at the City College Center for Worker Education in the Big
Apple, you see?
Otherwise known as N.Y.C. (mic drop)

ALISON DOBRICK is Associate Professor in the Department of Elementary and Early Childhood Education at William Paterson University of New Jersey. Dr. Dobrick also serves as Director of the William Paterson University Center for Holocaust and Genocide Studies.

Ali D, one L in my name
Teacher for life, won't graduate from the school game.
Professor and Mommy, Philosopher, and Wife,
I learn, teach, love, and focus on life!

JASON T. EBERL is the Semler Endowed Chair for Medical Ethics and Professor of Philosophy at Marian University in Indianapolis. He teaches and publishes on bioethics, medieval philosophy, and meta-physics. He's the editor or co-editor of *The Ultimate Star Trek and Philosophy*, *The Ultimate Star Wars and Philosophy*, *Sons of Anarchy and Philosophy*, *Star Trek and Philosophy*, *Star Wars and Philosophy*, and *The Philosophy of Christopher Nolan*. He's also contributed to books about Stanley Kubrick, J.J. Abrams, Harry Potter, Metallica, *Terminator*, *The Hunger Games*, *The Big Lebowski*, and *Avatar*. Not wanting to throw away his shot, he defended his doctoral dissertation in a rap battle to the tune of Eminem's "Lose Yourself."

My name's Dr. J and I likes me some Aristotle
I teach 'bout ethics within the hospital.
I'm usually more of a heavy metal guy
But Miranda's hip hop rocks, I cannot tell a lie.

CHERYL FRAZIER is a PhD candidate in philosophy at the University of Oklahoma. She does research in applied ethics and aesthetics, and is interested in the ways art can help us better understand the world around us. In addition to *Hamilton*, Cheryl has an almost unhealthy obsession with sloths, baby goats, and statement necklaces. She looks forward to the day where she can sell her kidney (first child, all her Earthly possessions, etc.) in exchange for tickets to see *Hamilton* in New York City, but in the meantime she's willing to wait for it.

> *I put the Fraze in Frazier, and I spells it my way.*
> *If I chose to, I'd write FrAzier with a capital A.*
> *But wait, that ain't like me, and I don't wanna be no fool*
> *And end up like Hamilton on the losing end of a duel.*

MAGGIE JACKSON holds an MA in Sociology from Goldsmiths, University of London, and will soon begin her PhD at The Ohio State University. Her academic work is largely concerned with representations of gender and sexuality where they intersect with media fandom, and involves quite a lot of scrolling endlessly through Tumblr. She has a tendency to alarm other drivers with her enthusiastic vehicular performances of "My Shot," and has never not cried during "It's Quiet Uptown."

> *"Sorry Ms. Jackson!" I've heard it before,*
> *I know all those words, hell, I wrote that score.*
> *I'm a nerd for Hamilton, no need to ask, bruh,*
> *But if you apologize to me again, Imma Outkast ya.*

MYRON JACKSON is Visiting Assistant Professor of Philosophy at Grand Valley State University. His work centers on the problems of philosophical anthropology and public philosophy broadly construed. His first forthcoming book is tentatively titled *Ironic American Exceptionalism: Visions of Open Selves.*

> *First name is Myron, comin' on like a siren.*
> *Last name is Jackson, and that's just the facts son.*
> *I do what I do with a mic or a pen*
> *Philosophizin' over and over again.*

TIM JUNG teaches English and Philosophy at Northside College Preparatory High School in Chicago.

> *I'm known as "Mr. Jung" and I've earned a bad rep*
> *Teaching high school in Chicago at Northside College Prep.*
> *When I'm not teaching English class, I run class like Socrates*
> *I'm corrupting the youth by teaching them philosophies.*

CHRISTOPHER KETCHAM earned his doctorate at the University of Texas at Austin. He teaches business and ethics for the University of Houston Downtown. His research interests are risk management, applied ethics, social justice, and East-West comparative philosophy. He has done recent work in the philosophical ideas of forgiveness, Emmanuel Levinas's responsibility, Gabriel Marcel's spirit of abstraction, space ethics, the ego in Buddhism and lots of chapters in Popular Culture and Philosophy volumes. Some of you can proudly take out a bill and say, "I graduated from the same college as he did . . ." Unfortunately, I am an alumnus from the college that graduated Chester A. Arthur. I have no hope in Hell of ever pulling out a bill with Arthur's face on it.

> *If I had a ten I'd be rich, rich, rich.*
> *If I had a twenty, don't need no money*
> *So, if I had a fifty, you know I'd get an itch*
> *But I'm broke, 'cause it come and go so quickly.*

DAVID LAROCCA is Visiting Assistant Professor in the Department of Philosophy at the State University of New York College at Cortland. Recently, he was Visiting Scholar in the Department of English at Cornell University, and Lecturer in Screen Studies in the Department of Cinema, Photography, and Media Arts at Ithaca College. His articles have appeared in *Afterimage*, *Epoché*, *Liminalities*, *Film and Philosophy*, *The Senses and Society*, *The Midwest Quarterly*, *The Journal of Aesthetic Education*, and *The Journal of Aesthetics and Art Criticism*. He has contributed book chapters on Michael Mann, Spike Lee, the Coen brothers, Tim Burton, Errol Morris, Werner Herzog, Sofia Coppola, *Star Wars*, *Girls*, and *Downton Abbey*. He's the author of *Emerson's English Traits and the Natural History of Metaphor*, and editor of Stanley Cavell's *Emerson's Transcendental Etudes*, *The Philosophy of Charlie Kaufman*, *The Philosophy of War Films*, and most recently, *The Philosophy of Documentary Film: Image, Sound, Fiction, Truth*. More details at <www.davidlarocca.org>.

> *How does an exile, scholar, son of a gun and a 'Merican,*
>   *adrift in the academy*
> *In a for-profit state, haunted by fate, a wanderer in doubt, in debt,*
>   *grow up to be an adjunct and a father?*
> *The unfathered father with ten dollars—Didn't get a lot farther*
>   *by working a lot harder*
> *But by singing with his daughter.*

JENNIFER L. MCMAHON is Professor of Philosophy and English at East Central University in Ada, Oklahoma. She has expertise in existentialism, aesthetics, and comparative philosophy. She's published numerous essays on philosophy and popular culture, most recently in *The Philosophy of Documentary Film* (2016), *Buddhism and American Cinema* (2014) and *Death in Classic and Contemporary Cinema* (2013). She's edited collections, including *The Philosophy of Tim Burton* (2014) and *The Philosophy of the Western* (2010). When seized with existential angst, she picks up her laptop and attempts to write her own deliverance (or distraction) one popular culture essay at a time.

> *I don't have a philosophy professor back in my family tree*
> *But that didn't matter; philosophy, she came for me*
> *And truth once you see it and all the places it can be found*
> *Truth once noticed turns the whole world around.*
> *Philosophy showed me she's not just a preoccupation for the elite*
> *No, philosophy was built for us to carry her to the street.*

LISA MAXINE MELINN is to the theater what her brother ADAM is to philosophy. Or rather, theater is to Lisa what philosophy is to Adam. They've been singing and attending musicals together all of their lives. By different paths, they've both found their way into teaching at the college level. Discovering *Hamilton* brought them together in a way that no other musical has done since they were children, memorizing every lyric on their mother's *Hair* LP. They've been collaborating ever since. In this sibling set, Adam is somewhat an Angelica, to Lisa's Peggy.

> *The name is Lisa. Lisa Maxine.*
> *Since the age of five acting's been my dream.*
> *Working as a playwright and a teacher as well,*
> *But damn it, writer's block is my creative hell!*
> *I got big dreams so I gotta earn some bank . . .*
> *Un-deux-troix-quatre-cinq!*

> *In Philly Adam Melinn dropped the ethics and aesthetics*
> *Now he's chillin' in China as a Professor of rhetoric.*
> *The siblings have been Melinn, Lisa, and Adam*
> *Been rhyming together, since their mother first had 'em.*
> *With passion for language, for teaching and art*
> *They've united Lin-Manuel Miranda with Sartre!*

AARON RABINOWITZ grew up in theater. It was his first love, shortly before philosophy. Today he's lucky enough to teach philosophy at Rutgers during the year, and theater during the summers, at the same camp where he grew up. Aaron also hosts the philosophy podcast Embrace the Void. His areas of philosophical expertise are ethics,

Eastern philosophy, and selfhood. He is thankful that dueling is illegal, so that he can enjoy a life of flourishing.

> *I see the suffering of minds, encumbered by chains.*
> *I feel the slings and the arrows that tear at their brains.*
> *My bro Moses he knows this ain't all we're destined to*
> *So I strung these words together as a ladder for you*
> *We're climbing together, to escape Plato's caves.*
> *They call me Aaron the Rabi, cause I'm freeing these slaves!*

BENJAMIN ROSS is a PhD candidate at the University of North Texas and a member of the Maria Kannon Zen Center in Dallas, Texas. Having no self, he may also have written some fiction and published on the philosophy of technology, but he cannot be sure.

> *They call me Benjamin, but it should be Benja-max,*
> *Speaking truth to power and questioning their "facts"*
> *My last name is Ross like that "Friend" from TV*
> *But he, unlike me, don't do philosophy*

JACQUELINE MCMAHON SMITH, after having worked as a criminal prosecutor for the Brooklyn District Attorney's Office and the NYS Attorney General, is an attorney for the New York City Police Department. Although she graduated from Wesleyan University a few years ahead of Lin-Manuel Miranda, she feels a kinship with him in a shared love for art, music, and their alma mater. She is currently working on a mystery novel set in Brooklyn in the late 1980s.

> *I remember that night, I'll never forget that night for the rest of my days*
> *I remember my friends, they were tripping over themselves with envy and praise.*
> *I remember those seats, so rare, so close, like a dream that you can't quite place*
> *But Lin-Manuel, I'll never forget that night I saw your face.*
> *You shook me up, my dreams unfurled, Hamilton—it rocked my world*
> *I grew up on old-school hip-hop, never wanted it to stop*
> *Studied the law, music, and art; got a job, played the part*
> *But through it all I have preferred, to communicate-the written word.*

CHAD WILLIAM TIMM is an Associate Professor of Education at Simpson College in Indianola, Iowa. For fifteen years he taught Howard Zinn's radical history to high school students, which on more than one occasion nearly got him fired. Once, after reading excerpts from Howard Zinn's *A People's History*, a group of his students organized a sit-in at the state Capitol calling for an end to the war in Iraq. Seeing his students take what they learned in class to "the room where it happens" certainly made him proud.

> *We can't escape our perspectives in the accounts we write*
> *Whether we're black, or brown, or yellow, or white.*
> *If "History is written by the victors" is true*
> *Then you gotta understand what the losers wrote too.*

KATELYN BOTSFORD TUCKER is a high school and middle school teacher in Connecticut. She holds a Master of Arts in Teaching from Sacred Heart University and a Master of Arts in American Studies from Fairfield University. She enjoys quoting *The Federalist Papers* and rapping the "Cabinet Battles" to her students, her husband, and her two children.

> *Katelyn Botsford Tucker is too hard to rhyme.*
> *Are you still waiting in the Hamilton ticket line?*
> *People paying top dollar to see the show.*
> *Don't be jealous, yo, I won my ticket to go.*

ANDREW T. VINK is a PhD student in systematic theology at Boston College. He holds MAs in philosophy and theology from Marquette University. His research interests are related to questions of social suffering, political theology, and philosophy of religion.

> *Son of Maryland, Andy V's my name*
> *Of philosophical and theological fame.*
> *Worked real hard, rose above my station*
> *Now I'm fighting for everyone's liberation.*

RACHEL WALL is a trained teacher and lover of math and philosophy problems, who balances this out with her ability to flawlessly rap all the lyrics of Hamilton. For real.

> *Now listen to the sounds of emcee Wall*
> *As I philosophize about the nature of race to you all.*
> *Who cares if George Washington is portrayed as non-white?*
> *We shouldn't start to shudder and to sweat at the sight.*

ANDY WIBLE is a full-time philosophy instructor at Muskegon Community College where he frequently duels administrators, teaches a variety of philosophy classes, and writes on issues in biomedical ethics and businesses ethics as well as LGBTQ rights.

Andy is first, followed by Wible
I enjoy nonfiction, so I don't read the Bible.
Ethics and LGBTQ issues are my study
Simplicity is for mathematicians—I prefer things muddy.

THOMAS WILK is a PhD candidate in Philosophy at Johns Hopkins University. Tom's long been interested in the Founding Fathers and their biographies, and even chose excerpts of John and Abigail Adams's letters to be read in his wedding ceremony. Tom didn't get hooked on *Hamilton*, however, until his own "young, scrappy, and hungry" two-year-old son, Sam, followed the rest of the world into an obsession with the cast recording. When he's not listening to Sam sing "The Work! Work! Song" or "The World Turned Upside Down Song" on constant repeat, Tom teaches introduction to philosophy, ethics, human rights, critical thinking, and logic as an adjunct instructor at Gettysburg College, George Washington University, Goucher College, and the US Naval Academy. He resides in Alexandria, Viginia, with his partner Kate; son Sam; and Plato, their beagle.

In Western PA I was born and raised
Johns Hopkins is where I spent my PhD days
Rappin' 'bout ethics, morals, and language.
My name's Tommy Wilk, that's my advantage.

Index